MUSLIMS IN THE
UNITED STATES

MUSLIMS IN THE UNITED STATES
THE STATE OF RESEARCH

KAREN ISAKSEN LEONARD

Russell Sage Foundation • New York

The Russell Sage Foundation

The Russell Sage Foundation, one of the oldest of America's general purpose foundations, was established in 1907 by Mrs. Margaret Olivia Sage for "the improvement of social and living conditions in the United States." The Foundation seeks to fulfill this mandate by fostering the development and dissemination of knowledge about the country's political, social, and economic problems. While the Foundation endeavors to assure the accuracy and objectivity of each book it publishes, the conclusions and interpretations in Russell Sage Foundation publications are those of the authors and not of the Foundation, its Trustees, or its staff. Publication by Russell Sage, therefore, does not imply Foundation endorsement.

Library of Congress Cataloging-in-Publication Data

Leonard, Karen Isaksen, 1939–
    Muslims in the United States : the state of research / Karen Isaksen Leonard.
        p.   cm.
    Includes bibliographical references and index.
    ISBN 0-87154-530-6
    1. Muslims—Research—United States. 2. Islam—Research—United States.
    I. Title.

E184.M88L46 2003
305.6'971073'0722—dc21   2003043100

Text design by Suzanne Nichols

RUSSELL SAGE FOUNDATION
112 East 64th Street, New York, New York 10021
10 9 8 7 6 5 4 3 2 1

Contents

vi   Contents

About the Author

Karen Isaksen Leonard is professor of anthropology at the University of California, Irvine.

═ Preface ═

THE September 11, 2001, terrorist attacks on New York City and Washington, D.C., and their consequences catalyzed a wide-ranging interest in Islam and in Muslim communities in America. The histories and current debates surveyed here are compelling and highly relevant not only to scholars but to a broader readership as well. I wrote this bibliographic essay—an interpretive overview of American Muslim histories and the state of the research on Islam and Muslims in the United States—for the Russell Sage Foundation in the summer of 2002 with the goal of providing a useful research tool for exploring this large body of social science research. My hope was to make the material as interesting and important to the reader as I find it to be and to demonstrate its relevance to broader questions in American history about the ways in which religion, freedom, and justice relate to each other and to the nation-state.

The number of published sources and the complex ways in which they relate to each other defeated my intention to be brief. Despite its length, the density of scholarly references, and the focus on theoretical and inter-disciplinary scholarly concerns, the essay is intended to be accessible to students and general readers as well as scholars. By providing a concise summary of significant historical and contemporary work on Muslims in the United States, my hope is to stimulate scholarly research and facilitate comparisons with research on Muslims elsewhere in the non-Muslim world. I have not included everything written about Muslims in the United States and sometimes chose just one or two pieces to represent an author. Some scholarly work comes up again and again, and some is referred to only once, but the amount and quality of research already done augers well for further research in this area.

Beginning with historical materials in part I, I discuss in chapters 1, 2, and 3 the ways in which national origin, language, sectarian affiliation, race, class, and gender have structured Muslim communities. The same variables have influenced debates about Islam, Muslims, and the sources of Islamic religious authority in America.

Chapters 1 and 2 sketch the development of Islam and Muslim communities in the United States from the early slavery era right down to the post–September 11, 2001, present. The United States is a nation of immigrants, and many of the Muslims discussed here are fairly recent immigrants. However, members of long-established populations, including many African Americans, have become Muslims. As chapter 1 shows, the interactions of indigenous African American Muslims with immigrant Muslims raise some of the most fascinating issues in the evolving history of Islam in America. Decisions to become active citizens and to mobilize politically have posed significant challenges for American Muslims, both before and after September 11, 2001, and the increasing participation of American Muslims in national politics is reviewed in chapter 2.

Chapter 3 surveys important historical issues that remain to be addressed, focusing on African American Muslims, many smaller and less well-known Muslim immigrant communities, and Muslims who are secular or nonreligious in orientation. Sources of tension within various Muslim communities in the United States and sources of tension between these communities and the wider public stand out in the historical materials.

Part II, chapters 4 through 7, building on the historical materials, move to the contemporary scene and integrate published research findings on a range of topics, highlighting important research issues. I have tried to organize the discussion topically, although numerous studies bridge topics and are discussed wherever they are relevant. Chapter 4 goes into greater depth on the diversity of American Muslim identities and affiliations—the ways in which Muslims self-identify and are identified by others. Issues of national origin, language, sectarian movements, race, and class are discussed more specifically here, as well as issues of generation, gender, and sexuality. Chapter 5 locates Muslims in the United States and in the world, reviewing the public and domestic spaces for the enactment of Muslim identities. Mosques in America have received the most attention, but transnational, cosmopolitan, and global spaces and networks are also important determinants of personal and community identity for many American Muslims, and I review the work being done on all of these topics.

Chapter 6 turns to specifically religious or Islamic discourses and practices, beginning with a review of scholarship on Islamic views of state and society in the United States, on the competing sources of religious authority in this country, and on the changing relationships between Islamic legal cultures and national or ethnic cultures among

American Muslims. The chapter ends with a look at the issues concerning Muslim women and the family in the American context. The scholarly research shows the social and political significance of the debate over these issues, which are important to the future of pluralism or cosmopolitanism in America.

Chapter 7 assesses the scholarly work on the mutual accommodation and integration between Muslims and non-Muslims in the United States. Muslims are now important participants in ongoing dialogues about religion, freedom, and justice and their relationship to civil religion and the American nation-state. I review the research on Muslim political organizations and institutions; on the kinds of mosques, religious beliefs, and practices that have been identified as "American"; and on the production and transmission of Islamic teachings in the United States. Turning to research on the aesthetic, or expressive, culture among Muslims in this country and the trends scholars see among young American Muslims, I highlight the current changes and innovations that provide evidence that distinctly "American" Muslim communities and identities are developing in the United States.

Finally, in chapter 8, I suggest some research agendas that would further our knowledge about Muslims in the United States. I do this comparatively: first and very broadly by contrasting the state of research on Muslims in Europe and Muslims in the United States; then by contrasting Muslim groups in the United States. After looking at the ways in which Islamic studies and religious studies scholars are moving closer together and also informing various American Muslim activists, I return to the impact of September 11, 2001, on scholarly research on American Muslims. In conclusion, I suggest the importance of Islam and Muslims for American religious and political history in the twenty-first century. I draw here, quite selectively, on scholars and theorists of changing patterns of religious affiliation and practice, ethno-racial affiliation, and cosmopolitanism and pluralism in the United States.

Writing as a non-Muslim secular scholar, I marshal and use a wide range of scholarly sources as I understand and evaluate them. My background is in the history and anthropology of South Asia (India, Pakistan, Bangladesh, Sri Lanka, Nepal, and Afghanistan). In particular, I have studied Hyderabad, formerly a princely state and now the capital city of Andhra Pradesh in modern India. My interest in American Muslims developed as part of a project on the Hyderabad diaspora, so Hyderabadi and other South Asian Muslim immigrants are my point of entry to the study of Muslims in the United States. My limitations should be kept in mind, particularly by readers whose expertise lies in religious studies, American studies, and African American and Arab American history, all fields I wish I knew much better for purposes of this book.

Other writers on the state of research on Muslims in the United States would almost certainly present the material differently. Some would define "Muslim" more narrowly, but as an anthropologist, I include and discuss here all who self-identify as Muslims. Unlike those who see the striving toward a universal umma, or community, as the overarching narrative for all Muslim experience, I see the persistence of asabiyya, group solidarity and experience (groups based on national origin, language, race, and/or ethnicity), as a very important theme. Yet I see emerging American versions of Islam, a theme that structures this bibliographic essay and brings the many sources reviewed into meaningful dialogue with each other.

I want to stress, however, that many of the sources reviewed here have not been in meaningful dialogue with each other, and the reasons for that will become apparent. They include academic disciplinary and "area studies" boundaries, as well as boundary-setting by various groups of Muslims themselves. It is not my view that all Muslims in the United States, or scholars of them, should necessarily all be talking to each other or brought into substantial agreement with each other. Yet it is interesting to see where the silences and boundaries have been and to reflect on what might be gained or lost by breaking them.

Confronted by materials concerning Muslims of very diverse backgrounds, I called on many other scholars for assistance. I want to thank colleagues who sent me references I might otherwise have missed: Zain Abdullah, Huma Ahmed-Ghosh, Syed Faiz Ali, Ali Asani, Edward Curtis IV, Josh DeWind, Robert Dannin, Marcia Hermansen, Jamillah Karim, Stewart Lawrence, Ann Chih Lin, Lawrence Mamiya, Paul Numrich, Aly Remtulla-Kassim, Garbi Schmidt, and Andrew Shryock. I also thank those who commented on earlier versions of the essay: Zain Abdullah, Barbara Al-Bayati, Syed Faiz Ali, Louise Cainkar, Edward Curtis IV, Marcia Hermansen, Sally Howell, Ivan Light, Bill Maurer, Paul Numrich, and Andrew Shryock. The comments of the three anonymous readers for the Russell Sage Foundation were especially helpful.

Other individuals and institutions have assisted me. Not knowing Arabic, I have elected to use simplified transliterations in most cases, as is becoming the practice in Islamic American English, or Islamic English. Although many scholars use Shi'a as a noun (it is both singular and plural) and Shi'i as an adjective, in the interests of a wider readership and Islamic English, I am simply using Shi'a in this book. For some proper names and words less commonly used in English, however, I have tried for accurate transliterations, using the open quote (') to signify ayn, and the close quote (') to signify hamza, following the *Chicago Manual of Style* recommendation. I thank Barbara Al-Bayati for help with those transliterations. Rhonda Higdon helped track down sources and get them from the library. The University of California Humanities Research Institute funded "Muslim Identities in North America," a major conference I coordinated in May 2000 at the Irvine campus. Finally, I have benefited greatly from several meetings and conferences on Muslims in the United States and in Europe organized by the Social Science Research Council (SSRC) and by the SSRC and the Russell Sage Foundation. I thank Stephanie Platz and Suzanne Nichols at the Russell Sage Foundation, Stephanie for asking me to write the original bibliographic essay, and Suzanne for helping turn it into a book. While thanking all of these people and institutions, I acknowledge that any remaining errors of fact or interpretation are, of course, mine.

= PART I =

HISTORICAL OVERVIEW OF MUSLIMS IN THE UNITED STATES

═ Chapter 1 ═

The Development of Ethno-Racial Muslim Communities in the United States

MUSLIMS in North America come from many places, including the United States. Their histories are varied, and their identities diverse and changing. Processes of individual and community identity formation and change like those we are witnessing now in the United States are not new to followers of this major world religion.

Within a century of the birth of Islam in seventh-century Arabia, there were contending interpretations, social groups, and sources of legal authority within the evolving Islamic community. Yet an identifiable "core" Islamic way of thinking and acting, based on the example and teachings of the Prophet Muhammad (570–632 C.E.), developed over time. This core comprises the five "pillars" of Islam: the profession of faith (there is no God but Allah and Muhammad is his Prophet); the offering of prayers five times a day; alms-giving, or zakat; fasting for the month of Ramadan; and the obligation to go on pilgrimage to the sacred center, Mecca, once in one's life if one can afford it. Islamic law, or shari'a, was eventually represented by several major legal traditions or schools, but it developed on the foundations of the Qur'an, delivered from Allah to the Prophet Muhammad by the Angel Gabriel, and the collected traditions, the hadith.

Islam is not a monolithic entity; its beliefs and practices are not the same throughout the world. An early battle (at Karbala in 680 C.E.) over the Caliphate—the political leadership of the rapidly growing Muslim community—produced a lasting split between Sunni (the majority) and Shi'a Muslims. The former vest leadership in friends of the Prophet, and the latter in his family. There are many other divisions within Islam. (See appendices 1 and 2 for some important organizational features of Old World and American Islam mentioned in this essay.)

3

As Islam moved to new places and confronted older religions, Muslims conquered or coexisted with them and their non-Muslim adherents (Asad 1986; Bulliet 1994). Such regional interactions in the Middle East, Africa, Central Asia, South and Southeast Asia, China, and now North America have shaped the ways in which this decentralized and nonhierarchical religion is practiced throughout the world. The religion has no centralized clergy, and mosques operate independently of each other.

Thus, Muslims in the United States understand and practice Islam in ways strongly shaped by the American historical context. The umma, or universal Muslim community, may be the goal sought by Muslims, but the reality is that asabiyya, or group solidarity and experience, shapes their everyday lives. Muslims in the United States have been defined and redefined by voices both internal and external to Muslim communities. Those definitions reflect, among other things, the complex relations among members of the ruling class and those being ruled in the American political context. Situating Muslim communities in the socioeconomic structure of the United States is crucial to their analysis, as is tracing their transnational networks and affiliations.

Muslims now constitute an important part of North American society. Islam may be the fastest-growing religion in the United States, poised to displace Judaism and become second only to Christianity in number of adherents. Its growth is mainly due to the rapid influx of immigrants and their relatively high birthrate, but the number of African American, Euro-American, and Hispanic converts is increasing too. It is difficult to know exactly how many Muslims there are in the United States: in 1990 estimates ranged from 1.2 million to 4.6 million; in 1992 the American Muslim Council put the figure between 5 million and 8 million (Nu'man 1992, 11). The U.S. Census Bureau collects no information on religion, and there are no reliable nationwide surveys that can estimate the Muslim population comparable to those done by the National Jewish Population Survey.[1]

The American Muslim "community" at the turn of the twenty-first century is strikingly diverse, and the number of Muslims in various categories is debated. One attempt to categorize and count Muslim Americans (Nu'man 1992) put African Americans at 42 percent, South Asians at 24.4 percent, Arabs at 12.4 percent, Africans at 6.2 percent, Iranians at 3.6 percent, Southeast Asians at 2 percent, European Americans at 1.6 percent, and "others" at 5.4 percent. Another report (Ba-Yunus and Siddiqui 1999) put "Americans" at 30 percent, Arabs at 33 percent, and South Asians at 29 percent. There are also differences of belief and practice between Sunni and Shi'a, as well as among Shi'a groups like the Ithna 'Ashari (most Iranis) and the Nizari Isma'ilis (followers of the Aga Khan). There are those whose Islamic identity is contested, groups like the

Ahmadis and the Druze (Haddad and Smith 1993). Then there are the Sufis, whose charismatic Sunni and Shi'a leaders teach mystical strands of Islam; the Sufis in the United States are from very diverse backgrounds, and many are Euro-American converts (Hermansen 1997). (Appendix 1 gives some idea of the major divisions and groups among Muslims.)

The three largest American Muslim groups—African Americans, Arabs, and South Asians—are very different from each other. The identities of African Americans, who constitute a large percentage of the Muslims in the United States, have been historically shaped by race and class struggle. Although there were Muslims among the Africans brought to the United States as slaves, the religion did not survive slavery times. African American Muslim history starts again in the early twentieth century, when blacks migrating to the North encountered religions new to them and drew upon them to create alternatives to Christianity and white America. The largest immigrant groups are Arab Muslims and South Asian Muslims. The Arabs—coming from Lebanon, Syria, Palestine, Egypt, Iraq, Jordan, Morocco (and in smaller numbers from other North African states, Saudi Arabia, and various Persian Gulf states)—are far more diverse in terms of national histories and colonial pasts. Arabs have been coming to the United States since the late nineteenth century, but until the 1960s the majority were Christians. South Asian Muslims, from India, Pakistan, Bangladesh, and Afghanistan, have a largely shared subcontinental history, and most have come since the 1965 Immigration and Naturalization Act. While Arabic-speakers often dominate as imams, or clerics, in mosques and educational settings, South Asians have a higher socioeconomic profile and are arguably more privileged in American society.

African American Muslims

The first Muslim "immigrants" to the United States were African Muslim slaves (Diouf 1998; Austin 1997), but many accounts of Muslims in America either overlook them or do not put them first. Although at least 10 percent of the African slaves were Muslims (Austin 1984), they have been historically neglected most likely because "there is no evidence of any African Muslim slave family that survived slavery and maintained Islam as a way of life" (Nyang 1998, 10–11; but see Gomez 1994).[2]

In the early twentieth century, some African Americans learned about Islam and developed their own versions of it. We know less than we would like about the founders of these movements, Noble Drew Ali of the Moorish Science Temple in 1913 (Curtis 2002a, 47, questions this date) and W. D. Fard and Elijah Muhammad of the Nation of Islam (NOI) in 1930 (see appendix 2). These movements have been separatist ones and are best explained, not by the spread of Islam to the United States, but by American religious history and African American economic and social history, and particularly by contacts between blacks and immigrant Arabs in Detroit and elsewhere (Nance 2002).

The fascinating history of these early-twentieth-century African American Muslim movements is only now being set out clearly. These movements owed much to the dynamic pan-African movements at the turn of the century and to the 1893 World's Columbian Exposition in Chicago, which featured mosques and practicing Muslims as part of the exposition and the Parliament of Religions.[3] Furthermore, like movements in Turkey and Iran that blended Freemasonry with Islam, the Moorish Science Temple and the Nation of Islam both drew on Masonic and Shriner rituals, symbolism, and members (Allen 1998; Schmidt 1998, 37–40; Zarcone 2000; Dannin 2002a, 15–34; Curtis 2002a, 45). Noble Drew Ali wrote his own *Holy Koran*, drawing on esoteric texts published in the 1920s, while Elijah Muhammad became more familiar with "Old World" Islamic teachings and texts. Both movements rejected the Negro or slave identity: Noble Drew Ali declared that "Moorish Americans" were Asiatics, and Elijah Muhammad proclaimed his followers to be "Asiatic-Blacks" (Essien-Udom 1962, 34; Marsh 1984, 45; Curtis 2002a, 56–64).

The best intellectual histories of African American Islam are by Edward Allen Jr. (1998), Robert Dannin (2002a, 1996b), and Edward E. Curtis IV (2002a); along with Aminah Beverly McCloud (1995, 1996), Richard Brent Turner (1997), and Mattias Gardell (1996), they and others show that this group of Muslims differs from immigrant Muslims in many respects and is also differentiated internally. Islam for African Americans was part of the landscape opened up by migration from the South between World Wars I and II, and it offered new possibilities for racial and national identification. African American Muslim history is part of the broader development of black nationalism and the search for roots and for alternatives to white Christian America; this growing collective consciousness fueled the movements of Edward Blyden, Marcus Garvey, and many others. Curtis (2002a) illuminates the meanings of Islam to key African American Muslim leaders, tracing the tensions between particularistic and universalistic visions of Islam in the thinking of Noble Drew Ali, Elijah Muhammad, Malcolm X, Wallace D. Mohammed, and Louis Farrakhan. Dannin (2002a) traces specific communities and mosques in both urban and rural settings, highlighting the passionate strivings for new ways of life and the evolving versions of Islam.

African American Islamic movements had some early input from South Asian Muslim missionaries to the United States, particularly the Ahmadiyyas, or Ahmadis.[4] Ahmadi missionaries from India started the long process of drawing these movements closer to dominant Sunni traditions by providing English translations of the Qur'an to African American Muslims and teaching them about the five pillars of Islam in 1920; the Ahmadis published the first English-language Muslim newspaper in the United States in 1921. The Ahmadi expansion overseas was formative for Islam in Nigeria, Trinidad, and other places besides the United States, and its significance cannot be overestimated, although its influence has diminished as its Islamic status has been challenged.[5] In the United States, African American converts were largely unaffected by overseas opinions of the Ahmadis (Lincoln 1961, 221; Turner 1997, 109–46). However, the partnership between African Americans and Ahmadis was a strained one from the start (Dannin 2002a, 97–103), and the strains are greater now that recently arrived well-off Pakistanis are in the majority (Walbridge and Haneef 1999).

Issues of racism continue to be crucial to African American Muslims. Many leaders of African American Muslim communities developed anti-white versions of Islam, and Louis Farrakhan of the Nation of Islam is still widely perceived as representing that separatist tradition (Mamiya 1988).[6] Not only whites but even occasionally "Brother Moslems from the East" were barred from temples (Essien-Udom 1962, 184–85). Malcolm X was the first prominent leader of the Nation of Islam to reject the Nation's separatist or racist teachings after his 1964 pilgrimage to Mecca, after which he also rejected Elijah Muhammad's leadership (Malcolm X and Haley 1965). In the short time before his assassination in 1965, Malcolm turned to pan-Africanism rather than to Islam as a vehicle for black liberation (Curtis 2002a, 88–99). The Middle East would also play an important role in African American cultural politics from the 1950s to the 1970s (McAlister 2001, 84–124).

It was Elijah Muhammad's son, Wallace D. Mohammed, or Warith Deen Mohammed, who aligned the Nation of Islam with mainstream Sunni teachings after his father's death in 1975. He redefined beliefs about the divinity of W. D. Fard and the prophethood of Elijah Muhammad, enjoined his followers to pray five times daily, changed the Ramadan fast from the Christian Advent season to the lunar month of Ramadan, and allowed whites to join the Nation. He renamed the NOI temples masjids, or mosques, took the title of Imam instead of Minister (he has studied Arabic and Islamic law), and disbanded the Fruit of Islam security force. Yet he continued to claim the right to interpret Islam in view of the circumstances in which African Americans lived, focusing on specifically black issues (Curtis 2002a, 108).

W. D. Mohammed still leads the larger part of the former Nation, now renamed the American Society of Muslims. In 1977 Louis Farrakhan split with W. D. Mohammed, reviving and continuing the beliefs and practices of Elijah Muhammad. Minister Farrakhan's Nation of Islam constitutes a small percentage of African American Muslims, but his public image looms large. Farrakhan has announced that he is joining the Islamic mainstream, although what this means exactly remains to be seen.

Farrakhan and many other African American Muslims focus on America's inner-city black populations, working to establish economic self-sufficiency and eradicate drugs and crime. Major efforts are devoted to converting and supporting African Americans in the prison system. African Americans were 12 percent of the U.S. population in the late 1990s but constituted 41.2 percent of the jail and prison inmate population. American prisons have been a major recruiting ground for Islam (Dannin 2002a, 165–87). Even in 1920 the first Ahmadi missionary, Mufti Muhammad Sadiq, was jailed almost upon arrival. Taken into custody allegedly because his religion promoted polygamy, he won a few converts in jail. In 1992 in New York State, Muslims were 17 percent of the state prison population and over 30 percent of the African American prison population; in 2000, 32 percent of the African American prison population was Muslim (Lotfi 2001, 241–42; Dannin 1996b; Dannin 2002a, 166).

In fact, most converts to Islam in the United States are African American and male (Bagby, Perl, and Froehle 2001, 22). Because so many American black men have converted to Islam in prison, a special concern for many African American Muslims has been maintaining civil and religious rights within the prison system. The pioneering efforts of African American Muslims to secure the rights to pray, to receive the services of imams, to eat halal (Islamically slaughtered or prepared) food, and other religious rights in prisons have led to broader claims on American society by other Muslims in other arenas. Long-standing African American efforts to secure legal rights and access to societal resources thus have significantly benefited incoming immigrant Muslims (Moore 1995), yet the indigenous and immigrant communities confront major historical differences as they work together in the United States.

The African American Muslim communities remain quite distinctive (McCloud 1995; Allen 1998; Dannin 2002a). They often hold ambivalent or antagonistic views toward the U.S. government, Christianity, and other racial or ethnic groups, including Muslim immigrants. Because Islam is seen as a defense against racism, as a new and separate collective identity in the United States, many African American Muslims argue that asabiyya (group solidarity and experience) must be given priority over the umma (the universal Muslim community) at this stage in African American Muslim life. They do not readily accept the customs or authority of immigrant Muslims (McCloud 1995, 4–5, 10–11, conclusion; Turner 1997). African American Muslims—"new Muslims"—are engaged in self-definition and dislike being defined by the "new

Americans" or immigrants (Dannin 1996a, 159, 169). It remains to be seen whether the new but growing group of Hispanic or Latino converts will be equally distinctive.[7]

Arabs and Arab Muslims

The first Muslim immigrants who retained their religion in America came from the Greater Syria region of the declining Ottoman Empire, especially Lebanon, in the late nineteenth century. Part of an Arab immigrant group that was largely Christian in the early decades, their accounts emphasized religious persecution and lack of freedoms under Ottoman rule as well as economic stresses in the Mount Lebanon area. Most immigrants were relatively uneducated men of modest means, from rural areas; they found work in factories and mines and in peddling. Some sent for their families, and others married locally, founding Arabic-speaking communities across North America, with salient concentrations in major urban areas like New York, Chicago, Boston, and Detroit. Most probably viewed themselves as sojourners—temporary or economic migrants who would return home when conditions became more favorable (Abraham and Shryock 2000, 51–53).

But World War I and the restrictive National Origins Quota Act of 1924, which favored the immigration of northwestern Europeans to the United States, effectively separated many early Arab immigrants from their homelands. The First World War and the ending of the Ottoman Empire brought major changes to the homelands. Turkey, shorn of its empire, became a secular state under Mustafa Kemal Ataturk, who abolished in 1924 the Caliphate in Istanbul, that long-lasting symbol of pan-Islamic political authority. The new League of Nations sanctioned mandates in the Middle East, establishing European powers there. France, which already held North Africa, assumed control of Syria and Lebanon. Britain took over in Iraq, Palestine, and Transjordan; it already held Egypt. The Balfour Declaration of 1917 announced the future establishment of a Jewish homeland, Israel, which was duly carved out of predominantly Muslim Palestine in 1948.

In the United States, Christian and Muslim Arabs were initially viewed by outsiders as a single community—as "Turks" and later as "Arabs"— but they viewed themselves as Lebanese or Syrian-Lebanese. Both categorizations emphasized national origin rather than religion. Only after almost one hundred years did a division between Christian and Muslim Arabs become salient in the identity politics and the public, organizational life of the Arab community.

The scholarly literature reflects this shift, focusing first on Arabs and more recently on Muslims, but both labels are used, and sometimes confusingly. One periodization discusses two major waves of Arab immigration: from 1870 to World War II and from World War II to the present (Suleiman 1999, 1). Yvonne Haddad and Adair Lummis (1987, 13–14) propose a second periodization for all Muslim immigrants; they describe five waves of immigration, the first three of Arabs. In this second scheme, the first wave was from 1875 to 1912 and consisted mostly of uneducated, rural, young Arab men from Lebanon and present-day Syria. The second-wave immigrants, from 1918 to 1922, were mostly the Arab relatives of the first wave, although some urban people came as well. The third wave, from 1930 to 1938, was primarily made up of relatives of all the previous Arab immigrants. Muslims from not only the Arabic-speaking countries of the Middle East but South Asia, the Soviet Union, Eastern Europe, and other places immigrated in the fourth wave, from 1947 to 1960. Many in this fourth wave were urban elites seeking higher education and better opportunities, and many were refugees. The fifth wave began in 1967 in response to the U.S. Immigration and Naturalization Act of 1965, which reversed the historic preference for European immigrants. That immigration wave extends to the present and has included highly educated professionals as well as skilled and semiskilled workers.

Another periodization proposed for all Muslims sees three waves: two waves of Arabs from the late nineteenth century to World War II and from World War II to 1965, and then a third, post-1965 wave that has expanded to include sixty to one hundred nationalities (Lawrence 1999, 23). These wave breakdowns are based on the immigrants' relationship to religious practices. The first wave established some twenty mosques but was essentially concerned with preserving cultural values (Naff 1985, analyzed in Lawrence 1999, 23). The second wave, including some students and urban entrepreneurs, may have stimulated religious consciousness and mosque-building to some extent, but the third wave, with large numbers of women and children, did this far more. Also, the third wave took place in the midst of major international events: the 1967 Arab-Israeli War, an oil crisis in the Middle East, the fall of the Shah and Ayatollah Khomeini's triumph in Iran. These events increased religious consciousness and pressures toward orthodoxy among both new and old immigrants and also led to foreign sponsorship of activities in the United States (Lawrence 1999, 24–25).

It has been argued that the early Arab category was largely unremarked by the larger society (Naber 2000). Early scholarly writing either followed the "Arab" categorization or focused on the national-origin labels—Lebanese or Syrian-Lebanese—preferred by the people themselves (Abraham and Abraham 1983; Naff 1985). Arabs were treated in contradictory fashion in terms of eligibility for naturalized citizenship

(Samhan 1999; Joseph 1999). People from the Middle East were "white" in successive census racial classifications, but in 1910 the Census Bureau classified them as "Asiatic" by nativity. (Turkey, seat of the Ottoman Empire, was then called Asia Minor.) Arabs were twice denied citizenship and declared not to be "free white persons," in 1909 and 1914 (the latter case involved a "Syrian of Asiatic birth"), although both decisions were reversed on appeal. The second reversal on appeal came in 1923; ironically, this was the same year in which Asian Indians (including Muslims), previously deemed eligible as Caucasians, were declared "not white in the popular meaning of the term" and therefore ineligible for U.S. citizenship.

Large Arab American communities developed in Michigan as Arabic-speaking immigrants and refugees from many different places settled there. The ways in which Lebanese, Palestinian, Yemeni, Iraqi, and other Arabs are simultaneously "on the margins" and "in the mainstream" have been captured by Nabeel Abraham and Andrew Shryock in a comprehensive volume, *Arab Detroit* (2000, 27) (see especially Shryock 2000). The book is notable for its inclusion of poems and memoirs and its emphasis on "themes of imagination, transcendence, and personal growth." The volume shows Old World identities becoming "Arab American" ones as village politics gives way to multi-ethnic coalition politics, living in ethnic neighborhoods is superseded by living any-where, protective families become open families, religious conservatism turns into religious liberalism, and speaking mostly Arabic changes to speaking mostly English (Abraham and Shryock 2000, 22). Abraham (2000) traces changes over the decades in mosque discourses and prac-tices, from "isolationist" discourses and practices to "integrationist" or "American" ones, and sometimes back again. An interview with an immigrant husband and American-born wife (both of Lebanese ances-try) also points to the tensions between the two trends (Howell 2000a).

Interestingly, Shi'a from Lebanon and Iraq, minorities in the Arab world, are majorities in Arab Detroit. Liyakat Takim (2002) states that the Shi'a participated jointly with Sunnis in Detroit until the late 1930s, then established their own clubs; they finally established mosques in the 1960s. Abdo Elkholy (1966) also speaks of social clubs rather than mosques in his description of the scene in 1959.[8] Linda Walbridge (1997, 18–19 passim) describes the Shi'a in Dearborn at the end of the twentieth century, delin-eating class and national-origin differences that place the Lebanese eco-nomically above Palestinians and Yemenis. The newest arrivals, des-perately poor Shi'a refugees from Iraq after 1991, are embarking on the path traveled by earlier groups (but with variations; see Walbridge and Aziz 2000).

A national-level Arab American identity began to develop after Egypt's nationalization of the Suez Canal in 1956 (Elkholy 1966) and emerged strongly in the 1960s in reaction to the humiliating defeat of the Arabs in the 1967 Arab-Israeli War. The Association of Arab American University Graduates (AAUG) was founded that same year, and the National Association of Arab Americans (NAAA) followed in 1972. Both the American-Arab Anti-Discrimination Committee (ADC), founded in 1980, and the Arab American Institute (AAI), founded in 1985, undertook political and legal work supporting Arab Americans. The AAUG, after a long decline, ended in 2001, and the NAAA was merged into the ADC in the late 1990s. The ADC and the AAI now represent Arab Americans; Arab and Muslim cultural, religious, and political interactions with the American legal system continue to command special attention (Al-Hayani 1999; Moore 2002b).

A specifically Muslim identity, expressed in national organizations that transcended local mosques and communities of national origin, began to develop among Arabic-speaking Americans in the 1950s and 1960s (see appendix 2). This move was led by the earlier Lebanese immigrants and by newly arrived Muslim foreign students. The Federation of Islamic Associations (FIA) was formed by Lebanese immigrants in 1953, and the Muslim Students' Association (MSA) was formed by Muslim foreign students in American universities in 1963 (Haddad and Lummis 1987, 5; Muhammad 1984, 211). The FIA included Muslim associations in Canada as well as in the United States, and this broader North American base was adopted by the MSA as its student leaders graduated and formed the Islamic Society of North America (ISNA). The FIA, MSA, and ISNA were initially led by Muslims from Arabic-speaking backgrounds. Certain Arab American leaders were organizing as members of a specifically Muslim community by the 1980s, when Muslims had become the majority among Arab immigrants and many more Muslims had immigrated to the United States from around the world.

South Asian Muslims

Immigrants from British India, mostly peasants from the Punjab, began to arrive in the United States around 1900, but Asian immigration was stopped by federal legislation during and after World War I (the Barred Zone Act of 1917 and the National Origins Quota Act of 1924). The few Punjabi Muslims who came married primarily Mexican American women, as did their Sikh companions (Leonard 1992). In India, Mahatma Gandhi and Jawaharlal Nehru mobilized the people against colonial rule, but as Britain prepared to grant independence in the 1940s, the nationalist movement split along religious lines. Citing Muslim fears about living in a Hindu-majority India, Muhammad Ali Jinnah's Muslim League demanded a separate Muslim state consisting of Muslim-majority areas. Britain made this concession, granting independence to not one but two states, India and Pakistan, in 1947. Pakistan's western and eastern provinces were separated by one thousand miles of India, and although many Muslims migrated to Pakistan, India still had a very large Muslim minority (some 12 percent). Traumatic violence occurred along both frontiers between Pakistan and India at the time of partition, and the Muslim-majority state of Kashmir acceded to India, an outcome still contested by Pakistan.

In 1946, just one year before Indian and Pakistani independence, the United States enacted the Luce-Celler Act; extending citizenship through naturalization to Indians, this legislation was still limited by the quota system set in place in 1924 and so produced few new immigrants. Large numbers of Indian and Pakistani immigrants began arriving only after the major changes in U.S. immigration policy in 1965. Immigration statistics and the census show a sharp rise in the number immigrating from India and Pakistan in the late 1960s, from Bangladesh after 1970–1971 (when it split off from Pakistan), and from Afghanistan after the Soviets invaded it in 1979 (Leonard 1997, 171–73).

Despite the large numbers of incoming South Asian Muslims, scholarly studies of Muslims in the 1970s and 1980s still focused on Arabic-speaking Muslims based on the East Coast and in the Midwest. However, scholars who were documenting considerable adaptation on the part of the earlier Arab Muslims noticed a new group of highly educated Pakistanis in upstate New York. These immigrants stood out as the most "conservative" Muslims in beliefs and practices (Haddad and Lummis 1987, 30–33, 123–24, 127), and the shift in sources and numbers of Muslim immigrants seemed to signal an interruption in a pattern of Muslim "assimilation," or accommodation, to American society (see also Abraham and Abraham 1983, 1–3).

South Asian Muslims are no longer overlooked. They are probably the largest single group among American immigrant Muslims; almost all of the immigrants to the United States from Pakistan, Bangladesh, and Afghanistan, and perhaps 12 percent of those coming from India, are Muslim. (India's population is about 12 percent Muslim.) These immigrants can be seen as separate national-origin communities, given the political conflicts among them, but they constitute a single diasporic population in many ways. The United States is an important site of reconnection between these South Asians. They share memories of British colonialism, the partition, the birth of Bangladesh, and the Soviet invasion of Afghanistan. These historical events may be remembered and interpreted differently by the immigrants, and the ease of transnational travel and communication gives them little chance to forget divisive home-land politics, yet they do often come together, particularly in Muslim American religious and political arenas.

Another unifying factor is that the South Asian Muslims, like the new South Asian immigrants generally, are relatively homogeneous in terms of socioeconomic class. In the U.S. census, the immigrants from India (others do not have a separate census classification) indicate the characteristics of the broader group. (Eighty percent of American South Asians are from India and Pakistan, the former outnumbering the latter by about ten to one.) In 1990 Indian immigrants had the highest median household income, family income, and per capita income of any foreign-born group, and they also had the highest percentage with a bachelor's degree or higher and the highest percentage in managerial and professional fields (Leonard 1997, 77–78). Although appropriate nationwide statistics are not readily available, a careful study of southern California ethnic groups shows that Indians and Pakistanis are ahead of "Arabs" with respect to education, occupational level, and household income (Allen and Turner 1997, 57, 71, 135, 136).

Not surprisingly, these post-1965 Indian and Pakistani Muslim immigrants are conspicuous and powerful in American Muslim religious and political arenas. Most of them have been educated in the English language since childhood, and Muslim Indians, Pakistanis, Bangladeshis, and Afghans often have strong religious orientations.[9] Indian Muslims are accustomed to being a minority in a secular democracy, and to varying degrees, all South Asians come to the United States with experience in democratic politics, particularly student politics. In contrast, Muslims from most Middle Eastern countries have had little experience with democratic processes.

South Asians, like Arabs, have defied easy racial classification, and their placement has changed over time. Despite the setback in 1923 (when the U.S. Supreme Court classified them as nonwhite and ineligible for citizenship, a ruling that would not be reversed until passage of the Luce-Celler Act of 1946), South Asians in the United States today are often perceived as white (unlike South Asians in the United Kingdom and Canada). There is disagreement about this, and many South Asians either claim nonwhite status or feel that others perceive them as nonwhite, yet it is undeniable that some are often treated or classified as white. One indication is that Asian Indians are the least residentially clustered (that is, the least segregated from whites) in several studies (for example, Allen and Turner 1997, 231). Another indication of South Asians' white status was the controversy that arose among Indians when Indian businessmen claimed minority status for preferential purposes (Fornaro 1984, 28–32). Perhaps, as has been argued for American Jews, the persistence of racism in the United States and the presence of African Americans contribute to classifications of many South Asians as white (Boyarin and Boyarin 1997, xi).

South Asian immigrants are also frequently classified as "Asian American," an increasingly important pan-ethnic category in the United States. Asian Americans, commonly misperceived as a "model minority," are a rapidly rising proportion of the U.S. total population (they will become 8 percent by 2020), and Asian Indians are the third-largest Asian American group, after Chinese and Filipinos (Leonard 1997, 68–69). South Asians themselves, including Muslims, are often ambivalent about their self-placement or placement by others in this category, and the category sometimes expands to include West Asian and Middle Eastern Muslims—but more often it does not (but see Lawrence 2002, who argues for the expansion).

I turn now to the late-twentieth-century efforts by Muslim religious and political leaders to bring these diverse communities and histories closer together.

= Chapter 2 =

Converging Histories in the Late Twentieth Century

IF THE construction of the category of "Muslim" in the United States is relatively recent, the emergence of new religious and political spokespeople drawing American Muslims together at the end of the twentieth century is even more recent. The decision to become an American citizen orients new immigrants to the future of the United States and of Muslims as part of its body politic. As Muslim immigrants have become "new Americans," their consciousness of other Muslims in the United States has sharpened.

Some Muslims have organized on the basis of religion, bridging differences among Muslims. Arabic-speakers tend to have greater proficiency in Arabic and in fiqh and shari'a (jurisprudence and Islamic law), so they may dominate in many mosque functions and in teaching Arabic and the Qur'an. Muslim professionals immigrating from South Asia, however, have been instrumental in building local mosques and mobilizing Muslims on religious and political issues, both regionally and nationally. African American Muslim movements remain relatively isolated, although key leaders and communities have been increasingly involved in coalition-building.

Citizenship and Political Participation

Many post-1965 Muslim immigrants elected to stay in the United States and become citizens, joining the indigenous African American and long-settled Arab American Muslims and making efforts to work together as Muslims. A gradual shift from Arabic-speaking leadership of Muslim Americans to South Asian leadership—or at least to shared leadership—is suggested by appendix 2, which provides an overview of major institutions and organizations developed by American Muslims over the decades. Major Muslim American organizations have been sorted into three categories, based partly on chronology and partly on constituent populations and leaders. (The categories are not mutually exclusive.)[1] "African American Muslim Organizations" are major groups that developed indigenously without benefit of strong links to the historical Islamic world. "American Islamic Organizations" are chiefly groups of immigrants that emphasize religious education, spiritual regeneration, and da'wa (conversion or outreach) activities. Finally, "American Muslim Political Organizations" are also chiefly immigrant groups but ones that emphasize political rather than religious activities. These political organizations advocate the participation of Muslims in American electoral politics and are the most broadly based groups: they draw from not only the first two categories but from the "unmosqued." Haddad and Lummis (1987, 8) estimated that only 10 to 20 percent of American Muslims attend mosques regularly; while dated, their figure still serves as a baseline.

Vigorous organization-building at the end of the twentieth century changed the political goals, leadership, and sources of support within the emerging American Muslim community. These politicization efforts, which were based on the East Coast or in the Midwest, began with the founding of the Federation of Islamic Associations (FIA) and the Muslim Students' Association (MSA). Gradually the FIA was superseded by the growth of the MSA and its transition into the Islamic Society of North America (ISNA) in 1982. The ISNA today is a multipurpose umbrella organization that focuses on religious issues and publishes a bimonthly journal, *Islamic Horizons*.[2]

American scholars and the media contributed to the politicization of Muslims by highlighting overseas events in Muslim countries in the 1970s and 1980s. In the 1980s and 1990s media stereotyping changed markedly: negative images of Arabs were replaced by negative images of Muslims, a change that occurred simultaneously with changes in the social and political affiliations of large numbers of Arabs in the United States from secular-nationalist affiliations to religious ones (Cainkar 1999). Events abroad brought increasing numbers of Muslim refugees to the United States: Afghans after the Soviet invasion of Afghanistan in 1979, Lebanese after the civil war in the 1970s and Israeli invasions of Lebanon in 1982, and Iraqi Shi'a after the Persian Gulf War of 1990 to 1991. Also in the 1970s and 1980s, the continuing civil rights movement drew attention to the separatist groups within African American Islam. African American Muslims and immigrant Muslims continued to have little contact in the United States, but by the 1980s Arab sponsors abroad frequently worked with Wallace D. Mohammed of the Nation of Islam, choosing him to be America's "Muslim representative" on numerous occasions (Mohammed 1991).

Further political shifts occurred at the end of the twentieth century as the national-origin communities reached out to other Muslims and the American public. In the 1980s, abandoning a stance that had favored only temporary residence in the United States, immigrant Muslim leaders and organizations began advocating that Muslims take citizenship and participate in mainstream politics. National leaders had earlier opposed such participation, or given it only qualified support (see, for example, Khan 2002, 8–11). American Muslim discourse began to position Islam as a partner with Judaism and Christianity in the development of Western civilization, emphasizing the religious teachings and values shared by these three monotheistic religions and implicitly opposing the "clash of civilizations" thesis being formulated by Samuel Huntington (1993) and others. In establishing national offices with professional staffs, the American Muslim organizations instituted bureaucratic procedures and moved toward electoral and mass, rather than elite, politics.

In the 1990s South Asian Muslims assumed leadership positions in the newly organized American Muslim political coalitions, often taking over from Arab Americans and reinforcing the expansion of goals and audiences (Leonard 2002a). In 1988 the Muslim Public Affairs Council (MPAC) was established by the multi-ethnic Islamic center of Southern California in Los Angeles and began putting out *The Minaret* (Campo 1996). In northern California a year later, in 1989, the American Muslim Alliance (AMA) was established by a political scientist of Pakistani origin. On the East Coast the American Muslim Council (AMC) was established in 1990 in Washington, D.C., under Arab leadership, and in 1994 it was also Arab leaders who founded the Council on American-Islamic Relations (CAIR) in Washington, D.C. In 1999 these four organizations agreed to work together on occasion as the American Muslim Political Coordinating Council (AMPCC).

In the late 1990s American Muslim organizations began to move away from non-American Islamic influence and sources of funding. Saudi Arabia and some Persian Gulf states had been leading supporters of earlier Islamic activity in the United States; Egypt, Saudi Arabia, Iraq, and Pakistan were major funders, for instance, of the Islamic center in Washington, D.C., which opened in 1957 (Abdul-Rauf 1978). However, according to Akbar Muhammad (1984, 213), American Muslims were not "dependent on external aid or . . . controlled by their foreign donors." Conflicts among and within developing American Muslim organizations stemmed from politics outside the United States, such as Sunni-Shi'a differences heightened by the Iranian Revolution of 1979 and the Iran-Iraq War. Other conflicts involved the differences between the Salafiya or Wahhabi puritanical orthodox movement based in Saudi

Arabia and the Gulf states and the Ikhwan ul Muslimeen, or Muslim Brotherhood movement, based in Egypt (Poston 1992, 32; Johnson 1991, 111–24). Since the 1990–91 Gulf War and rising Islamophobia in the United States, American Muslims have increasingly minimized foreign funding and seen "outside interference" as unwelcome. In the late twentieth century, internal organizational conflicts have been increasingly focused on politics within the United States, many arising from tensions between modernizers and traditionalists (Taha 1987; Leonard, forthcoming a).

As immigrant Muslims built a firmer foundation in the United States, African American Muslims, especially those in W. D. Mohammed's American Society of Muslims, also strengthened their position in mainstream American politics and society. Indeed, they came to be nationally recognized. In 1991 Siraj Wahaj (the African American imam of Masjid al-Tawqa, the mosque in Brooklyn, New York) offered the first-ever Muslim invocation in the U.S. House of Representatives (see Smith 1999, 195–96), and a short time later W. D. Mohammed did the same in the Senate. The prominence of these and other indigenous or African American Muslim leaders is reflected in immigrant efforts to involve them in the new religious and political organizations.

At the opening of the twenty-first century the four leading American Muslim political organizations are the AMA, the AMC, MPAC, and CAIR. They engage in political lobbying and encourage Muslims to run for electoral office. The AMA and AMC were (in early 2000) led by South Asians, while MPAC and CAIR were led by Arabic-speakers; the AMPCC's initial leader was the AMA's leader, a Pakistani American academic. A smaller organization, the National Council on Islamic Affairs (NCIA), founded by an Arab Muslim activist in New York, merged into the AMA in early 2000. The then-head of the AMA and AMPCC, Dr. Agha Saeed (2000), said the merger marked "the beginning of a new phase of American Muslim politics, a phase of convergence and consolidation of organizations with similar agendas, and reflects the growing maturity of our community."

A landmark meeting of Arab and Muslim American organizations in early 2000 linked the venerable American-Arab Anti-Discrimination Committee (ADC) to the newer organizations, bringing together the four major Arab American and the five largest Muslim American organizations in Washington, D.C., to coordinate work on the future of Jerusalem, civil and human rights, participation in the electoral process, and inclusion in political structures.[3] As can be seen from this ordering of their priorities, those who dominate the major political organizations have emphasized foreign policy issues, such as Bosnia, Kosovo, Palestine, and Kashmir.

Even when, in 2000, the American Muslim groups mounted a coalition effort to swing the "Muslim vote" to the Republican presidential candidate, George W. Bush, foreign policy issues dominated their thinking. Supposing that Bush and his running mate, Richard Cheney, were more favorable toward Palestine and more negative toward the "secret evidence act" (provisions of the 1996 Antiterrorism and Effective Death Penalty Act, used primarily against Middle Easterners and Muslims; see Moore 1999) than were the Democrats Al Gore and Joseph Lieberman, national Muslim leaders swung their support to the Republican ticket. CAIR reported that 80 percent of Muslims it polled favored the independent candidate Ralph Nader (an Arab Christian of Lebanese descent), but Muslim American support shifted after Bush declared himself opposed to secret evidence in a debate with Gore in Michigan. The decisive meeting occurred on September 30, 2000, at the fifth annual national convention of the American Muslim Alliance, held in Irvine, California. Immigrant Muslims dominated this meeting; very few African American Muslims were present and their interests were not really considered. At both the Republican and Democratic national conventions in 2000, incidentally, Islamic prayers were offered for the first time (Khan 2002, 6–7), broadening the symbolic boundaries of America's civil religious culture.

Another way of reviewing the converging Muslim histories in the United States is by focusing on the characteristics and views of the leaders. As they rose to prominence at the end of the twentieth century, these new spokespeople attempted to define the community in ways that emphasized their own role and marginalized those other spokespeople and groups less like themselves. While some imams in mosques and scholars of fiqh (Islamic jurisprudence) in the United States continue to exemplify high standards of Islamic learning, many of those in leadership positions in mosques and in the increasingly powerful political coalitions are typically doctors, engineers, and other professionals. These are educated men (and in a few instances, women) without classical training in Islamic history and law, yet they are eager to understand their religion, and they see it as central to their modern identities. Richard Bulliet (1994), in his final chapter, perceptively and sympathetically discusses the efforts of such Muslims to interpret their faith.

These new spokespeople and their ambitions signal a wider role and mainstream audience for Islam in the United States. By "presenting Islamic doctrine and discourse in accessible, vernacular terms," they hope to reach a wider public and, to that end, have reframed Islamic discourse "in styles of reasoning and forms of argument that draw on wider, less exclusive or erudite bodies of knowledge" (Eickelman and Anderson 1999, 12). Professionals with educational qualifications in medicine, engineering, architecture, and business—the fields in which so many post-1965 Muslim immigrants to the United States have been trained— turn to their disciplines when explicating Islam (see, for example, Haider 1996, 37). Doctors and engineers are publishing short general books intended for English-reading Muslim and non-Muslim audiences (for example, Hassan Hathout 1995; Athar 1994; Maher Hathout 2002), and professionals and academics are reconfiguring Islamic financial practices (Maurer, forthcoming). These well-educated professionals are even being criticized for their leadership of mosques, characterized as having medical, business, or computer technology training rather than "knowledge and wisdom" (Abdullah 1998, 14).

The extent to which these new spokespeople actually involve those of Muslim heritage in religious and political movements is difficult to ascertain. Since the clergy and mosques have been decentralized for most of Islamic history, and since mosque-attenders are estimated to be a minority of American Muslims, neither religious nor political developments can be equated with what is going on in America's mosques. While "unmosqued" Muslims are presumably beyond the reach of imams and other mosque leaders, these more numerous and less observant Muslims are possibly being reached through the new political organizations and popular Muslim media by the new spokespeople, whom some call "professional Muslims" (Schmidt 1998, 189–93). All of these trends are reflected in the reinvigoration of Islamic discourse by the Western-educated spokespeople and the new media (the Internet in addition to print, radio, TV, and recording technologies).

Modern technology has reinforced the authority of the confident new spokespeople, who have little knowledge of the traditional Islamic legal schools and their rigorous methods of decisionmaking. Satisfied with their own more literal-minded readings of the Qur'an and hadith, they often oppose ijtihad (the interpretations reached by fiqh scholars), which would arguably encourage flexible adaptations to the American context and revitalize Islamic law and culture (Abou El Fadl 2001a, 1–42; Khan 2002, 84–86). It should also be noted that Sufism, the mystical strand of Islam, has been increasingly attacked and marginalized in the United States by the post-1965 immigrant professionals. Many professionals have been influenced by puritanical Islamic movements that rely on the Qur'an, hadith, and sunna (tradition), especially the Wahhabis from the Middle East and Deobandis from South Asia. (Deoband is a theological school in north India.)

These new American Muslim spokespeople are eager to learn about and control the boundaries of the American Muslim community. They are conducting national surveys of Muslims, defining their survey population as they do so. In April 2001, a highly publicized national survey of mosques was released through CAIR (Bagby, Perl, and Froehle 2001).[4] The survey deliberately omitted some Shi'a (the Isma'ili followers of the Aga Khan), as well as the Nation of Islam (Louis Farrakhan's group) and the Ahmadis.[5] Also significant was the survey's definition of a mosque as any organization that sponsored Friday prayers and other Islamic activities; thus included were many groups of young Muslims on campuses. But the survey failed to include the many largely African American Muslim groups in American prisons.

Boundaries were also drawn in the first systematic poll of American Muslims designed to cover participation in public life (Project MAPS 2002). Commissioned by Project MAPS (Muslims in the American Public Square), this poll was conducted by Zogby International in November and December 2001. This pioneering effort omitted Nation of Islam and Ahmadi mosques when selecting initial sites for local telephone books from which to select Muslim names. Then, when taking an additional sample of African American Muslims to compensate for their Anglo-American or non-Muslim surnames, the poll-takers weighted African Americans at 20 percent of the American Muslim population; many would consider this a serious underestimate. Probably to affirm the unity of all Muslims, the poll made no attempt to ascertain respondents' sectarian affiliations within Islam.[6]

Before September 11, 2001, the stance of the political leaders of American Islam was overwhelmingly optimistic; indeed, they envisioned a major role for Muslims in the United States. A physician from Pakistan wrote about religious and family values, stating that "Muslims believe in the same values for which this country [the United States] was founded. . . . They feel closer to the founding fathers than what America has become" (Athar 1994, 7). The African American Muslim leader W. D. Mohammed had already expressed such views in the 1980s (Curtis 2002a, 123–24). Indeed, American Muslims seemed destined to play a special role in leadership of the international Muslim umma. Murad Wilfried Hofman, an internationally known European convert to Islam, wrote that Muslims could make "an essential contribution to the healing of America" by becoming more visible and ceasing to "cast doubt on the compatibility of Islam, democracy and human rights." Furthermore, arguing that Muslims in North America had a "head start" over those in Europe since most already were citizens or were becoming citizens and could therefore participate in public life, Hofman (1999, 20–22) wrote: "Muslims all over the world are looking with high expectations toward the Ummah in the United States and Canada. Its dynamism, fresh approach, enlightened scholarship and sheer growth is their hope for an Islamic Renaissance worldwide. Perhaps the mujaddid of the 15th Islamic century and the second millennium of the common era will be an American Muslim, insha Allah." Mohommed A. Muqtedar Khan (1998a, 68), a young Indian American Muslim political scientist with a Ph.D. from Georgetown, wrote euphorically:

> But internally, [the United States] is the most Islamic state that has been operational in the last three hundred years. Internally, it is genuinely seeking to aspire to its ideals and the growing cultural, material and religious health of American Muslims is the best testimony to my claim. This debate, the existence of a Muslim public sphere where Muslims can think freely to revive and practice Islam is its gift to Muslims. [It is] something unavailable in most of the Muslim world.

Omer Bin Abdullah (1995, 27), a Pakistani American physician, echoed Khan's sentiments: "All that we need is unity among Muslims."

After September 11, 2001

The trajectory along which American Muslims were moving was changed dramatically by the events of September 11, 2001. The directions taken since that day have reversed earlier tendencies on the part of American Muslim political organizations to narrow the boundaries of the community and to emphasize foreign policy issues at the expense of domestic ones. These new directions reopen the boundaries and also draw more widely on the religion's rich, long-standing traditions of humanistic and legal scholarship. Importantly too, the new directions are being strongly shaped by non-Muslim politicians and the media in the United States. This new interaction between American Muslims and the state is drawing Muslims, perhaps paradoxically, more closely into national political life.

The murderous attacks on the Pentagon and the World Trade Center of September 11, 2001, and the growing evidence that the explosions had been triggered by Islamic extremists put American Muslims under the spotlight. President Bush began meeting with religious leaders almost immediately and visited the Islamic center mosque in Washington. A young American Muslim, Shaykh Hamza Yusuf, was one of six religious leaders, and the only Muslim, to meet with the president at the White House on September 20 to pray, sing "God Bless America," and endorse military action. Yusuf lamented that "Islam was hijacked on that September 11, 2001, on that plane as an innocent victim." A Euro-American convert with Sufi leanings, Yusuf held no office in national Muslim political organizations.   •

A clear pattern emerged as the White House and the American media learned more about Islam, Muslims, and American Muslims (for more details, see Leonard 2002b). The government and media looked for Muslim leaders who would "denounce fundamentalist hatemongering" and they found them, often outside the organized American Muslim political community. Those I have called the new spokespeople found themselves on the defensive as scholars, journalists, and others outside the Muslim political organizations freely offered comments and advice. Proclaiming their loyalty and tempering their previously strong and outspoken criticisms of U.S. foreign policy, American Muslim leaders were immediately confronted with the American bombing of Afghanistan, a worsening situation in Israel and Palestine, and continuing uncertainties about the next targets of the "war on terrorism."

Journalists, talk show hosts, and the like sought out moderate Muslims, urging them to speak up and to deplore and repudiate the violent acts and those who would justify them in any way. American-born Muslims and Muslim women were preferred over immigrant men. Oprah looked for Muslim "soccer moms" for her daytime television show and ended up with two immigrant women, an Arab and a Pakistani. A respected scholar, John Esposito from Georgetown's Center for Christian-Muslim Understanding, told American Muslims at a fund-raising banquet for CAIR in Los Angeles on October 6, 2001, that they had to put forward more women and young people who spoke unaccented American English to articulate their community's message. "Unless you tap the next generation, you are not going to make it through the next few months," he said, suggesting that, by using representatives who spoke English as Americans did, Muslims would not appear to be a predominantly foreign group. (Muslim organizations did not make conspicuous efforts to follow this advice, in my observation.)

Despite the media preference for American Muslims, African American Muslims were not prominent among those invited to speak out. W. D. Mohammed did speak out to his own followers, and his messages differed from those of immigrant Muslims. In the October 12, 2001, issue of his *Muslim Journal,* he talked of fighting and dying for the U.S. flag and the need to "claim your share of America." Earlier, on October 5, he had also advised women followers to avoid putting themselves unnecessarily in danger by their dress: "Sisters . . . should not be able to be distinguished from anybody else out on the street . . . [and should] stay in the house."

Strikingly, the American Muslims who commanded national attention immediately after September 11 were not drawn primarily from the ranks of leaders of national American Muslim organizations. The leading figure was Shaykh Hamza Yusuf. Born Mark Hanson, this codirector of the Zaytuna Institute in the San Francisco Bay Area converted to Islam at age seventeen. Widely traveled, he has studied with Islamic scholars in Algeria, Morocco, and Mauretania. Never centrally engaged in American Muslim political organizing (although often a featured speaker at national conventions), the Shaykh is a charismatic speaker with a rock-star-like following among second-generation American Muslims. He produces numerous, widely circulated video- and audio-cassettes, and his public appearances, often with other popular speakers like Siraj Wahaj, always generate enthusiastic audiences.

Yusuf's words about Islam having been hijacked were repeatedly quoted and paraphrased, and his views welcomed by the president, the media, and the American public. Young American Muslims, many of them already his fans, circulated by e-mail his interviews and speeches more than those of any other Muslim leader, especially his interview with Richard Scheinin in the *San Jose Mercury News* on September 16 in which he called the World Trade Center attackers "enemies of Islam" and "mass murderers, pure and simple":

> I think that the Muslims—and I really feel this strongly—have to reject the discourse of anger. Because there is a lot of anger in the Muslim . . . world about the oppressive conditions that many Muslims find themselves in. . . . We have to move to a higher moral ground, recognizing that the desire to blame others leads to anger and eventually to wrath, neither of which are rungs on a spiritual ladder to God. It's times like these that we really need to become introspective.

Answering the reporter's questions about the meanings of jihad, martyrdom, and suicide in Islam, he ended by saying, "If there are any martyrs in this affair it would certainly be those brave firefighters and police that went in there to save human lives and in that process lost their own." His words resonated widely with the American public.

In other newspaper, radio, and TV interviews, Yusuf stressed that contemporary spokespeople for Islam in the Middle East and the United States had studied (like the hijackers) sciences, medicine, and engineering rather than the humanities, philosophy, literature, and theology. He urged the Muslim world to stop blaming the West for its problems and to become introspective. He talked about oppressions in the Muslim world that were cultural, not Islamic, and of the advantages of living in the West, urging Muslims who were not happy there to leave. He was "fast becoming a world figure as Islam's most able theological critic of the suicide hijacking," according to Jack Sullivan in *The Guardian* on October 8, 2001. Sullivan asserted that "many Muslims find his views hard to stomach, but he is advising the White House on the current crisis." He also reported that Yusuf's detractors had dubbed him a "collaborator" and Bush's "pet Muslim."

Others called upon and cited in the mainstream media were Professor Ali Asani, Professor Khaled Abou El Fadl, Shaykh Muhammad Hisham Kabbani, and Professor Mohommed A. Muqtedar Khan. What these men had in common was their outsider or marginal status with respect to American Muslim coalition politics. Asani, an Islamic studies professor at Harvard and a member of the Aga Khan's Shi'a community (one of the groups excluded from the 2001 study of American mosques cosponsored by CAIR), criticized American Muslim spokespeople for using incendiary language in private while speaking of peace to the American public. He also praised American pluralism as essential to encouraging the true spirit of the Qur'an and undermining "exclusivist" and repressive versions of Islam. In an interview with Jake Tapper for *Salon* on September 26, 2001, Asani voiced a "general concern among Muslim intellectuals about how not only CAIR but some of these other organizations are claiming to speak in the name of the Muslim community, and how they're coming to be recognized by the government as spokespeople for the Muslim community in the U.S."

Khaled Abou El Fadl, holder of UCLA's chair in Islamic law, was already well known for his independent views (developed in three scholarly books), particularly his views about women in Islam and his long-standing criticisms of the science-trained new spokespeople. When the national and local media turned to him after September 11, he spoke of the "crumbling of the Islamic civilization [that] has removed the established institutions to seriously challenge the extremists." Quoted in the *Los Angeles Times* on September 24, 2001, he maintained that "extremist theology is a combustible brew of puritanism, ethical and moral irresponsibility and rampant apologetics."

An even more controversial figure within the American Muslim community, the Sufi Shaykh Muhammad Hisham Kabbani, found his American career resurrected after September 11, 2001. A representative in the United States of the powerful Naqshbandi-Haqqani Sufis based in Cyprus, Kabbani was one of those striving for ascendancy in American Muslim politics in the late 1990s. He had successfully presented an individualistic and moderate form of Islam to Americans and was aggressively "calling" Americans to Islam, from Euro-Americans to gang members in urban ghettos. In 1999, however, he had alienated the Sunni mainstream immigrant leaders by branding 80 percent of the American Muslim population "extremists" in a widely reproduced speech to the U.S. Secretary of State's Public Forum. After September 11, Shaykh Kabbani was "back in the spotlight as never before" as "the Muslim who dared to blow the whistle on his brethren."[7]

Mohommed A. Muqtedar Khan, a younger Indian-origin political scientist known for his enthusiastic modern views, had been trying to establish himself as a political philosopher. His forceful website essay after September 11, "A Memo to American Muslims" was immediately circulated by e-mail, quoted in newspaper editorials, and reprinted in many venues.[8]

> Muslims love to live in the U.S. but also love to hate it. . . . As an Indian Muslim, I know for sure that nowhere on earth, including India, will I get the same sense of dignity and respect that I have received in the U.S. . . . If . . . Sept. 11 had happened in India, the biggest democracy, thousands of Muslims would have been slaughtered in riots on mere suspicion and there would be another slaughter after confirmation. But in the U.S., bigotry and xenophobia has been kept in check by media and leaders. . . . It is time that we acknowledge that the freedoms we enjoy in the U.S. are more desirable to us than superficial solidarity with the Muslim world. If you disagree then prove it by packing your bags and going to whichever Muslim country you identify with.

The media blitz has produced a range of different reactions as PBS, NPR, and all of the commercial TV stations have taken hard and frequent looks at Islam and at American Muslims. Leaders of the Muslim political groups, like ISNA's vice president, Ingrid Mattson (a convert and a scholar of Islam), have had opportunities to speak out. Copies of the Qur'an have sold out in bookstores all over the United States, and many Islamic centers and mosques have held open houses. Some Muslims see an opportunity, citing the increased media time and contact with the government, while others see a major setback for Islam in the United States. Concern about profiling by religion and national origin has grown steadily, and younger American-born Muslims—like Asma Gull Hasan, whose book (2000) about growing up Muslim in the United States has a youthful following, and Altaf Husain, president of the MSA—are more ready to express outrage as they feel suspicion and discrimination directed against them (Schmidt 2002b).

With a wide range of reports and opinions being bandied about, the American Muslim organizational leaders tried to seize center stage—only to attract media attention to some of their earlier rhetoric critical of the United States and its foreign policy. Such rhetoric, designed for private and known audiences of cobelievers and intended to instill pride and a sense of mission, sounded very different when moved into the public arena and absorbed by a wider audience. American Muslim leaders had previously been reluctant to criticize certain Muslim governments, but many now found it possible to do so; at the same time, they tempered their words about the United States.[9] The 2001 convention of the AMA (the 2000 one had started the endorsement of Bush and Cheney) called for a more evenhanded approach to foreign affairs while expressing concern about potential civil rights abuses, and it had as its logo the Islamic crescent combined with the Stars and Stripes.

The new political spokespeople for Muslims in the United States have faced internal difficulties since September 11. With the U.S. bombing of Afghanistan and ongoing problems there and in the Middle East, they have faced concerns from community members about Afghan and other Muslim civilians and about America's broader war aims. Muslims previously uninvolved in political organizing have been galvanized into action; at least one new national organization, also led by doctors and other professionals, was formed to combat "extremism." A debate began about what is being said in American mosques, and by whom. Whose views were more "immoderate" before September 11—the "traditional," foreign-born imams employed in American mosques or the Western-educated members of the boards of directors that run the mosques? Some writers in community papers argued that the "moderate" members of the boards should hire only American-educated imams who are fluent in English and can talk to the media and to other Americans. Other writers have criticized the members of the boards of directors who employ the imams, arguing that such board members, educated in fields like medicine, engineering, and computers, have inadequate knowledge of Islam yet do not let the imams speak out (see Leonard 2002b). There is some agreement that the best plan would be to train young people in American schools to become both imams and board members. There has been no noticeable shift, however, to younger (or female) American Muslim leaders on the part of most American Muslim political organizations.

At the time of writing, the beginning of 2003, American Muslims and the leaders of American Muslim political organizations face many challenges. Most organizations have long had American citizens as officers and avoided foreign funding, yet they are resigned to setbacks while being "investigated." CAIR, MPAC, and other groups increasingly allege that the civil rights of Muslims and Arabs have been violated, and there clearly have been such violations. The political leaders are still competing with each other, as before, despite the formation of AMPCC.

The established political leaders are also competing with the newest spokespeople, men and women who have been largely selected by the media and the American public and who are often the very people the political leaders have attempted to marginalize in the past. These newly elevated coreligionists are not the builders of political movements; they both speak for and represent a wider range of Islam's sectarian, intellectual, artistic, and legal traditions than do the political spokespeople. There are pressures on the political spokespeople, even from their own followers, to broaden their constituencies to include more generations and put more emphasis on American values, training, and political issues. And most seriously, tensions between the goals of American Muslim political leaders and those of U.S. political leaders are certainly growing, even as both sets of leaders try hard, even desperately, to work together.

I return to the current predicament of American Muslims at the end of this book, relating it to the increasing polarization between religious conservatives and liberals in the United States and to the competing concepts of pluralism and cosmopolitanism in American multiculturalism (Wuthnow 1988; Hollinger 1995). But now, having sketched Muslim history in the United States in broad outline, let us look more closely at issues that call out for further research.

═══ Chapter 3 ═══

Historical Research Issues

T HREE sets of issues are most significant for further research and theory-building. First is the set of issues related to African American Muslims and their Islamic movements. Black Islamic legitimacy is often called into question by immigrant and other Muslims, yet they are a key group in the American context. Second, a survey of the many smaller national-origin and sectarian (non-Sunni) communities now establishing themselves in the United States opens up a wider range of interpretations of Islam and raises gender issues and questions about sources of religious authority. Finally, any discussion of the "unmosqued" or invisible Muslims must confront issues of identity and classification.

African American Muslim Histories

Empirical questions abound about the various African American Muslim movements, since the sources available come chiefly from within the movements or from the FBI (Curtis 2002a; Evanzz 1999). The origins of founding figures like W. D. Fard and Noble Drew Ali are still elusive, and the early years of the movements, particularly of the Moorish Science Temple, are poorly documented (but see Nance 2002). The field is highly politicized, and access has been difficult.[1] Some researchers who have amassed bodies of material are reportedly reluctant to publish it, since the "Islamic authenticity" of the movements might again be questioned.

Theorizing about how to anchor these movements in their American context, let alone a global Islamic context, has varied widely. Early scholars like E. U. Essien-Udom (1962) and the pioneer analyst of Black Muslims, C. Eric Lincoln (1961), related these movements to racial struggle and emphasized the shedding of names and habits derived from slavery. The racial theme has continued to be central; contemporary scholars stress, for instance, the disproportionate number of African American men involved with the American justice and prison system.

All of these movements can also be related to larger international or global movements, to the contemporary pan-African movements, and to early-twentieth-century esoteric religious syncretisms. Also clearly relevant were Christian missionary efforts in Africa and elsewhere, Ahmadi missionary efforts, the wide-ranging influences and counter-influences generated by interactions of the Masonic Orders with Turkish and Iranian Islamic movements, and the rising nationalisms in Asia and consciousness of them in the United States. More recently, African Americans have developed connections with Saudi and Persian Gulf Muslims, with African Muslims (particularly West African Sufis), and with Muslims in the Caribbean.

Although many accounts of African American Muslim movements are descriptive, the theoretical perspectives taken by researchers often reflect the scholarly conversations of their times. Clifton Marsh (1984, 3, 104) analyzed the Nation of Islam as a black nationalist social movement designed to alleviate African American socioeconomic problems and as a separatist movement growing out of conditions from 1914 to 1930 (World War I and the Depression), and he traced its transformation into a religious movement increasingly aligned with orthodox Islam. Martha Lee (1988, 2), focusing on the Nation of Islam as a millenarian movement, wrote of its cosmology: "At its core was millenarianism, the belief in an imminent, ultimate, collective, this-worldly, and total salvation" as the white world fell and the black millennium rose. At the same time, she saw that the Nation's economic efforts lifted the membership out of the lower class and fostered a sense of identity and political community. Lawrence Mamiya (1988, 202–3) saw the Moorish Science Temple and Nation of Islam movements as "new religious movements"; comparable to those in Japan, they arose at a time of general societal crisis and were produced by oppressed people whose needs had been largely ignored and who were looking for ultimate meaning, identity, and destiny.

At the turn of the twenty-first century, race, class, and gender concerns dominate much of the work on African American Muslims. The late C. Eric Lincoln highlighted the male bonding in the movements and pointed to Louis Farrakhan's ability to attract black middle-class men and others beyond his primarily urban, working-class, Muslim constituency. Lincoln also emphasized the special plight of young black men through alienation, criminalization, and incarceration (Lincoln 1996, 89–90, 124–28). Robert Dannin (2002a, 3–4; 2002b) focuses on black men as patriarchs, community-builders, and prison inmates; he also relates the conversion narratives he collected to both "up from slavery" and Islamic hijra (migration) narratives.

Looking at African American Muslims as those "who have not experienced Islam in the context of comprehensive institutional orthodoxies,"

Gregory Starrett (1999, 57, 59) shows how a W. D. Mohammed group in the Carolinas is developing a Muslim identity—constituting a body of knowledge and interpretive traditions—as households purchase religious media, books, and videotapes and share them with others in the mosque. As he says, these sources or communities of knowledge are often in competition with one another. Susan Palmer and Steve Luxton (1997), coming from literary criticism, see the charisma of the founder of the Ansaaru Allah community and his postmodern narrative strategies as responsible for the success of this new black nationalist religion. The Ansaaru Allah movement has global dimensions, with followers in Trinidad, England, and Canada, and it draws upon Israelite, Egyptian, and Nubian materials as well as Islamic ones; the analysis of Dwight York, the founder of a black nationalist new religion, and his followers as explorers of "postmodern blackness" is persuasive.

Echoing current scholarly concerns with the local and the global, Curtis (2002a) frames African American Muslim movements in tension with "Old World" Islam, in tension with the civil rights movement, and in tension with the Afrocentric movement as either particularistic or universalistic. Yusuf Nuruddin (1998) analyzes tensions among traditional Islam, Afrocentricity, and the American way. Louis DeCaro (1996, 169), in a religious biography of Malcolm X, feels that Lincoln's classic study of the Nation of Islam overestimated its religious legitimacy, while Herbert Berg (1998, 1999) tries to establish Elijah Muhammad as an interpreter of the Qur'an (mufassir). Melani McAlister (2001) analyzes the change from closeness to tension between African Americans and American Jews and the increasing salience of the Middle East and Islam to the construction of black identities. She relates these to the challenges to Christianity's Eurocentric heritage and links with imperialism posed by political events in the Middle East like the 1967 Arab-Israeli War. Other researchers pay less attention to such tensions by analyzing only a single movement or mosque. There are few transnational studies, although Dannin (2002a), Metcalf (1996), Walbridge and Haneef (1999), and Starrett (1999) include instances of transnational travel, communication, and interaction.

The scholarly focus has usually been on the leaders rather than the followers, and on men rather than on women. Men like Elijah Muhammad, Malcolm X, and Louis Farrakhan have thus received much attention as the builders of mosque-centered residential and economic communities in urban America. Ordinary African American Muslims, however, and their experiences with Islam are covered in two outstanding recent books. Robert Dannin's *Black Pilgrimage to Islam* (2002a) is a fascinating series of ethnographic reports, ranging from Cleveland, Ohio, to Brooklyn, New York, and from the rural community of Jabul Arabiyya in West

Valley, New York, to the New York State prison system. Dannin raises issues seldom written about among American Muslims of any background. In his discussion of gender and sexuality issues, he presents Naima Saif'ullah, a woman Islamically married and divorced four times and a municipal health outreach worker who helps her clients deal with sexual transmitted diseases. The other book, a collection of interviews by Steven Barboza (1994), brings to life both major and minor figures in African American Islam, including men and women involved in polygynous marriages. Barboza's compelling profile of Tarajee Abdur-Rahim highlights her efforts to deal with AIDS in the African American Muslim community (158–72).

Recently, there have been two notable cultural studies of African American Muslims. Edward Curtis (2002b) shows that Elijah Muhammad used Islamic ritual as a means of saving black men and women from emasculation, violation, and contamination. Jamillah Karim (forthcoming b) considers Islamic concepts of beauty by examining images of women in the magazine *Azizah*. Material on clothing the body Islamically, some of it advertisements, abounds in American Muslim journals and newspapers. These new research vistas recall other studies in American culture, such as Robin Kelley's (1994) study of Malcolm Little (later Malcolm X) and zoot suits, the lindy hop, and hep cultural lingo in post–World War II black cultural politics.

Historical material on African American Muslims is still being brought to light. As Michael Gomez (1994, 709–10) points out, both Noble Drew Ali and Elijah Muhammad were born during a time when Islam might still have been practiced by African-born Muslims. Such linkages, when discovered, can be theorized in different ways depending on a scholar's field, from religious studies to literature on social movements, immigrant adaptation, or transnationalism. The potential impact of such discoveries on the development of American Muslim popular culture could make African American Muslims an even more meaningful bridging community for immigrant Muslims.

The Smaller Immigrant Communities

The broad historical overview in chapter 1 of Muslims in the United States was organized along geographic and linguistic lines (American, Arab, South Asian), and it was also implicitly focused on Sunni Muslims, the dominant or mainstream tradition in Islam. Most studies of the smaller sectarian or national-origin Muslim communities in the United States are microlevel studies, and as Stewart Lawrence points out (1999, 26), among the many local case studies, few are comparative. Aminah Mohammad-Arif (2000, 193–210) has looked at the smaller groups in

New York City. There are many studies of some small, highly educated communities, but few studies of other small communities.

The historical story for the earlier Muslim immigrants to the United States was usually one of adaptation to or integration with American society. Today, by contrast, the increasing numbers and the prevalence of family migration have encouraged the development of separate sectarian or national-origin communities. Theoretical issues are thus grounded primarily in migration studies, religious studies, and the emerging field of transnational or global studies. The striking differences among these smaller communities emphasize the importance of context. What were the contexts in which such differences developed? Does the U.S. context encourage maintenance of these differences or does it encourage change? If change, in what direction?

Like those working with African American Muslim groups, scholars interested in these smaller sectarian or national-origin communities often justify their explicit emphasis on asabiyya rather than on movement toward an international Islamic community. For example, in the case of the majority Shi'a group, the Ithna 'Ashari, keeping apart from the Sunnis, Linda Walbridge (1999, 62) says, has preserved a rich religious tradition that would undoubtedly have to be compromised if the two groups were to join. She also points to the Ithna 'Ashari sense of well-being and collective mental health, based on preserving this distinctive community (Walbridge 1997, 202). Liyakat Takim (2002, 224), while stating that the increasing number of Shi'a has promoted fragmentation along ethnic, cultural, and even national lines, thinks that such "ethnicization" does provide different ways of adapting to the United States (2002, 224) and is therefore somewhat advantageous.

The Shi'a minority, thought to be some 15 percent of Muslims worldwide and 15 to 20 percent of Muslims in the United States (Takim 2002, 219; Smith 1999, 30), is represented in the United States by many quite distinct communities. They all relate themselves historically to the political split at Karbala in 680 C.E. with the Sunnis over the succession to the Caliphate; they all share a primary allegiance to the Prophet's descendants; and most of them are enjoined to pray three rather than five times a day. With the increasing number of immigrant Muslims, and of Shi'a among them, both written and oral sources agree that Shi'a separation from Sunnis has grown rather than diminished in the United States. As a minority in most Muslim countries, Shi'a had traditionally been allowed to practice taqiyya, or dissimulation and secrecy, to avoid persecution; that is, they could be Sunnis outwardly while privately following Shi'a practices. But in the United States, Shi'a communities need not do this. Many are very high-profile, have established separate mosques and organizations, and conspicuously observe Muharram. (For Shi'a, the month of Muharram is primarily one of mourning for Husain's martyrdom, and emotional majlises, or lamentation assemblies, are held in mosques and homes.)

Shi'a Muslims have a greater reverence for their leading religious scholars as representatives of divine authority and earthly guidance than do Sunnis (Sachedina 1988; Elkholy 1966, 78; Takim 2002, 220), and subsequent differences over succession to the leadership (Imamate) have produced further divisions among them. Most notable is that between "Twelver" (Ithna 'Ashari) and "Sevener" (Isma'ili) Shi'a (see appendix 1). The Twelver Shi'a believe that the twelfth Imam went into hiding in 873 C.E. but still guides his community through designated leaders and will reappear. Twelver or Ithna 'Ashari sacred places and religious schools are centered in Iraq and Iran. The Seveners split off in 765 C.E. over the issue of which son of the sixth Imam should become the seventh Imam; since they favored Isma'il, the first son, they are termed Isma'ilis. Some Isma'ilis are in the Middle East, but more are in South and Central Asia. Yet another branch of the Shi'a, the Zaydis, followed a son of the fourth Imam, Zayd, who contended for recognition as the fifth Imam. This branch was based in Yemen, and small groups also live in Syria, Lebanon, Iran, and Pakistan (Haddad and Smith 1993, 4). Also based in Yemen is the Ja'fari Shi'a school of law (named after the sixth Imam, before the split between the Twelvers and the Seveners).

The Ithna 'Ashari Shi'a immigrants from Iran, Iraq, and Lebanon interact in the United States in some ways and not in others. The Iraqis and Lebanese tend to share mosques and interact socially, while the Iranis, many of whom are not religious, remain separate. The religious schools in Iran and Iraq train mujtahids, or religious scholars, who are typically organized in a hierarchy, with a top-ranked marja' taqlid whose proclamations on law and ritual are authoritative. Maraji' are religious and judicial authorities, not state representatives, and followers give one-fifth of their savings to them as tithes. At any one time there may be several maraji' competing for followers. Ithna 'Ashari immigrants in the United States continue to recognize and follow contenders for the position of marja' taqlid, who in turn extend their teachings and authority overseas.[2]

The Ithna 'Ashari Shi'a constituted a U.S. Shi'a Council of Ulama in 1993 (but have not constituted a National Fiqh Council like that started by Sunnis through ISNA). The seventy-member Shi'a Council of Ulama has an executive committee that meets annually, and a regional council was formed in 1996 in the Washington, D.C., area, but neither council has strong leadership or funding (Takim 2002). This U.S. council recognizes the three leading maraji' figures: Ali Khamenei in Iran, Seyyed Muhammad Fadlallah in Lebanon, and Ayatollah Ali Sistani in Iraq. Khamenei represents the militant Hizbullah (Islamist) movement, and his followers are a minority in the United States. Fadlallah and Sistani represent the apolitical Da'wa (reform) movement started by Baqir as-Sadr in Iraq. (To some extent they also represent Abul Qasim Khui of Iran, who resided in Iraq for many years.) Walbridge (1999) shows that the followers' allegiances do not coincide with national origins.

There are competing new spokespeople among the Shi'a in the United States, as among the Sunnis. The well-educated and younger followers of Fadlallah in the United States are engineers and scientists who want rational, scientific explanations and ideas presented by their religious leaders in accessible language; they are not reluctant to challenge even a marja' taqlid with their own readings of the Qur'an (Walbridge 1999, 59–61). They sound like the new spokespeople described earlier, the builders of Muslim political coalitions in the United States. Yet the Shi'a are less active than Sunnis in such national coalition-building and inter-faith dialogues. Although Shi'a have traditionally become law-abiding citizens of the countries in which they live, they have been politically inactive because they deem all governments in the absence of the twelfth Imam to be illegitimate (Takim 2002, 225–27). Their nonparticipation also stems from the nature of the ordinary Shi'a ulama (clerics) in the United States. These specialists are largely imported and seldom conversant with English. A seminary set up in the United States in 1980 has not helped, since it continues to train ulama as though they were in Iran or Iraq. In contrast to these traditional religious leaders, Shi'a scholars in the United States such as Mahmud Ayoub, Abdulaziz Sachedina, and Seyyed Hossein Nasr are highly educated and speak about interpretations of Shi'a Islam that are relevant to American life, such as new ways of considering women's rights, relations between the ritually pure and the impure (non-Muslims), and pluralism (Takim 2002, 223).

Standing out from among the Sevener Shi'a are the Nizari Isma'ilis, followers of the Aga Khan. They alone (among all Shi'a in fact) recognize a living Imam, and they accord him a high degree of divine authority.[3] The transnational Nizari Isma'ili community, over 15 million people in some twenty-five countries worldwide (Williams 1988, 186), stands out in other ways as well. Its followers include speakers of Arabic in the Middle East, speakers of Persian or Tajik in northeast and central Asia, and speakers of Gujarati, Sindhi, and Punjabi in India and East Africa. The Indian branch is called Khojahs; once a Hindu caste, it was converted to Islam in medieval times by missionaries from Iran. These Nizaris retained both beliefs and practices associated with Hinduism: interpreting Ali, the Prophet's son-in-law and first Imam, as the tenth avatar of Vishnu (Asani 1987, 33); marrying endogamously; and continuing to observe Hindu customary law and marriage rituals. Isma'ilis and Sufis also share many beliefs, and at times they seem to have shared leaders.

Both Shi'a and Sufis see union with God as the ultimate goal of the spiritual life. In the nineteenth century Sufis claimed Isma'ili Imams as members of the Ni'matullah Sufi Order, while Isma'ilis claimed Shah Ni'matullah as an Isma'ili leader (da'i or pir) (Ruthven 1997, 374–76).

When political disturbances in Iran in the 1840s sent the Isma'ili Imam to Bombay, India, cases tried in the British Indian court system helped consolidate his authority and establish an Islamic as well as an Indian identity for the community. Yet the Nizari Isma'ili identity is an Islamic identity distinct from that of the Sunnis and also from that of the Ithna 'Ashari Shi'a (Asani 1987, 35–36; Williams 1988, 193–94; Ruthven 1997, 378–80). Emphasizing the inner spiritual teachings rather than ritual, Nizari Isma'ilis generally do not observe the month of fasting or practice the hajj (pilgrimage); since their Imam is alive, they do not observe the mourning period of Muharram either. They call their mosques jamatkhanas (meeting places), and nonmembers are not allowed to enter them. Their prayers are different from those of Sunnis and in India and East Africa (where many Nizari Isma'ili merchants and traders migrated) were conducted in Gujarati or Sindhi. Burial grounds, schools, and health clinics are separate from those of other Muslims, and the community contributes to such projects in addition to paying a tithe (once 10 percent, now 8 percent of earnings) to the Imam (Ruthven 1997, 382–91; Kassam-Remtulla 1999).

Having a living Imam whose word is authoritative has enabled these Isma'ilis to undertake flexible adaptations to changing conditions. Aga Khan III (1885–1957) urged followers to adapt to their host countries and to secure modern educations in English or French. Encouraging women to wear Western dress, pursue higher education, and become active in community institutions, he issued a firman (order) in 1899 that "in our Isma'ili faith women and men are exactly equal" (Ruthven 1997, 389). The institution of mut'a, or temporary marriage,[4] permissible among Ithna 'Ashari Shi'a, is not permitted among Nizari (or other) Isma'ilis. Isma'ili women must be present and sign their own marriage contract at their wedding. (Fathers often do this for other South Asian Muslim women, for example.)

Prince Karim Shah, Aga Khan IV, succeeded his grandfather as Imam in 1957 at the age of twenty. A student of Islamic history at Harvard, he now lives in Aiglemont, France, and is guiding his followers closer to mainstream Islam. Prayers are now in Arabic and selections from the Qur'an are included (changes made by Aga Khan III in the 1950s and strengthened by Aga Khan IV). In the jamatkhanas, the symbolic throne of the Imam has been removed, and only two pictures of the Imam are allowed (changes made by Aga Khan IV in the 1980s). The Institute for Isma'ili Studies in London promotes a standardized and increasingly

Islamic course of study for Isma'ili students.[5] Aga Khan IV continues to emphasize education and women's rights. The Aga Khan University in Karachi, Pakistan, the Aga Khan Foundation in Geneva, Switzerland, the Institute for Isma'ili Studies in London, and other Nizari Isma'ili institutions employ multinational staff of very high caliber. The community overall is highly educated, highly endogamous, and highly efficient in its international outreach efforts. Such efforts are directed primarily to community members—for example, in Pakistan's northern territories, and more recently in Afghanistan and Central Asia, where followers have come forward as the Soviet Union fell.

In the United States many of the more than forty thousand Nizari Isma'ilis are twice or thrice migrants, having moved from India or Pakistan to East Africa, Britain, or Canada, and then to the United States. In North America most are professionals and businesspeople who came from East Africa as refugees in the 1970s or from Pakistan (Nanji 1983, 157; Williams 1988, 187). The Aga Khan formulated a constitution for Nizari Isma'ilis in the United States in 1977, setting up a national council with an executive committee and regional councils, all run by well-educated professionals. Women have their own organizations but are also well represented in the broader structures.[6] In 1986 the Aga Khan introduced one constitution to govern all of his followers, replacing regionalism with a vision of a pan-Isma'ili global community. Significantly, a pioneering youth program for Muslim immigrant youth in the United States, designed with the support of the Aga Khan Foundation, is entitled "Al Ummah: An Experience in Islamic Living"; nowhere in the handbook is the designation "Nizari Isma'ili" mentioned, although the term "jamatkhana" is used once to designate the place of worship and the young men and women are pictured in shorts engaging in physical and artistic activities (Ross-Sheriff, Dhanidina, and Asani 1996).[7]

The Bohras are another Isma'ili group converted long ago from Hindu merchant castes; they are Gujarati-speakers, but their Gujarati-language religious texts are written in Arabic script and they claim to be more Islamized than the Khojahs (Engineer 1980, 161). The majority group is the Daudi Bohras. (Others, the Sulaymanis and Aliyas, seceded from the main group in the sixteenth and seventeenth centuries.) Not numerous but present in the United States, the Bohras are split internally over reforms that have been proposed by community leaders but are opposed by the priesthood in India. Issues raised by reformers include undue reverence to the da'i, or head of the community (he is not considered an Imam), and the tendency for the position to become hereditary. Reformers also object to a mandatory oath of allegiance and the payment of (extra or non-Islamic) taxes and tithes to the da'i. Unlike the Nizari Isma'ilis, the Bohras emphasize the hajj to Mecca but also pilgrimages to Kerbala and Najaf in Iraq (where the tombs of Imam Husain and Hazrat Ali are located (Engineer 1980, 156–63)).

The Druze, an eleventh-century split-off from the Sevener Shi'a, sometimes invoke the Shi'a taqiyya, or right to conceal one's faith and follow highly esoteric beliefs and practices. They believe in the virtual divinity of the then-Caliph and Imam Al Hakim (Ruthven 1997, 372), and they define jihad as purely spiritual in nature. Coming from the mountains of Lebanon and parts of Syria, these immigrants were a small part of the early Arab immigration. In the early years when Druze women were forbidden to leave Lebanon, some intermarriages occurred with American Christians. But the community became well organized and known as a highly endogamous and rather secretive community headed by the Shaykh al-'Aql in Lebanon and his representatives in North America. The Druze have long been regarded—and regarded themselves—as separate from other Muslims, even perhaps a separate religion (Haddad and Smith 1993, 34, 28–29, 23–24; Smith 1999, 64).[8] According to some, however, they increasingly claim a Muslim identity in the United States.

The Ahmadi missionaries from South Asia came in the 1920s and worked with African American Muslims, and there is now a sizable Ahmadi immigrant community in the United States. The messianic Ahmadiyya movement began in 1889 in colonial India in the Punjab, where Hindu revivalists, Muslim ulama, and Christian missionaries were contending for followers. It was founded by Mirza Ghulam Ahmad, who announced that he was the mahdi (the rightly guided leader from the Prophet's family whose arrival will establish God's just rule on earth). Accusations that he claimed to be a prophet himself, denied by at least some of his followers, persist and make the group's status as Muslims uncertain, since Muslims affirm Muhammad as the "seal of the Prophets," the last or final one. In many books and articles, Ghulam Ahmad developed distinctive beliefs (for example, he was opposed to jihad as holy war, and he taught that Jesus remained on earth and journeyed to Kashmir), and the community developed as an endogamous one centered on a particular village. Ghulam Ahmad's ancestors, for service to the Mughals and the Sikh Maharajas, had been rewarded with the village estate of Qadian; therefore the Ahmadis are sometimes termed Qadianis.[9]

Most Ahmadi immigrants have come from Pakistan, which declared in 1974 that Ahmadis were non-Muslims. Unable to call themselves Muslims or practice Islam in their homeland, well-educated, professional Ahmadi immigrants vigorously represent Islam in the United States but are often opposed by other post-1965 immigrants. Interactions between the new immigrants and the long-standing African American Ahmadis are also complicated by class, cultural, and racial differences.

The African American Ahmadi mosques were established in inner-city locations, but the immigrant Ahmadis often live in the suburbs and want mosques there. Ahmadi women play major roles within the mission (Haddad and Smith 1993, 72–73; Smith 1999, 73–75; Ahmed-Ghosh, forthcoming); however, compared to the often-single African American women in the established Ahmadi mosques, the immigrant women seem culturally conservative and constrained by traditional family roles. African American men and immigrant men do not work together easily, and the former are no longer prominent in the movement (Walbridge and Haneef 1999).

Sufis, followers of charismatic pirs (teachers) of mystical and meditative techniques, are becoming more numerous in the United States and are exceedingly difficult to classify. Sufism was and is an important part of Islam, represented among both Sunnis and Shi'a and spread throughout the Islamic world. Representing the romantic or mystical side of Islam, it invokes poetry, music, and dancing to achieve higher degrees of spiritual awareness and moral excellence, even a sense of union with the divine. As one well-known Sufi qawwali (song) put it in a Hindi movie from India in the 1970s, "Which is greater, the love of knowledge or the knowledge of love?" The Sufi answer is, of course, the latter. The American writer Peter Lamborn Wilson (1993, 7–8) invoked Jalaluddin Rumi, the thirteenth-century Persian poet and founder of the Mevlevi Order of dervishes (mystics, popularly known as "whirling dervishes") and his saying, "Wherever a caravan journeys, love is its Mecca," to convey the spirit of Sufism's "heterodox or even heretical moments."

Although many American Sufis are members of mystical orders rooted in the traditional Islamic world (see appendix 1), others come out of twentieth-century European and American syncretistic religious movements and may not even call themselves Muslims. The former tend to be led by immigrants and the latter by Euro-Americans who see Sufism as one way of reaching the universal truth that underlies all religions.[10] Marcia Hermansen (1997) calls the former movements "hybrids" and the latter "perennials."[11] Since the movements are many, the followers are usually small in number, and comparative or analytical work on them is lacking, I will point here to only a few major Sufi figures in the United States who teach Sufism as part of the Islamic tradition. (For "pop" Sufism and Euro-American movements with few links to Old World Islam or Muslims, see Wilson 1997 and Jervis 1997.)

In the United States, Sufi movements that require members to become formal Muslims, practice Islamic ritual, and observe some aspects of dress codes include the Bawa Muhaiyaddeen Fellowship (founded by a Sri Lankan Singhalese teacher in 1971) (Webb 1994), the Helveti-Jerrahi Order (brought by a Turkish Shaykh in 1980), and the Naqshbandi-

Haqqani Order (headed by Shaykh Nazim al-Kibrisi in Cyprus and, in the United States, by his son-in-law, Shaykh Muhammad Hisham Kabbani, discussed earlier as a post-9/11 figure). There are also Shi'i tariqas (orders) in the United States (Hermansen 1997, 164–65). In most of these cases, followers tend to be white, middle- and upper-middle-class Americans, although some immigrants and African Americans also join, and in all these cases traditional Islamic standards are "somewhat relaxed" because of "overriding Western cultural practice" (Hermansen 1997, 158; see also Hermansen, forthcoming b). Younger teachers with Sufi inclinations, like Shaykh Hamza Yusuf (see chapter 2) may themselves be Euro-American converts to Islam.

I turn now to communities of Muslim immigrants who represent major parts of world Islam but are still insignificant on the American Muslim scene. Most of these communities are distinctive because of their national origin rather than their sectarian affiliation. Many of these communities were started by foreign students, chiefly young men who stayed and married American non-Muslims. For example, one study (Nu'man 1992, 13) estimates that 5.1 percent of American Muslims are Muslims from Africa, but they come from many different countries. Perhaps only the Somali political refugees constitute a significant African Muslim presence (Nyang 2002, 255; Lindkvist 2002), although Sufi orders such as the Murids and Tijaniyya from West Africa have been attracting African Americans since the 1990s (Hermansen 1997, 156, 166; Dannin 2002a, 255–56). According to Victoria Ebin (1990, 27–28), the Murid movement is particularly attractive to African American women.

Some recent studies of West African Muslim immigrants see them as transnational and intercultural agents of global restructuring. Rosemary Coombe and Paul Stoller (1994) look at Songhay vendors from Niger, considering them less in their role as Muslims than as vendors of Malcolm X goods in Harlem. An "informal economy" study of the Wolof from Senegal who are peddlers, taxi drivers, and laborers in New York City again sees these migrants as filling an economic niche in the United States (Perry 1997). They are from two Sufi orders often in conflict at home, the Murids and Tijaniyyas, but in the United States the Wolof present a united front.[12] Zain Abdullah (forthcoming) looks at West African Muslims in New York and their interactions with other Muslims in the city. Joann D'Alisera (2001) analyzes Muslims from Sierra Leone who are taxi drivers and food vendors, the latter usually women, in Washington, D.C., with some attention to their Muslim identity. The Sierra Leoneans, while finding themselves practicing Islam differently than advocated by some other Muslims in the city, displayed items that proclaimed their Muslim identity in the belief that mainstream Americans would value religious people—at least this was their view before September 11, 2001.

Indonesians, from the largest Muslim country in the world in terms of population, and Malaysians, from an important and successfully modernizing Southeast Asian Muslim country, are not yet numerous in the United States and have hardly been studied (They form part of the 2 percent, Southeast Asian, category; Nu'man 1992, 13.) Muslims from Bosnia, Kosovo, Central Asia, and northwestern China have attracted public notice largely for political reasons, but again they have not been studied. The small Indo-Chinese population of Chams in Seattle is barely mentioned (Adeney and DeMaster 1994, 196, 201–3). Albanian Muslims, from the only European Muslim-majority country, were part of the early Ottoman immigrant population in the Dearborn-Detroit area, where they established both a Sunni mosque and a Bektashi Sufi tekke, or retreat. Frances Trix (1994) deftly shows the ways in which these institutions and their Albanian members and leaders have changed over time in the American context, reflecting both Albanian nationalism and Albanian regionalism.

Few Muslims have settled in rural America, although because no one has studied the distribution of post-1965 immigrant doctors in rural areas, their numbers may be larger than suspected (Syed Ali, personal communication, 2002). Jonathan Friedlander's (1994) studies of Yemeni agricultural workers in California's Central Valley trace these male sojourners of the 1950s. Most went back to Yemen, but some settled down and married Hispanic women; by the late 1970s, others had brought their families. The story here is similar to that of the early Punjabi Muslims in California, with intermarriage and adaptation in the early decades and then changes in the direction of the homeland religion and culture as the population increased (Leonard 1992). More recently, Friedlander (2000) reported that tentative attendance by Delano Yemenis at a Bakersfield multi-ethnic mosque has stopped, and the Yemenis are building their own mosque closer to home. Through powerful photographs and text, he shows the earlier and basically ethnic identity of California's rural Yemeni farmworkers changing as they build a mosque and become "more religious."

Finally, much information about smaller Muslim communities, both immigrant and indigenous, can be found in studies of particular U.S. localities or regions (for a summary, see appendix 3). Many of these studies reveal details of interaction or lack of interaction among Muslims and other members of the localities. Then there are small but growing numbers of indigenous Latino and Native American converts (Smith 1999, 66–68) who might or might not form communities of their own. Newspaper stories on these converts are available, but I know of no scholarly studies.

The "Unmosqued" and
Other Invisible Muslims

The U.S. census does not have a question about religion, but this "invisible Muslim" category is surely a large one. It includes Muslims who are not affiliated with Islamic religious institutions and organizations; since Muslims need not go to a mosque to pray, some of these may be religious but practice privately. It includes Muslims by birth or lineage who have become nonreligious or who do not identify themselves primarily by their religion. It is likely that many descendants of early immigrants, and particularly of those who married non-Muslims, fall into this category, since historical studies frequently found conversion to Christianity or a falling away from Islam occurring among the early Muslim immigrants and their families.[13] There are undoubtedly many individuals of Muslim background who do not mark themselves by wearing a beard or the hijab (head scarf) but who proudly identify with Islamic civilization and culture or with the ethnic or national cultures of their ancestors.

No one is sure how many Muslims in the United States either do not go to mosques or go to them rarely. The most-quoted estimate is 80 to 90 percent (Haddad and Lummis 1987, 8), but this figure is controversial: many Muslims think mosque-attenders are a higher percentage today.[14] Most scholars have concentrated on mosque populations, using mosques as entry points for research on Muslims. This is true even of surveys intended to give a broader picture of America's Muslim population (Lovell 1983, 93; Ba-Yunus and Siddiqui 1999, 36). Stewart Lawrence (1999) pointed to the lack of large-scale survey research that would capture Muslims not affiliated with mosques, yet the "first systematic American Muslim poll" in the fall of 2001 also sought interviewees in the vicinities of mosques and Islamic centers (Bukhari 2002).[15]

There is a definite need to survey the broader Muslim population, partly to ascertain regional differences within the United States. Yvonne Haddad and Adair Lummis (1987) carried out a pioneering study of religious attitudes, concentrating on five mosques.[16] They did not include Muslim populations in three important national centers: New York, Chicago, and Los Angeles. Moreover, their commitment to keep even the mosque names and locations confidential lessens the continuing usefulness of the results. Attempting to compensate for the omission of the West Coast in the earlier study, Kambiz GhaneaBassiri (1997, 13–15, 18, 115–16) did a survey of Muslims in Los Angeles in 1993–94, including African American Muslims. He distributed surveys chiefly at mosques, Islamic centers, and Islamic organizations and obtained 143 responses. His informants were 22 percent Iranian, 17 percent Pakistani, 17 percent

Arab, 15 percent African American, 10 percent Indian, and under 5 percent Indian, Turkish, and other. Like Haddad and Lummis (1987), he found that Muslims who dined with non-Muslims were more assimilated, and that the Pakistanis were often the most conservative; for example, Pakistani men and women often followed an Islamic dress code. But this was a nonrandom survey.

Attempts to survey Muslim populations in the United States have almost always encountered difficulties, from low rates of questionnaire return to lack of trust on the part of potential respondents (Haddad and Lummis 1987, 9–11; Poston 1992, 161; Walbridge and Haneef 1999, 129). The mosque survey sponsored in 2000 by leading Muslim organizations telephoned respondents, although the survey was conducted by mail among other congregations (Bagby, Perl, and Froehle 2001). The telephoning, however, presumably increased its randomness and reliability.

There are two national-origin populations of American Muslims that are more secular than religious: the Iranians and the Turks, set in one count at 3.6 percent and 2.4 percent, respectively (Nu'man 1992, 13). Both groups come from nations that underwent anti-Islamic modernization campaigns (under the Shah in Iran and Ataturk in Turkey). Their identities are rooted in their proud civilizational or cultural heritages, which are, of course, quite distinct from each other. The Iranians are Ithna 'Ashari Shi'a; the Turks are Sunni and Sufi in orientation. American immigrant populations of Iranians and Turks continue to reflect the long-standing historical tensions among these (and Arab and South Asian) Old World Muslim populations. Memories of the Safavids in Iran, the Ottomans in Turkey, and the Mughals in India—empires that arose in the eighteenth century and became major, competing world empires—remain strong.

Most Muslim Iranian immigrants came to the United States after 1979, fleeing the Iranian Revolution eventually consolidated under Ayatollah Khomeini in Iran, and they are secular people. A sociological survey showed that only 5 percent are religiously observant "always and often" and that 95 percent are "occasionally and never" observant (Bozorgmehr 1997, 398; see also Bozorgmehr and Sabagh, forthcoming). Like the Arabs earlier, Iranians of different religions see themselves more as a national-origin community (Sabagh and Bozorgmehr 1994). Ironically, other Americans probably see the Iranians as Islamic fundamentalists, or Islamists, because of media treatment of the 1979 revolution. It should be noted that the Iranian Revolution and its call for social justice for the oppressed is credited with inspiring some African American Muslims to become Shi'a (Sachedina 1994, 10; Kelley 1994, 157).

Studies of Iranians focus chiefly on the large numbers in California, as well as on their culture and ethnic entrepreneurship rather than their religion.[17] An important book about Muslim, Jewish, Armenian, Baha'i, Assyrian, Zoroastrian, and Kurdish Iranians in Los Angeles, *Irangeles,* edited by Ron Kelley and Jonathan Friedlander (1993), includes interviews and photographs as well as early articles by many scholars who have written extensively on this population, including Medhi Bozorgmehr, Georges Sabagh, Hamid Naficy, Arlene Dallalfar, and Kelley himself. A comparative overview (Bozorgmehr, Sabagh, and Der-Martirosian 1993, 82–86, 79) mentions some religious Muslims but states that "Iranian Muslims, given their strong identification with nationality rather than religion, are unlikely ever to become integrated into the non-Iranian Muslim community in Los Angeles." This is a "comfortable" if not wealthy Iranian community (Kelley 1993b, 250; see also Bozorgmehr and Sabagh 1988). Mary Elaine Hegland (1999, forthcoming) focuses on Iranian women in northern California and their difficult transitions to life in the United States.

The popular culture of Iranian exiles has attracted notice because of its abundance and vital relationship with mainstream American culture; the leading scholar here is Hamid Naficy (1993a, 1993b, 1998). Since 1980 Iranians have published at least eighty periodicals in Los Angeles alone, most but not all in the Persian language. They have also produced dozens of Iranian television programs, radio programs, films, music videos, and theatrical and musical performances. Almost all of these productions are secular in nature, opposed to the Islamic government in Iran, and intended to consolidate and maintain Iranian ethnic and national identity. Naficy (1993a, 360) concludes, however, that American "national popular culture tends to co-opt the ethnic and exilic subcultures."

There are few studies of Muslims from Turkey, perhaps the "most secularized" Muslim immigrants in the United States (Poston 1992, 29). Barbara Bilge (1996, 100–1, 102) has studied pre-1965 immigrants from Turkey, who tended to be either male students or professional military men who came for training after Turkey entered NATO. Many of these men married non-Muslim women; Bilge traced thirty-three such marriages over time. She carefully situated the men in a secular, nationalistic Turkey that at the time (as it still does today) suppressed Islamic movements, and the women in the United States just before a second wave of feminism rose. She found that affluent and working-class couples were more compatible than those in the ex-military group. She then found that Turkish cultural identity was most successfully transferred to the children of the affluent couples. She called the affluent Turks, chiefly doctors, "preadapted to life in America" by their schooling and ambitions and a "brain drain" (albeit a small one then) from Turkey, an insight perhaps applicable to many of the post-1965 Muslim professionals immigrating from other countries. Bilge (1994), in another, fuller study, focused on the Turkish voluntary associations in metropolitan Detroit and covered the history of the community, including information about housing, burial, and charitable societies, coffeehouses, orchestras, and Mevlevi and Bektashi dervish orders.

Kurdish immigrants from Iran, Turkey, and Iraq, most but not all of them Shi'a Muslims, have also come to the United States. Most Iranian Kurds are settled in the Los Angeles area, and most Iraqis are in San Diego. All three Kurdish populations speak Kurdish, but the three dialects are so heavily influenced by Persian, Turkish, and Arabic that they communicate in English. The Kurdish Shi'a women wear bright clothing, and there are no injunctions against their dancing in public (Kelley 1993a, 156–57). Their degree of religiosity is unknown, since they are not singled out in studies of Iranian or other Muslims.

Then there are many American Muslims self-defined as secular. Many religious Muslims do not accept the usage "secular Muslim," maintaining that it is an oxymoron. In my view, this is a deliberate attempt at erasure, and one that undoubtedly contributes to the invisibility of an important part of the American Muslim population. These secular Muslims do take pride in the high achievements of Islamic civilizations but do not identify themselves primarily through their religious heritage. For example, C. M. Naim (1995), an Indian American professor of Urdu and South Asian studies at the University of Chicago, writes movingly about the way he, a naturalized American, is often viewed and treated as a representative of a people, as an Indian, and more specifically, as an Indian Muslim. He evokes various aspects of his identity that are meaningful to him: his Indian homeland, its arts and architecture; his mother tongue; India's many and intertwined religions. Reminding us that immigrant-built religious institutions in the United States (in this case, Muslim mosques, Hindu temples, and Sikh gurdwaras) are new, without historical relationships to their localities or to each other, he questions the essentialization of religion and of religious identity that seems to be growing along with these institutions.

Many secular Muslims, like Naim, now have a heightened concern with Islam, a concern induced by identity politics in the United States and the politics of contemporary globalization. Sara Suleri (1992, 219), a Pakistani American professor of English at Yale, saw Salman Rushdie's novel *The Satanic Verses* (which led to the fatwa from Iran calling for his death in 1989) as a turning point for secular Muslims. Commenting on Rushdie's sudden (and brief) embrace of Islam in an afterword directed to him, she says: "We . . . were equally impatient with your earlier claims that you were *not* a Muslim as with your current declaration that you *are*. . . . Perhaps you have not realized that the Rushdie crisis forced many cultural immigrants like yourself finally to claim that they were Muslim."

These nonbelievers (they may be agnostics or atheists) often support pro-reform positions on behalf of believers. The argument, well made by Akeel Bilgrami (1993), is that both secular Muslims and devout Muslim moderates should oppose Islamists because of a fundamental commitment to an authentic self, a Muslim identity but one without a functional religious role. Rather, the identity serves other functions, such as defense against the "domineering colonial or post-colonial contempt" for Muslim culture. Instead of simply reacting defensively, Bilgrami urges moderate Muslims to become active agents in the reinterpretation of Islam: "It will prove to be the final victory for imperialism that after all the other humiliations it has visited upon Muslims, it lingered in our psyches in the form of *genuine self-understanding* to make self-criticism and free, unreactive agency impossible" (293, Bilgrami's emphasis).

By moving beyond the historical overview of the major Muslim groups in the United States to discuss distinctive research issues raised by African American Muslim movements, the many smaller national-origin and sectarian Muslim communities, and the unknown numbers of secular Muslims in as much detail as authoritative sources permitted, we now have a greater grasp of the differences among Muslims. Muslims from the "heartland" or Old World settings and from the United States itself are coming together in this country, and their efforts to work together can now be better appreciated. Also, all of the historical materials can now be drawn upon comparatively and analytically to discuss contemporary research issues in the following chapters.

═ PART II ═

CONTEMPORARY RESEARCH ISSUES

Chapter 4

Contemporary American
Muslim Identities

I N THIS chapter, I discuss the range of Muslim identities and affiliations
in the U.S. context and interactions among them. The American context now assumes greater importance in our story of Muslims. "All
identity is constructed across difference," wrote Stuart Hall (1987, 45),
and the configurations of sameness and difference in the United States
have important implications for American Muslims. The national white-
dominated version of cultural pluralism extends equal rights to immigrants as citizens and to ethnic communities without expecting them to
give up their "difference." Bourgeois law, argue Jane Collier, Bill Maurer,
and Liliana Suarez-Navaz (1997), constitutes people as equal before the
law but necessarily different in other spheres of their lives. The national
vision of cultural pluralism is the liberal legal vision that people not
only do not have to give up their differences but are expected to have
and maintain differences. In fact, as David Hollinger (1995) pointed out,
American concepts of multiculturalism have emphasized pluralism (re-
specting inherited boundaries and preserving ethno-racial groups) more
than cosmopolitanism (promoting multiple, changing identities and
favoring voluntary affiliations). Cultural diversity is taken for granted
and often celebrated, yet there is a laissez-faire approach to the maintenance of ethnic cultures along with a strong emphasis on individualism.
People must mobilize themselves to create and police ethnic or communal boundaries (Leonard 2000), and some American Muslims have been
doing just that.

As we have seen, however, there is more than one Muslim identity.
Muslim identities, like other identities, are characterized by instability,
construction in context, and reinterpretations of the past in the present
(Hall 1988, 1989). An American Muslim political scientist has added a
postmodern political identity to what he sees as the two traditional ingredients of Islamic pluralism: asabiyya (ethnicity) and the schools of fiqh

(jurisprudence) (Khan 1998b, 108): "Muslim society has not escaped the effects of post-modernity, [so] it too now manifests identity politics." In the North American context, Muslim individual and collective identities can draw upon national origin, language, ethnicity, sectarian affiliation, race, and/or class, and all of these can be crosscut by generation, gender, and sexuality.

Like other Americans, Muslim Americans probably display regional differences within the United States. Religious studies scholars have done some comparisons of regional differences among Christians and Jews (Tweed 1997, 11–12; Wuthnow 1988, 84–85). This is an unexplored topic for Muslims in the United States, perhaps because resistance to the concept of an emerging American Islam remains strong. One estimate places 20 percent of the U.S. Muslim population in California and another 16 percent in New York, with no other state having more than 10 percent (Nu'man 1992, 15). The obvious hypothesis would contrast East Coast, Midwest, and West Coast Muslims and predict greater changes in the postmodern direction on the California end of the continuum. Such predicted changes would be in line with those found in the general population by sociologists and historians of the family, using measures of individualism such as naming patterns that deviate from ancestral ones, marriages out of birth order and across racial, ethnic, and religious boundaries, and high numbers of widows living alone. Such measures also factor into generation, gender, and sexuality issues.

National Origins, Languages, and Sectarian Movements

Muslims in North America come from every part of the world, and although variables such as national origin, language, and sectarian community membership are not neatly correlated, scholars have often overlooked the complex effects of their combination. Muslim immigrants from any one country may represent more than one branch of Islam, and sometimes one group is fleeing from another (the Ahmadis from Pakistan, the Iraqi Shi'a from the ruling Sunnis). Muslim immigrants from any one sect or movement may come from more than one country, and sometimes they have a common language (the Nizari Isma'ilis)[1] and sometimes they do not (the Kurdish Shi'a). National-origin categories very often include more than Muslims and can encompass several languages. (Iranians and Indians of many religions have immigrated to the United States, and further, Indian Muslims can be native speakers of Urdu, Tamil, Malayalam, or other Indian vernaculars.)

The coalition-building efforts under way among American Muslims have involved structural and ideological linkages among groups of different national origins. Political scientists interested in American Muslim politics are few and typically look only at one national-origin group—for example, Arabs (but see Johnson 1991). National-origin politics does intrude into American Muslim politics (Leonard 2002b; Khan 2002), and there is a tension between the "diasporic" perspective and the "claiming America" view, a tension analyzed in Asian American studies (Wong 1995). In that field, the "claiming America" view focuses on the struggles of the early Asian immigrants (Chinese, Japanese, Korean, and Asian Indian), and the "diasporic" view focuses on the large numbers of post-1965 immigrants from Vietnam, Korea, the Philippines, Thailand, and other countries in South and Southeast Asia and their continuing relations with their homelands. The analogy in American Muslim studies, to my mind, would be between the long-established immigrant and indigenous Muslim communities and the post-1965 immigrants. Khan (2002) sees it slightly differently, analyzing contrasting commitments to American politics or foreign politics without respect to generations and terming those focused on foreign politics "isolationist," not "diasporic." However, for young American Muslims, the future more than the (diasporic) past shapes even their efforts to define and defend an Islamic world well beyond the United States, while "claiming America" might mean, for some among the upwardly mobile and confident new immigrants, redeeming it through conversion to Islam.

Analyses of African American Islam reflect this tension between the "claiming America" view and the "diasporic" perspective, sometimes even within a single analysis. W. E. B. Du Bois first emphasized this dualism, or "nation within a nation," aspect of African American thought (Essien-Udom 1962, 12). African American Islam, seen as black nationalism or black Islamic nationalism (the latter phrase used by Mattias Gardell), displays the same potential for double-consciousness, grounding itself in the United States and/or elsewhere. Gardell (1996, 8–9, 349), for example, who focuses on Louis Farrakhan's Nation of Islam, postulates an imagined community with the unique and corporate character of an African American Islamic nation and a "collectively articulated ambition to achieve political independence" as a divinely ordained "chosen nation." Yet Gardell carefully delineates the economic and social conditions that have inspired the black Islamic urban youth culture and terms them "of key importance for the future of the American project." thus locating the future nation within the United States. Gilles Kepel (1997, 75) notes that Farrakhan defended President Clinton during his first hundred days in office and spoke broadly about U.S. social problems. In his 1993 book, Farrakhan makes no reference to creating a separate black state, and the book as a whole falls in the "claiming America" category, with a final chapter entitled "A Vision for America."

There are at least three cases in the literature where the homeland or nation of origin presents something of a problem: the Nizari Isma'ilis, the Ahmadis, and the Palestinians. The Nizari Isma'ilis, who will be covered more fully in chapter 5 in the discussion of transnational or global identities, are clearly a kind of deterritorialized nation. They have a constitution, a titled leader, or Imam, with his own flag and throne, and a common secular language, English. The Aga Khan encourages Isma'ilis to become citizens of the nations in which they reside. In the United States it is clear that the identities being strengthened by a Nizari Isma'ili summer camp program are modern, Western ones, albeit rooted in pride in Islamic history and culture and with a slight emphasis on Sufi or self-strengthening ways of understanding Islam (Ross-Sheriff, Dhanidina, and Asani 1996).

Since their early history in the United States as missionaries from India, the Ahmadis have recently reappeared as exiles from their current homeland of Pakistan, where their recognized leader resides. (The Indian Ahmadis, however, see Pakistan as a hostile place where their coreligionists are persecuted.) The Ahmadi leader, like so many Shi'a leaders, encourages followers to become citizens wherever they have settled, and many Ahmadi emigrants have become citizens of the United Kingdom and the United States, countries in which they are free to assert their Islamic identity. Rather than trying to participate in American Muslim coalition politics—an arena in which other Muslims often turn against them—Ahmadis actively seek converts at the grassroots level, employing American approaches to proselytization such as "blitz" campaigns and citywide programs (Poston 1992, 113–14). In the United States they appear to be one of the most tightly bounded Muslim groups (Ahmed-Ghosh, forthcoming), and like the Nizari Isma'ilis (but less explicitly so), they form a stateless and transnational community.

For the Palestinians, it is their statelessness that poses the ongoing problem. Louise Cainkar's (1996, 53) study of Palestinian Muslim women in Chicago revealed the burden of statelessness and its emotional effects on their daily lives. These women felt unsettled; pained by tales of the suffering of family, friends, or Palestinians in general; and lonely because family members often had been dispersed. More recently, Cainkar (forthcoming) has found that Palestine remains the key focal point of the lives of both U.S.-born and immigrant Palestinians in Chicago, and May Seikaly (1999) found that Palestine is equally important for Palestinians in Detroit. Perhaps the most well-known Palestinian in the United States is Edward Said (who is a Christian, not a Muslim). His autobiography (Said 1999) captures some of this special sense of displacement (see also Said 1986).

The first thing to say about linguistic differences among American Muslims is that few scholars have analyzed them, although the second generation's transition to English is remarked upon in almost every study of immigrant Muslims. Attention is paid, again in microlevel studies, to the language used by imams for khutbas (sermons) in the mosques and for counseling purposes. Zain Abdullah (forthcoming) shows that West Africans in New York sought out mosques not dominated by English and founded their own mosques and Islamic centers in the 1990s so that imams or speakers could communicate in French or their own African languages. Walbridge (1997, 100–25) discusses not only the use of English or Arabic in Dearborn Shi'a mosques but the use of classical or colloquial Arabic and variations among sermons and styles of presentation. The use of "black English" and "rap" has been remarked among some of the African American Muslim groups—for example, the youthful Five Percenters (Nuruddin 1994).

Language is clearly a very basic and important marker of difference between African American and immigrant Muslims. Although the study of mosques released in 2001 (Bagby, Perl, and Froehle 2001) does not go into detail, it does state that 97 percent of the mosques use English "as the main language, or one of the main languages," for the Friday sermon, but that 47 percent of those using English also use one or more additional languages, usually Arabic or Urdu. (The call to prayer and the ritual prayer are traditionally in Arabic in all mosques.)

Scholars have paid some attention to the development of "Islamic American English." The phrase was coined by Garbi Schmidt (1998, 252–55), a Danish scholar, although Barbara Daly Metcalf (1996, xv–xix) had earlier discussed "Islamic English" in her edited volume. Both Schmidt and Metcalf credit Isma'il Al-Faruqi, a Palestinian immigrant who published a pamphlet on the subject in 1986 (and who founded the Association of Muslim Social Scientists and the Institute of Islamic Thought in Virginia, discussed later in the book). Whether "Islamic English" is really "American" or a broader development among religious English-speaking Muslims in many countries (C. M. Naim, personal communication, 2001) remains to be seen.

Certainly, immigrant and African American Muslims in the United States are incorporating Arabic phrases and Muslim terms of address into everyday speech, even with non-Muslims. Muslims in North America— or their answering machines—often answer the telephone with the greeting, "Asalam aleikum" (peace be with you), which either reflects the belief that all their callers are cobelievers or asserts their religious identity. I have heard a simultaneously globalized and localized message on the answering machine of an officer of a Los Angeles Pakistani association: it begins with "Asalam aleikum," gives a message in Urdu, and ends in English with, "Have an awesome day." (Whenever I recount this message, no one fails to place it in California, adding a regional dimension to the analysis.)

Despite the strong sectarian or national-origin differences among Muslims in the United States, few studies focus on conflicts based on them. Some Muslim organizations and institutions barely mention the differences, much less the conflicts, in their publications. Michael Fischer and Mehdi Abedi (1990, 271–88, 289–314) provide fascinating close-ups of conflicts over death and marriage rituals in Houston among Sunnis and Shi'a, Pakistanis, Arabs, and Iranians; Abedi's diary of the Ramadan observances in the Islamic Society of Greater Houston in 1984 also highlights conflicts. Hoda Badr (2000) also discusses conflicts in Houston. Ron Kelley (1994) discusses political conflicts in Los Angeles: Yemeni animosity toward Saudis; conflicts between pro-Khomeini Muslims and Iranian secularists; and mosque politics (Saudi conservative control of one, Palestinian "supra-religious discourse" in another, and Arab versus Indo-Pakistani differences in a third). Mohommed A. Muqtedar Khan (2002, 15–22) explicitly deplores ethnic and racial clustering among American Muslims in two separate essays in his book, the second one a rare public acknowledgment of the 2001 formation of a new largely African American group, the Muslim Alliance of North America (MANA, discussed later in the book). Robert Dannin (2002a) and Khalid Fattah Griggs (2002) publish details of conflicts among African American Muslim groups, Griggs treating the now-defunct Islamic Party in North America.

First-generation immigrants may strictly maintain sectarian differences in their new country, but the young people born in the United States may see these differences as baseless. Young Sunni Muslims with no experience of sectarian differences in their parents' homeland may even be ignorant of such divisions within Islam. Asma Gull Hasan (2000, 23, 26), a young second-generation American Sunni Muslim, was "unaware" that there were Shi'a Muslims until she met one in high school. Hasan, a popular writer on the "new generation" of American Muslims, thinks that sectarian divisions within Islam are no longer important, and that ethnicities (by which she means national origins) are what prevent unity among American Muslims. Other young Muslims born in the United States react with hostility to what they personally do not know to be Islam, denying both historical and contemporary validity to any number of Islamic movements (especially to African American, Ahmadi, Shi'a, and Sufi movements).

Race and Class

Scholarly work on Muslims and race has emphasized two issues: the old issue of African American Muslims and linkages between race, culture, and class; and the new issue of the racialization of Muslims.

With respect to African American Muslims, C. Eric Lincoln, as he does so often, sets key themes. First, he clearly links African American Islam to black religion in the United States and the contradictions posed by the coexistence of Christianity and slavery. Since slavery was apparently acceptable not only to God but to the white church establishment, the black church was always somewhat estranged from Christian "orthodoxy" as represented by the white church. "Hence, the salient tradition of Black religion has always been the sufficiency of its own insight" (Lincoln 1997 [1983], 226, 226–27). Thus, Lincoln argues, blacks moving from the black Christian churches to the Nation of Islam did not particularly value the notion of orthodoxy, and "further, since Islam is no stranger to the enslavement of Blacks, even in contemporary times, many of those who came to the faith . . . may well view Islamic orthodoxy as the Islamic counterpart of white Christianity. . . . Blacks . . . have learned to rely on feeling . . . rather than on the official formulas and prescriptions of the experts." It is this tradition of self-reliance and skepticism, Lincoln felt, with which W. D. Mohammed contended as he moved his community toward Islamic orthodoxy and that bolsters Louis Farrakhan in his independent stance. Robert Dannin (2002a, 16–17) argues, in contrast, that "the Black Church was not central to the spiritual life of all African Americans," and he sees the unchurched as liminal people, better able to reject "conventional sacerdotal and secular hierarchies" and move toward Islam.

Second, Lincoln (1961, 50) defines all black nationalist movements (including the Islamic ones)[2] as having three characteristics in common: a disparagement of the white man and his culture; a repudiation of Negro identity; and an appropriation of "Asiatic" culture symbols. This contention (disputed by Edward Curtis, personal communication, 2002) directs attention to W. D. Mohammed's changes in the Nation of Islam's ideas about race. Mohammed first opened the Nation to whites and then reclaimed a black identity by introducing the term "Bilalian" (after the Ethiopian Bilal Ibn Rabah, whom the Prophet Muhammad invited to be the first muezzin, or caller to prayer, in the earliest Muslim community in Medina). The name did not last, reportedly because immigrant Muslims found its emphasis on race objectionable (Mamiya 1982; Curtis 2002a, 120–21).[3]

The shifting concepts of race among African American Muslims are pertinent in two arenas: first, in the crucial interaction between African American Muslims and immigrant Muslims (primarily West and South Asian immigrants) and the nonconnection between "Asian" immigrant cultures and contemporary African American Muslim culture (despite the latter's earlier claims to be "Asiatic"); and second, in the relationships between indigenous and African immigrant blacks in places like

New York. As Zain Abdullah (forthcoming) shows, differences among Africans resonate with differences among Egyptian-led and African American–led mosques in the city. Thus, the Murids from Senegal, whose Sufism combines with a discourse of Negritude, prefer the black nationalist speakers at Masjid Malcolm Shabazz. The Sunnis from Ivory Coast and Guinea, however, prefer the pan-Islamic speakers at the Islamic Center of New York or the Mosque of Islamic Brotherhood (led by Egyptians and African American Sunnis, respectively).

Racism on the part of immigrant Muslims is not fully acknowledged and has been underexplored by scholars, but it does fuel tensions between African American and immigrant Muslims (McCloud 1995; Karim, forthcoming a). While Richard Brent Turner (1997, 109–46) saw the Ahmadi communities developed from the 1920s as multiracial models for American Islam, a national survey of Ahmadis showed the difficulties of integrating American and Pakistani members, and this despite the integrative efforts of the international khalifa, or leader (Walbridge and Haneef 1999). The difficulties can easily be generalized to the broader American Muslim community, and the tensions arise as much or more from cultural and class differences as from racial ones.

Class divisions within African American Islam need more attention. E. U. Essien-Udom (1962, 2–3) showed the pivotal role of early "race men"—educated African Americans who first identified with their people and then, moving into the middle class, rejected them, leaving it to leaders like Noble Drew Ali and Elijah Muhammad to recruit the "Negro masses." Mamiya (1982, 145; 1983, 245) has worked on class issues, employing Max Weber's ideas about the work ethic and morality and "elective affinity," or believers' selections of religious ideas based on their interests. Elijah Muhammad initially appealed to the black lower class but gradually developed a largely middle-class membership, as did his son W. D. Mohammed (who is a Republican). Since 1977, Louis Farrakhan has reclaimed the Nation of Islam name, Elijah Muhammad's teachings, and the lower-class base of the earlier movement. Mamiya (1983, 250–53) quotes a convert to the Nation: "I don't see Wallace's group as being concerned with the outcasts. They seem to me to be Arabicized intellectuals, spouting Arabic phrases at you." Mamiya predicts that the continuing anger and resentment of the black underclass will create a new generation of black Muslims in the United States.

The second issue with respect to race is what some see as the racialization of Muslims—their construction as a category that, if not racial as traditionally understood, is at least racial in that Muslims experience discrimination and are not given full access to opportunities (Naber, forthcoming). Even before the radical Islamist terrorist attacks of September 11, 2001, some had diagnosed a new surge of "racism" in the

United States that targets all Muslims; this analysis has only become more pressing in the aftermath of the attacks. But the analysis concedes that Muslims are targeted in ways that confound traditional racism. Well illustrating the confusion is a U.S. Department of Transportation memo issued in October 2001: it provided guidelines for airport security personnel in questioning "Arab, Middle Eastern, South Asian, Muslim and Sikh" passengers.[4] These are linguistic, national-origin, and religious categories.

According to Neil Gotanda (2002), there are three modes of racialist thinking in the United States: an East Coast model based on a black-white dichotomy, with immigrants as a third category; a fuller social stratification model taking the form of a sliding scale with whites at the top, blacks at the bottom, and Latinos and Asians in the middle; and an alternative to the second model, based on West Coast equations of the Chinese race and national origin, that allows conceptualization of race as a national-origin category as well as, or instead of, a biological category.

In fact, the confusion generated by these shifting conceptualizations of race is not new, as we saw earlier. The earliest Arab immigrants were called Turks and Asiatics, and the earliest African American Muslim leaders reinvented themselves as Asiatics. Then Malcolm X in 1958 called Arabs "a colored people" who "should and must make more effort to reach the millions of colored people in America" (Lincoln 1961, 172). When W. D. Mohammed tried emphasizing blackness to connect with early followers of the Prophet, he was rebuffed by "politically correct" Arabs and South Asians who wanted to downplay race. Moreover the national-origin game can be played so as to combine homelands with religion and claim a place of privilege in the United States. Many first-generation American Muslim immigrant leaders are making the argument that Muslims are followers of one of the three Abrahamic religions and thus partners in Western civilization; perhaps they, like the Jews earlier in the United States, are becoming white (Brodkin 1998). As Jews became "white," "Christian Civilization" was replaced in the discourse by "Western Civilization" and the "Judeo-Christian tradition," Daniel Segal points out (2002).[5] For the new Muslim spokespeople today the terms are "Western civilization" and the "Abrahamic tradition."

These new "racial" concepts resonate less with class than with national origin and culture, and perhaps they can be compared to the concepts of Tariq Modood (1988, 1994) and others in the United Kingdom who are now emphasizing cultural differences instead of racial and class similarities. However, these scholars and activists are using cultural racism to distinguish South Asians from West Indians and to justify breaking away from previous "black British" political alliances. Scholars and activists in the United States, in contrast, emphasize national origins, culture, and religion as constructing targets of "racism" based on "foreignness." They talk about ideological if not organizational solidarity with African Americans, having never quite put alliances into place as successfully as was done in the United Kingdom in the late twentieth century.

Turning from literature on race to that on class among Muslims, we discover once again that good census data are missing. (Religion is not asked for in the U.S. census.) We do have a good demographic portrait of Arabs in Detroit (Schopmeyer 2000), work on Arab American women's employment there (Aswad 1994; Read 2002), and an analysis of class (and gender) differences in ways of being Palestinian and Muslim in Chicago (Cainkar 1994). Other information is scattered in numerous studies focused on other topics.

The best information on class comes from two contemporary surveys of American Muslims, both tied to mosque populations.[6] These general portraits of American Muslims at the beginning of the twenty-first century include many indicators of class status (more indicators than some readers will want perhaps). The 2000 survey (Bagby, Perl, and Froehle, 2001) of 631 mosques (with imams, board presidents, or board members of 416 mosques responding) asked for percentages of members in various categories. Mosque participants were estimated to be 75 percent male, 33 percent South Asian, 30 percent African American, and 25 percent Arab. Forty-eight percent were thought to be college graduates, and 19 percent had no high school diploma; almost half were under thirty-five years old, and 11 percent were over sixty. Seventy-six percent had annual household incomes of $20,000 or more. (The median U.S. household income was $41,000.) Cross-tabulations show that the predominantly African American mosques, located in inner-city areas and financially stressed, contributed to these outcomes.

The MAPS telephone survey of Muslim individuals, conducted in November and December 2001 (Project MAPS 2002), has published simple distribution tables. Of the 1,781 respondents, 29 percent were based in the East, with 27 percent in the Central or Great Lakes region, 21 percent in the South, and 13 percent in the West. The ethnic breakdown was 32 percent South Asian, 26 percent Arab, 20 percent Afro-American, 7 percent African, and 14 percent other. Fifty-nine percent were men, and 41 percent were women; 69 percent were married, 19 percent were single (never married), and 11 percent were divorced, separated, or widowed. Half were thirty to forty-nine years of age, with about one-fourth younger than thirty and one-fourth older than forty-nine. Fifty-eight percent were college graduates, 24 percent had some college education, 12 percent were high school graduates, and 6 percent had less schooling. Income and occupation are the variables of most interest here: 28 percent earned more than $75,000 a year, 22 percent earned between $50,000 and

$74,999, and 50 percent earned less than that (with 10 percent earning less than $15,000). Twenty-two percent of the respondents were in professional or technical occupations, followed by managerial (12 percent), other (11 percent), medical and homemaker (10 percent each), and then a scattering of diverse occupations. Only 12 percent (of the immigrants?) surveyed had come to the United States before 1970.

Without census data, the picture is regrettably incomplete, but some of the historical divisions within the American Muslim community are still clearly reflected in these surveys. Decisions about the inclusion or exclusion of some African American Muslims and, in the second survey, the ceiling set for the African American percentage of the community undoubtedly influenced the results, as did the decision to exclude the reputedly high-achieving communities of Nizari Isma'ilis and Ahmadis. I will be drawing on both surveys in other contexts.

Generation, Gender, and Sexuality

I review here the scholarly work on generational and gender issues chiefly in family and community arenas, reserving discussion of these issues in mosques, in Islamic law, and among young American Muslims for later sections. I also review work on sexuality, homosexuality, and reproductive health. Work on generational and gender differences and sexuality among American Muslims requires acknowledging the importance to many Muslims of patriarchy, or male authority, and gender complementarity (differing male and female roles).

Many immigrant Muslims and some African American "new Muslims" uphold patriarchy and gender complementarity in family and community.[7] They perceive the dominant American values of gender equality and freedom of sexual expression as serious threats to a Muslim way of life, and indeed to all ordered social life. Barbara Aswad (1996, 64–66) and others, however, argue that it is not so much Islam as the rules and regulations of patrilineality and patrilocality (inheritance and residential patterns following the line of male descent) that distinguish Arab (and other immigrant) Muslim families from mainstream American bilateral families with inheritance and residential patterns following either male or female lines of descent.) (Aswad stresses that patriarchy can also be found in American families that practice bilateral inheritance and residential patterns, and there is ample evidence of that.)

These concerns with the maintenance of patriarchy and gender complementarity seem to be centrally connected to a fear of "American individualism," which is interpreted not as a moral ideal but as amoral egoism and a sign of family and societal breakdown (Taylor 1999, 159, n. 3). Whether because of religious teaching or cultural background, some

Muslim understandings of these significant and deeply personal issues are often at odds with the dominant culture in the United States and the directions in which American (and Western) society is moving. Expressions of sexuality, particularly homosexuality, in American society arouse alarm and apprehension among many religious Muslims.

Work on generational and gender issues among immigrant Muslims has been primarily descriptive, and it has been comparative only in the sense that research on one community is printed next to research on another community in conference or topical volumes (Haddad 1991, 2002). For example, issues of gender and generation are treated in this way in several volumes focusing on immigrant family life (Waugh, Abu-Laban, and Qureshi 1991; Haddad and Smith 1994; Aswad and Bilge 1996; Bozorgmehr and Feldman 1996). For indigenous Muslims, even descriptive studies of generational and gender issues are rare, although there are second-, third-, and fourth-generation African American Muslims. Studies of African American Muslim leaders seldom include details of generational or gender differences. Some of the narratives by or about converts, especially Carol Anway's (1995) account of her daughter's conversion and interviews with other American women converts to Islam, involve generational and gender dynamics.

Generational differences in immigrant Muslim communities have emerged in both private and public spaces, and in both settings language is a key marker of change. Many studies comment on the difficulties of transmitting religion and culture to young people who do not know their parents' languages well. The nonparticipation of Muslim youth in adult gatherings and in mosques or Islamic centers could be addressed by using English rather than the language usually spoken by immigrant or first-generation adults and preachers, but the older people were reluctant to give up their language, and the preachers often were not fluent in English (Sachedina 1994, 11). Karen Hunt Ahmed (2002), working with three generations of immigrant Muslims in Chicago, finds differences of self-definition among them, the last generation calling itself "modern" and "liberal."

Brief life stories of Muslim immigrants to the Dearborn-Detroit area, if not yet full life histories, have been published. Walbridge (1996b, 301–17) gives five vignettes on Muslims from Palestine, South Dakota, Yemen, and Lebanon: four first- and one second-generation, three women and two men. Nabeel Abraham, Shams Alwujude, Lara Hamza, and Hayan Charara, all born or brought up in the United States, give somewhat longer accounts of their lives (Abraham and Shryock 2000). Evelyn Shakir (1997) includes personal testimonies with her comments on Arab women's lives in *Bint Arab* (it means daughter of Arabs), and the stories are organized by generations, from one to three.

Robert Dannin (2002a) includes partial life stories of the pioneer African American Muslims El-Hajj Wali Akram of the First Cleveland Mosque (who moved from Ahmadi to Sunni Islam) and Sheikh Daoud Ghani (who founded the West Valley, New York, rural community of Jabul Arabiyya). Dannin tracked members of the second generation of Ghani's community. He also focused on Shuaib Abdur Rahman, whose account of his conversion, life in New York, and imprisonment for a holdup and murder highlights the conflicts between different groups of African American Muslims.

We have no clear picture of how generational cohorts might work in the African American Muslim mosques or prison populations, or whether mentoring by older Muslim men is part of the pattern of recruitment and support. One study shows that a younger generation of "disenchanted youth" in New York (a generational cohort) has made the Five Percent Nation a "potentially permanent feature of the black adolescent sub-culture" (Nuruddin 1994, 109–10, 121). This Nation of Islam splinter group thrives partly through its connection with rappers; rap music lyrics convey the group's ideology. This mix of black and male supremacist views is forcefully expressed in "streetology," "black talk," or American black English; the group is also called the Nation of Gods and Earths, the men being "Gods" and the women "Earths." Although there is a history of conflict between the Five Percenters and Sunni Muslims, there also seems to be a movement of the younger Five Percenter Muslims into the Sunni community as they grow older.

Systematic research on generational differences among immigrant Muslims has been rare as well. Abdo Elkholy (1966, 88–89, 93, 96–97), comparing immigrants in Detroit and Toledo, Ohio, looked at intergenerational relations and also at measures of assimilation or adaptation to American society. He saw differences in language and education, but he emphasized the attitude of the first generation: as happened in Detroit, the more the first generation "struggled to maintain domination," the more the second generation was alienated from it. In contrast, the more moderate or liberal Toledo Muslims gave over leadership to the second generation, and mainly to young women, keeping the generations closer and moving both toward assimilation. An interesting difference here concerned occupations. The Toledo Muslim immigrants were concentrated in the liquor business, owning liquor stores, bars, and restaurants,[8] and there was little change in this occupational pattern for the next generation. In Detroit a more working-class first generation did see a second-generation shift into new occupations.

Nabeel Abraham and Andrew Shryock also explicitly discuss generational differences, Shryock (2000) in an exploration of Arab family dynamics in Detroit, and Abraham (2000) in his personal accounts and analysis of Detroit's "American" mosque. Both play with the contrasts and interactions of Arab and American understandings of family, kinship, and community. Shryock (2000, 605) reminds us that the fourteenth-century Arab philosopher Ibn Khaldun called "jealous respect for kinship ties 'asabiya,' a term often translated as 'group feeling' or 'solidarity' but also as 'clannishness' and 'factionalism.' " He sees this emphasis on shared blood and origin playing both destructive and constructive roles in Arab Detroit.

Other researchers focus not on the first generation, which bears the brunt of the transition to a new context, but on the second, which deals more with identity conflicts. Conflicts often involve gender as well as generation, and many studies focus on the combination. For example—and again focusing on Arabs in Dearborn—Charlene Joyce Eisenlohr (1996, 251) interviewed Arab girls in high school and found that a major stress in their lives involved parental constraints: they could talk to boys but not date them. The parents trusted their daughters, however, and backed their educational efforts.

Generational and gender negotiations are part of marriage-making for many young Muslims in the United States. The early immigrants, many of whom married outside their religion and ethnic group, nonetheless tried to control the marriages of their children (often preferring that they marry first cousins). In Elkholy's (1966, 33) comparative study of Detroit and Toledo in the late 1950s, there were differences in the two communities' views toward mixed marriages and also in its incidence. In both communities the first generation was mostly opposed to women marrying non-Muslims. (Muslim men could marry non-Muslim women "of the book," usually meaning Christians and Jews, but Muslim women could not, because Arab society was patrilineal.) But in both communities a high number of young people married Christians, especially in the second and third generations. In Toledo such marriages were better accepted, but with the condition that the husband converted to Islam.

Although Elkholy (1966, 102) called Islam a male religion, in Toledo the "social religious role" was played so much by the women that he attributed the establishment of a mosque to their efforts. Women organized a ladies' auxiliary, taught Sunday school, and undertook many activities to support the mosque. Abraham (2000), writing about Detroit in roughly the same early period, also emphasized the significant role of women in mosque establishment.

Elkholy (1966, 124) further argued that the most religiously active members of the Toledo community had married outside the faith, and that Islamic organizations, including the Federation of Islamic Associations, were "the product of the mixed-marriage children." Some other observations support this, although again, systematic and comparative work is needed. Anglo American and African American women converts organized the first Islamic School in Seattle (Adeney and DeMaster 1994, 197), and an American convert and her daughter were the first to begin wearing the hijab in a Los Angeles Shi'a mosque, leading many Pakistani immigrants to take it up (Ron Kelley 1994, 147).

The reinforcement of patriarchy in the family and the community influences marriage negotiations and gender relations within marriages. For example, Laila al-Marayati, a doctor and leader of American Muslim women and the daughter of an Arab immigrant, spoke at the International Islamic Unity Conference in Los Angeles in 1996. She advocated writing good Islamic marriage contracts before marriage to ensure a woman's rights (such contracts specify mehr, a monetary settlement to the woman in case of divorce, and are enforceable in American courts) and urged mutual respect and flexibility within the family unit regarding work and domestic roles. Al-Marayati also mentioned that if a couple could not make a marriage work, divorce was acceptable in Islam. She was immediately challenged from the floor by both older and younger Muslim men, who recommended reinforcing traditional sex roles instead and keeping the family together; they blamed American society for causing problems for Muslim families.

Muslim marriage arrangements, marriages, and divorces are important issues, yet studies are few. There are no studies of mehr contracts or their enforcement among American Muslims. Divorce rates throughout the Muslim world are "difficult to ascertain" (Smith 1984, 95), but an exploratory (and contested) study (Ba-Yunus 1999, 42) indicates a high rate among Muslims in North America—33 percent of all marriages, third-highest percentage in the world behind the United States as a whole (48.6 percent) and the United Kingdom (36 percent). Divorce is usually initiated by the husband and is far easier for him. Under Islamic law, he need only pronounce, "I divorce you," three times (the triple talaq). (Although this is insufficient in the United States for a legal divorce, there are instances of it.) Women can divorce their husbands, but under Islamic law the fathers gain custody of the children. Then there is inheritance: in Islamic law, women generally inherit half the property inherited by men, but inheritance patterns in the United States are different, as Yvonne Haddad and Adair Lummis indicated (1987, 110–12). I am unaware of serious studies of divorce, child custody, and inheritance issues among American Muslims.

There is a range of marriage practices among Muslims in the United States. Marriage-making among immigrants differs from community to community and often involves skewed demographic patterns. Louise Cainkar (1991) shows that the preference of American-born Palestinian males for women from the homeland has left many U.S.-born Arab women without husbands. Contemporary marriage advertisements and marriage arrangement services show that many American Muslims continue to prefer endogamous marriages (by national origin, language group, sect, or caste). This may or may not involve bringing a bride or groom from the homeland, a practice sometimes questioned by the Immigration and Naturalization Service (INS). In cases of arranged marriage involving partners of South Asian origin, the bride and groom may not have met, whereas the INS assumes prior acquaintance between fiancés. Families sponsoring such transnational arranged marriages must secure letters from religious or academic authorities about the (often cultural) marriage practices in their communities.[9]

Marriage practices in the United States include "youth weddings" at which the bride, and sometimes the groom too, may be a teenager. Both Robert Dannin (2002a) and Denise Al-Johar (forthcoming) remark on such early marriages. Al-Johar did not work with African American Muslims, and in her study the reason for early marriages appears to be fear of daughters marrying outside the parental sectarian or ethnic group. Dannin (2002a, 252) did work with African Americans, and he reports on a thirteen-year-old and a fifteen-year-old who were married to each other in the Universal Islamic Brotherhood in Cleveland, the first of several such marriages planned there. Instead of fighting teenage sexual activity, this African American Muslim group accepted adolescent sexuality as inevitable and controlled it through marriage.

Muslim marriage practices in the United States include polygyny (having more than one wife). A man is legally permitted to have four wives under Islamic law (although he is enjoined to treat all wives equally, an expectation often cited as actually discouraging polygyny), but a man may have only one wife under American law. Some American Muslim men and women do marry Islamically, without benefit of civil or legal marriage, and they divorce that way too, the man pronouncing the talaq three times. Opportunistic use of either system of law can lead to confusion. For example, a woman who divorces her husband or is divorced by him under American law may find that, since he has not divorced her under Islamic law, she is still considered married by other Muslims in the United States and in her homeland (Ayyub 2000, 240). I have found only fragmentary published material on polygyny among immigrant and African American Muslims. Aminah Beverly McCloud (1995) pointed to some of the legal problems these practices cause for women, and Steven Barboza (1994) interviewed an African American imam and his three wives.

Robert Dannin (2002a, 234, 196–97 passim, 235) discusses some cases of polygynous marriage in detail. Dannin's work reveals the great importance given to the role of marriage in the African American communities he studied. Several times he cites informants quoting the Qur'anic saying that, in Islam, marriage is "half of your religion," and he talks about the role of the wali, a male guardian appointed by an imam (or sometimes the imam himself) to protect women and counsel them in their marriage choices. After a lengthy discussion of patriarchy, conversion, and adoption among Muslims, drawing on Middle Eastern and North African materials and making comparisons with Mormons in the United States, Dannin analyzes the wali among African American Muslims as an enforcer of the Islamic social order and a curb on female sexuality and self-determination (see also Fischer and Abedi 1990, 329; Mamiya 2001–2002, 39).

Introducing Naima Saif'ullah, a young woman who has married five times since converting, Dannin (2002a, 196–97) paints a vivid picture of the pressures on single African American women, many of whom are new converts, to marry a "brother," and often to do so polygynously:

> So many new Muslims in one place inevitably led to confusion and discrepancies in their understanding of Islamic worship. It was an extremely heterogeneous network that connected ex-convicts with former drug users in various stages of rehabilitation, abused women, and even formerly homeless men. African Americans had many different ideas about Islam, different reasons for converting, and various goals. . . . Conflicts arose frequently, particularly in relations between men and women. Despite efforts by some experienced and knowledgeable leaders . . . to maintain proper adab [etiquette], the mosque sometimes became a sexual arena where men were constantly on the prowl.

McCloud (1991, 180) and Hermansen (1991, 197–98) also discuss the pressures on single Muslim women to marry.

Dannin points out that Naima is atypical—most Muslim women have stable monogamous relationships—but by focusing on this woman's experiences, he shows that sexuality and marriage are crucial in both positive and negative ways to African American experiences with Islam. Dannin describes the difficulties of interviewing Muslim men who were maintaining more than one household and notes that some women in plural marriages supported their households by receiving Aid to Families with Dependent Children (AFDC) benefits, since the state did not legally recognize more than one spouse. (This became harder after 1995, when a more rigorous and limited welfare program was enacted.) Finally, he describes women who were unhappy in their marriages going to imams to ask them to persuade their husbands to divorce them so they would not embarrass the community by "going downtown" to attempt a civil court settlement. In Dannin's material, adab means "etiquette between men and women": a wife put "in adab" has been verbally repudiated, and under shari'a law the divorce will be final if there is no sexual contact for three menstrual cycles (Dannin 2002a, 196, 201, 205). Dannin's detailed material and theoretical analysis suggest the great need for research in this area.

Another issue is the practice of mut'a. Fixed-term marriage, or "pleasure" marriage, is permitted in Shi'a Islam. Mut'a is a temporary marriage contracted between a man and an unmarried woman to legitimate sexual relations between them. The contract specifies the duration of the marriage and the amount of money she is to be given; women may form only one such marriage at a time, but men may contract as many as they wish (Haeri 1989). Children of these marriages are legitimate and can inherit, but the wife has no right of inheritance from the husband. Such marriages, notably among the Shi'a Ithna 'Ashari, do occur in the United States, although systematic study of them is lacking. In Dearborn, Michigan, students or men not yet able to marry but wanting sexual relationships, older Lebanese women without resources, and possibly young Lebanese women desirous of sexual relationships have engaged in mut'a marriages. The practice was prevalent enough that the imam at the local Islamic Institute wrote a booklet about it (Walbridge 1996a; Berri 1989). In Houston, Texas, an Iranian Shi'a seeking to understand the different discourses of African American Muslims interviewed an African American woman convert who had experienced several mut'a marriages (Fischer and Abedi 1990, 314–22).

The small but well-off and conspicuous Nizari Isma'ili Shi'a community takes stances toward marriage that are, as a whole, very different from those of other Muslims, both Shi'a and Sunni. For its members, marriage is a contract between two consenting adults to which the woman herself must consent. Although this is the ideal for all Muslims, among some, perhaps chiefly South Asians, it is often the bride's father or another man who answers on her behalf. The rights of Nizari Isma'ili women are very well established in the areas of marriage and inheritance. In reforms accomplished chiefly under the Aga Khan III, polygyny, child marriage, and mut'a marriage are prohibited, divorce by repudiation by the husband is prohibited, and widows may remarry (Asani 1994; see also Kanji 1990, 13).[10] The situation for the Druze is somewhat similar. Both men and women are highly educated and considered equal, and polygyny, talaq divorces, and mut'a marriages are prohibited (Haddad and Smith 1993, 31).

The Daudi Bohras, once a Hindu merchant caste like the Nizari Isma'ilis, also disallow mut'a marriages, but they have not made major reforms like those of the Nizaris in marriage and divorce practices. Apparently responding to the Iranian Revolution of 1979 and a heightened consciousness of Shi'a orthopraxy, they have instead instituted a strict Islamic dress code of beards and white kurta (shirt), pajama (pants), and sherwani (coat) for men, and burqa (full-length cloak) and veil for women. They have also instituted certificates of orthopraxy, identity cards either green (in full compliance with the dictates of the da'i or Syedna), yellow (largely in compliance), or red (noncompliance in some major area, like not having a beard, not keeping a halal household, or drinking alcohol). These details come from a study of Bohras in India (Blank 2001, 180–93, 191). The only remark on expatriate Bohras is that over 50 percent of expatriates pictured in a who's who of leaders throughout the world had "nontraditional" appearances in the 1970s, prior to the issuing of the "modern" dress code.

I know of no large-scale quantitative studies of second-generation immigrant Muslim marriage patterns. One study of some thirty young Muslims from many ethnic backgrounds in Houston, Texas, finds clearly delineated movements beyond national-origin and ethnic groups to a broader range of potential spouses as well as a broader range of marriage practices (Al-Johar, forthcoming). Many studies remark briefly on marriage trends. For example, among young Iranian Muslims in Los Angeles, the trend is toward freedom of choice, although parental constraints continue to play roles (Hanassah 1993, 227).

Although sexuality is discussed again as an element of "expressive culture" in chapter 7, some introductory remarks seem in order here, since sexuality covers issues of marriage and family, reproductive health, adolescent sexuality, homosexuality, and women's roles.[11] The normative or elite view is that there is "a more positive sexual attitude in Islam than in traditional Christianity" (Roy 1996, 75). Muslim men and women are to enjoy sex within marriage; that is, sex is viewed very positively, and both husband and wife are entitled to satisfaction.[12] As we have seen, polygyny and temporary marriage are allowed in addition to monogamous marriage (although these practices, arguably, favor husbands). Contraception is allowed if there are good reasons for it, and so is abortion before the fetus acquires a soul (within 40 to 120 days of conception, depending on the school of law; see Green and Numrich 2001, 67). Sex before marriage, however, is prohibited, and many Muslims believe that dating leads directly to sexual activity (Athar 1995).

Homosexuality is forbidden in Qur'anic verses, but such relations have venerable histories in Muslim societies. Stephen Murray and Will Roscoe (1997) very effectively decenter the dominant Eurocentric model of gay and lesbian history, and certainly homosexual relations are practiced by some Muslims in the contemporary United States. Scholars of Islamic law generally regard homosexuality as a crime, not just a sin, but it is not a hadd crime (one with a set punishment), and judgment can be exercised as to the penalty. Since proof of such relations has been difficult to establish under Islamic law, jurists allegedly often urge repentance (Duran 1993, 183–84).

While the laws in most Western countries have gradually been secularized—so that sexual matters are now generally left to individuals subject to adulthood, free consent, and privacy—Islamic law has not changed in this way. Although few Muslim countries actually implement the shari'a fully, in legal systems close to the ideal, sexual relationships that violate shari'a constitute criminal offenses. Thus, the shari'a differentiates between nikah, or legal sex (it also refers to the marriage contract), and zina, or illicit sex, and there are two categories of offenses: defined ones with set punishments (hadd), and lesser ones for which authorities can decide punishments. Extramarital sexual intercourse (except by men with concubines and slave girls, a detail rarely if ever relevant today) constitutes zina, a hadd offense punishable by one hundred lashes if unmarried and by stoning to death if married. Zina requires strong proof; in testimony, that of one man equals that of two women (Roy 1996, 76–78, 95). Muslims in the United States, subject not to shari'a but to U.S. civil and criminal law, are generally very conscious of the sharply contrasting ways in which the two legal systems define and discipline sexual behaviors.

There is little material on issues of reproductive health and sexuality among American Muslims, although two interviews with African American women working to educate other Muslims about AIDS and other sexually transmitted diseases show the need for this (Dannin 2002a, 189–213; Barboza 1994, 158–72). Tarajee Abdur-Rahim's interview with Steven Barboza, entitled "Under the Prayer Rug," is especially poignant. Arab Americans in Dearborn have been shown to have less knowledge than the general population about the actions that transmit HIV or about treatment (Kulwicki and Cass 1996, 217–19). On Islamic approaches to health, again, little has been written (Waugh 1999; Smith 1999, 137–39) besides brief magazine articles, but some work is under way (Hermansen, forthcoming a).

This chapter has reviewed research on Muslim identities, attributes, and achievements by looking at their constituent elements, such as national origin, language, sectarian affiliation, race, class, generation, gender, and sexuality. Now we need to locate Muslims in the American landscape and examine the ways in which some Muslim identities are signified and enacted in domestic and public spaces.

═ Chapter 5 ═

Muslims in the
American Landscape

T HE IDENTITIES discussed in the last chapter can be displayed in private
homes, work sites, schools, mosques, and a variety of public spaces.
Some Muslims mark themselves as Muslim externally, wherever
they may be. There are spaces in the United States that are marked as
Islamic ones, especially mosques, and they have received much scholarly
attention. Transnational or global spaces and networks also shape personal and collective identities for many American Muslims. This chapter
looks at research on those spatial locations and, to some extent, the nature
of the communities developed in and across them that are important to
contemporary Muslim identities and affiliations in the United States.

Public and Domestic Spaces

Beginning with some grand ideas about Islamic space in America or
America as Islamic space, we have authors likening the United States to
Medina, the city to which the Prophet Muhammad journeyed in 622 C.E.
to establish the first Muslim community. The analogy captures Muslims'
optimistic hopes for the future of Islam in the United States (Metcalf 1996;
Schmidt 1998). Robert Dannin (2002b, 59) has likened the concept of hijra
itself, the migration to Medina, to experiences particularly significant for
African Americans: the Middle Passage to slavery, the Underground
Railroad to freedom, the Great Migration north from 1916 to 1930, and the
civil rights movement of the 1950s and 1960s. He sees the westward
expansion of Islam as perhaps its "greatest" migration and African American Muslims as an integral and interactive part of this recurring alle-
gory of spatial mobility, this drive to create a "self-sustaining symbol of
Islamic space."

Scholars of religion have looked at the settlement patterns of new
immigrants and their religious institutions in the United States, assessing

the religious dimensions of changing urban landscapes. Some see Jews, Christians, Hindus, and Muslims sharing localities, developing ethno-racial enclaves that, arguably, enhance the diversity of American neighborhoods (Livezey 2000, 133, 138). Thus "Indo-Pakistanis" in Chicago remained fairly homogeneous in the midst of a very diverse area, and without publicly promoting the "racial integration" of the area, they made commitments to remain in Rogers Park and maintain its diversity (Livezey 2000, 156–58). Lowell Livezey, following David Hollinger (1995), calls this "pluralist" rather than "cosmopolitan" multiculturalism, since the Muslims and other religious groups are looking inward rather than reaching out to each other or to the city as a whole. Livezey sees the groups as "building capacities of moral discourse and responsibility" within their communities (158–59).

Scholars are relating changing religious landscapes to the new American metropolis. Paul Numrich (1997, 59, 64–65) argues that the tendency to create ethnic residential enclaves in Chicago has given way to a socio-economically polarized settlement pattern that is also differentiated by religious affiliation. Two-thirds of the city's mosques (fifteen of twenty-two) are majority Indian or Indo-Pakistani. Numrich focuses on the north side Muslim Community Center, the oldest Indo-Pakistani mosque in the Chicago region.[1] Through comparison with Indo-Pakistani non-Muslim religious institutions, he shows that Muslims worship in less "desirable" municipalities in terms of income and crime statistics, an argument he develops further in a longer version of this article (Numrich 2000a, 261), in which he states that "Indo-Pakistani Christians and Muslims lag behind fellow ethnics (Hindus, Sikhs, etc.) in establishing religious centers in the suburbs." He concludes that socioeconomic status is now more important than ethnicity in explaining the location of residences and religious establishments. In a third article, Numrich (2000b, 204–5) examines institutionalized religions in the suburb of Naperville, west of Chicago, an "edge-city technoburb" with an Indo-Pakistani Islamic center and afternoon school whose status is somewhat marginal (or marginalized).

New religious landscapes are being delineated in other American cities. Barbara Weightman (1993, 3) has done a spatially oriented study of Los Angeles. Although she focuses on Christian spaces, she mentions five Islamic centers and eighty-two mosques in southern California and many other new institutions. Such studies by sociologists, geographers, and religious studies scholars are characterized by broad-brush mapping of institutions and membership characteristics, and as yet such projects have produced little qualitative work on the religious communities.[2]

American Muslim institutions and organizations map themselves onto the American landscape in interesting ways. A political project aimed at educating the American public about Islam and also at unifying American Muslims named itself Muslims in American Public Square, suggesting the community's entry into the political arena; its acronym is MAPS. Such entry involves adopting public symbolism, and many of the national Muslim political organizations include an American flag design as part of their masthead or logo (added by some after September 11, 2001), and the American flag hangs in some Islamic religious spaces—for example, in Nizari Isma'ili jamatkhanas and in W. D. Mohammed's American Society of Muslims mosques.

More materially grounded work on the Muslim presence in American public and domestic spaces focuses on mosque and school designs, the external markings of believers working and moving in public spaces, and domestic decorations and practices. Gulzar Haider (1996), a Pakistani Canadian architect who often works in the United States, has written about the changing mosque styles over the decades. Mosques in the United States began in houses and storefronts, and when mosques began to be built, their adherents initially wanted them to blend into the landscape. By the end of the twentieth century, however, Muslims wanted their mosques to be statements of Islamic identity—for example, through architecturally striking minarets and domes.

Analyses of visual images of Islam in American landscapes include an innovative study of the Muslim World Day Parade and storefront mosques in New York (Slyomovics 1996). The parade claims public space for Muslims, its signs and banners prominently featuring slogans and texts and its floats featuring scale models of the Ka'ba in Mecca, the Dome of the Rock in Jerusalem, and the Medina mosque in which the Prophet is buried. The texts and visual symbols seem intended to educate non-Muslims about important Islamic messages and sites. Most storefront mosques function as temporary quarters, often unmarked, according to Susan Slyomovics, and are likely to be transferred to purposefully built mosques and school buildings in New York. Abdelhamid Lotfi (2001, 238–39), who also studied storefront mosques, comments on their visual markers, including the use of the color green. Omar Khalidi (1998), writing only about structures designed to be mosques or cultural centers, traces strictly traditional designs, reinterpretations of tradition, and entirely innovative architecture in American mosques. Like Slyomovics, he comments on the gendering of space in the mosques. Robert Dannin (1996b, 131) analyzes prison mosques as spaces of "order, community, and purpose" for primarily African American Muslim inmates.

Some work has been done on the domestic spaces of African American Muslims by Aminah Beverly McCloud (1996, 68), who states that believers consider the outside community to be dar al-harb (house of war) and the domestic space to be dar al-Islam (the house of Islam).

African American Muslims control and organize domestic space to enhance shared spirituality with other Muslims and see the outside as a space of intolerance and racism. African American Muslims feel free to draw on anywhere in the Muslim world for interior design, dress, and food; they also implement their own sets of gendered practices in domestic space.

Little other work has been done specifically on the display of Islamic identities in homes, schools, and work sites. Sally Howell (forthcoming) includes material on home decoration among Arabs in Detroit, and fragmentary remarks about home decorations occur in other sources. Joann D'Alisera (2001) remarks on the display of Islamic symbols and messages by Sierra Leonean street food vendors in Washington, D.C., but she has noticed a decline in these displays since September 11, 2001. Zain Abdullah (forthcoming) describes Senegalese Murid space along New York's West 116th Street, its restaurants and shops marked in many ways with religious symbols, especially the name of Touba, a holy city established by the founder of the Murid Sufi order. New York City's mayor proclaimed July 28 Cheikh Amadou Bamba Day, and there is a parade. William Lockwood and Yvonne Lockwood (2000) discuss Arab (Christian and Muslim) food and foodways in public and private sectors in Detroit, ending with descriptions of Thanksgiving feasts.

Spatial aspects of schools, work sites, and public arenas have received little scholarly attention. There may have been no significant adaptations of American work sites for Muslim prayers, for example, but occasionally issues related to being able to pray at work or wear religious attire at work arise in the media and courts. Funeral homes and cemeteries have adapted to Muslim clients in particular ways—aligning the graves toward Mecca, for instance, and allowing men to wash the unembalmed body and bury it quickly (Leonard 1989–90; Husain and Vogelaar 1994, 249). Participants in public events that are religious in nature or primarily attract Muslims adapt the hall, auditorium, or restaurant to their needs, perhaps enforcing gendered seating or, if that proves difficult, seating by family parties.

A case can be made, I think, that non-Muslims are increasingly being invited, to varying degrees according to the community and the nature of the occasion, into Muslim spaces in the United States. Thus, friends from work or school or the neighborhood may attend a wedding, a funeral, or the celebration of a child's bismillah (the initiation of a child's education in Arabic, traditionally at the age of four years and four months) or ameen (his or her first completed reading of the Qur'an), all of which are events marked to some extent by religious rituals and displays. Here the non-Muslim adapts to the conventions of the sponsors, perhaps removing shoes, covering the head (women), and observing gendered seating arrangements. These patterns of interaction deserve scholarly attention.

Mosques: Spatial and Identity Issues

Mosques are important sites for the development of Muslim identities in the United States, and I discuss them here as a topic connecting issues of race, class, gender, and generation to issues of public and domestic spaces. We need to consider both the difficulties encountered by Muslims establishing mosques in the United States and the mapping of mosques in time and space. Sometimes difficulties with mosque-building come from within the "Muslim community," which may have disputes over design features or the choice of a firm to employ. The Islamic Cultural Center in New York City took almost forty long years from start to dedication (Ferris 1994, 218–19). Much more often, however, difficulties have come from non-Muslim opposition.

Scattered accounts and a concentrated discussion by Kathleen Moore (1995) attest to the initial resistance of non-Muslims to mosque-building. Moore surveyed legal cases that had won rights for Muslims in this area (and in other areas). A few examples show the kinds of conditions imposed by local authorities. In southern California's Granada Hills, the Los Angeles City Council directed the Islamic center of Northridge to ensure that its new mosque reflected the local Spanish architectural styles; this was one of forty-four conditions, the most restrictions ever placed on a place of worship in the city (Ron Kelley 1994, 162). The plans for the King Fahd white marble mosque built in Culver City in Los Angeles, primarily with Saudi patronage, drew initial criticism because it would reflect light too brightly.[3]

To map America's mosques in time and space, I draw again on the survey of U.S. mosques done in 2000 as part of a "national portrait" interfaith project involving American congregations of forty different denominations and groups.[4] Of the 431 responding mosques, the earliest mosque was founded in 1925, but only 2 percent were founded prior to 1950, and only 13 percent prior to 1970. Half the mosques were founded by 1980 and half after 1980; the survey also stated that over three-fifths of the mosques had been founded since 1979 (Bagby, Perl, and Froehle 2001, 23, 24, 25, 26). Mosques have shifted locations: 69 percent of those founded more than ten years ago have moved. Four-fifths of the mosques are in metropolitan areas, with one-fifth in towns or rural areas. A breakdown by town, suburb, city neighborhood, and inner city, cross-tabulated with ethnic groups, shows that predominantly African American mosques are heavily concentrated in the last two city locations (62 percent and 27 percent), while predominantly South Asian and Arab mosques are more evenly distributed. Most mosques (55 percent) were purchased, and only 26 percent were actually built as mosques. Fifteen percent are rented, and 4 percent are provided by universities or businesses.

Moving from issues of legal entitlement, architecture, timing, and space to issues of race, class, generation, and gender, the 2000 survey provides fascinating data about mosques. The mosque representatives reported that their mosques are very ethnically diverse: almost 90 percent are attended by South Asians, African Americans, and Arabs, and only 7 percent are attended by only one ethnic group. However, 24 percent of the mosques have 90 percent membership from one ethnic group; these 24 percent and the 7 percent of mosques with only one ethnic group are African American mosques (Bagby, Perl, and Froehle 2001, 3, 19, 13–14). Thirty-one percent of the mosques were attended by two major ethnic groups, the most frequent combination being South Asian and Arab. While the number of regular attenders has increased at 75 percent of the mosques, suburban mosques have grown the most and inner-city mosques the least (and remember that the largest proportion of inner-city mosques are African American). Some characteristics of mosque-attenders were reported earlier when discussing class, and we should note here that 40 percent traveled more than fifteen minutes to reach their mosque, indicating that residential and mosque patterns are not well correlated (Bagby, Perl, and Froehle 2001, 16, 16–17; cf. Numrich 1997, 2000a). One in three of regular attenders was a convert, a percentage that correlates well with the estimated 30 percent of African American Muslims and 1.6 percent of white American Muslims in the study. Most converts in the mosques were African American men.[5]

Ethno-racial differences showed in other ways (Bagby, Perl, and Froehle 2001, 32, 33, 41, 44, 59, 62, 35–36). Although representatives of most of these mosques surveyed in 2000 felt that Muslims should participate in American institutions (77 percent) and the political process (72 percent), between 65 and 70 percent of all mosques agreed "somewhat" or "strongly" with the statement that "America is immoral"; African American mosques felt that most strongly. African American mosques were also least supportive of political participation (77 percent supported it, compared to 95 percent and 98 percent for the South Asian and Arab-dominated mosques). Despite this, it was African American mosques that believed most strongly in da'wa, or outreach activities, and were most likely to interact with politicians, engage in interfaith dialogues and social service projects, and visit schools and churches. (The Arab and South Asian–Arab mosques were slightly ahead of African American mosques on the measure of interactions with the media). African American mosques were also most active in providing cash assistance, counseling services, prison programs, food and clothing assistance, tutoring, and antidrug, anticrime, and substance abuse programs, presumably because of greater needs. (African American mosques have the greatest financial difficulties.) Seventy-one percent of the mosques had a regular weekend school, and 21 percent had a full-time Islamic school. Most of the full-time Islamic schools were elementary schools in large, mixed South Asian and Arab mosques in suburbs or city neighborhoods in the American South.

Differences in the 2000 survey among mosques with respect to formal leadership also show striking correlations with dominant ethno-racial groups (Bagby, Perl, and Froehle 2001, 46, 49, 50–52). Eighty-one percent of the mosques had an imam. In half of those 81 percent, the imam was the religious and organizational leader of the mosque; in the other half, the imam was a spiritual guide, leading prayers and teaching Islam. Ninety-four percent of the mosques had an executive committee or board of directors; 59 percent of all mosques were run by these decisionmaking bodies, while 28 percent were run by imams and 11 percent by another leader. Two-thirds of imams who were mosque leaders were African American; most imams who were not mosque leaders were Arab (49 percent) or South Asian (29 percent), and most mosque leaders who were not imams were South Asian (46 percent) or Arab (38 percent). Imams who were and were not mosque leaders and other mosque leaders differed in terms of general and Islamic education but were homogeneous with respect to age, averaging between forty-two and forty-eight.

We have no reports on generational patterns in immigrant or indigenous mosques, of either the membership or the leadership. A key question is whether second or later generations are taking up leadership positions. In some cases, second-generation immigrant Muslims are conspicuous among leaders, and in other cases first-generation and incoming immigrants continue to be leaders, as board members and as imams. W. D. Mohammed did claim his father's African American Muslim community and central mosque in Chicago, but I do not know if there are patterns of inherited leadership in other groups (perhaps among Sufis, but they are not centered in mosques).

Turning to gender issues in mosque settings, the mosque representatives in the 2000 survey reported that for the Friday prayer, some 78 percent of participants were men, 15 percent were women, and 7 percent were children. (The survey did not ask about Sunday, the day many researchers have reported the highest attendance at mosques, particularly women's attendance.) In two-thirds of the mosques, women prayed behind a curtain or partition or in another room. Since in a similar survey conducted in 1994 only 52 percent of the mosques reported this practice, the 2000 study concludes that gender segregation is growing (Bagby, Perl, and Froehle 2001, 9, 11, 56). And while 69 percent of the mosques with a governing board allow women to serve on the board, women have served during the last five years on boards in only 72 percent of those that permitted it; again, this compares badly with the 1994 survey.

The mosque survey done in 2000 offers no more data on gender, but separate articles based on the survey provide further details (Mamiya 2001–2002; Bagby 2001–2002). Ihsan Bagby (2001–2002, 207, 211, 216–17) singles out African American mosques and comments that the issue of women's involvement in mosques is a major difference between African American Muslims and immigrant Muslims.[6] Bagby divides mosques into immigrant and African American, and the latter again into what he terms "historically sunni African-American masjids" (HSAAM), and W. D. Mohammed's (then-named) Muslim American Society (MAS), which is based in the South and includes 56 percent of African American mosques in its membership. Bagby then notes that HSAAM Muslims have recently formed the Muslim Alliance of North America (MANA) to unite and formulate "a more authentic, normative form" that does not give up the critical stance toward American society characteristic of early African American Islam (as MAS has done). Pointing out that in the Prophet Muhammad's mosque there was no barrier between men and women, Bagby reports that in immigrant mosques 13 percent of the Friday prayer attenders are women but in African American mosques 21 percent are women (and in MAS mosques 24 percent are women, while in HSAAM ones, 17 percent are women, reflecting the latter's higher percentage of immigrant participants). In 81 percent of immigrant mosques, women pray behind a curtain or in another room, but in only 30 percent of African American mosques do women do this. (Only 16 percent of MAS mosques have this practice, and 45 percent of HSAAM mosques.) The percentages of the types of mosques allowing women to serve on the governing board are also sharply different. The new HSAAM category and MANA signal an important new initiative, one apparently partly inspired by disagreements about gender issues. Khan (2002, 19) quotes its mission statement as aiming "to pursue an agenda that reflects the points of view and experiences of the indigenous Muslims of North America. . . . And by indigenous, we mean all Muslims raised here in America."[7]

Other sources indicate diverse patterns of women's participation in mosques. Scholars of African American Islam tend to criticize "the Muslim world's misrepresentation of gender relations in Islam," seeing most immigrant practices as cultural rather than religious (McCloud 1995, 157). African American Muslim women in the First Cleveland Mosque were enfranchised in 1944 by the Uniting Islamic Society of America (UISA).[8] This was part of an inclusionist movement, and two women were appointed to the constitutional subcommittee of the developing organization. The UISA women's society featured Muslim fashion shows and built alliances among Muslim women, especially those in Cleveland and Pittsburgh. The UISA effort to build a national Muslim community failed, partly because of disagreements between indigenous and immigrant Muslims about assimilation and women's rights (Dannin 2002a, 51–53). Hoda Badr (2000) shows how the Islamic Society of Greater Houston's advocacy of English as the dominant language in mosques and women's lesser competence in that language has helped keep Muslims there fragmented.

Women's service on boards and as imams is an issue more contested than their seating in mosques. In southern California the election of a woman around 1990 to one mosque's board of directors was opposed by some of the men, while in another mosque women are prominent participants and hold an annual Islamic fashion show (Ron Kelley 1994, 147–48). Although it is generally held that women may not be imams, two women (who are almost certainly African American) are among the thirty-two imams or Muslim chaplains who work in the New York State prison system (Barboza 1994, 156–57). Women participate a great deal in Nizari Isma'ili governing institutions, and Asma Gull Hasan (2000, 25), a young American Muslim woman (a Sunni of Pakistani background and a second-generation American), writes enthusiastically of supporting the rumored appointment of Aga Khan IV's daughter to succeed him as head of the Nizari Isma'ilis.

Among the Ithna 'Ashari Shi'a, gender issues call for interpretations from the maraji' taqlid, and these have proved important in sanctioning innovations that increase women's participation in religious activities. When closed-circuit television was introduced so that women, seated behind a partition or separately, could watch a male speaker deliver a religious lecture, opposition in some Shi'a centers in North America was overcome by the ruling of the marja' that this practice was religiously commendable. An even more innovative move is the inclusion of female students in the Shi'a seminary in Medina, New York, where they are receiving training traditionally reserved for male students. The young women will become prayer leaders and preachers in Islamic institutions (Sachedina 1994, 11–12). Some who argue that Iraqi Shi'a are more progressive than Iranians cite an Iraqi-based Shi'a mosque in Pomona, California, where women are not seated in a different room for prayer and sometimes address the mixed congregation (Ron Kelley 1994, 156). Iraq has been a far more secular country than Iran, a difference that reminds us to look again at homelands when assessing immigrant discourses and practices in the United States.

Transnational, Cosmopolitan, and Global Identities

Muslim immigrants settling in the United States and around the world are becoming transnational in significant ways, and indigenous American

Muslims are studying and working abroad, making strong connections with Muslims and Islamic institutions in other countries. In chapter 4, I introduced David Hollinger's (1995) distinction between pluralism and cosmopolitanism as competing interpretations of America's commitment to multiculturalism or cultural diversity. Some scholars make a distinction between cosmopolitanism and transnationalism at the global level as part of an ongoing debate about class and global subjectivity. Thus, Pnina Werbner (1999, 19–20) defines "cosmopolitans" as people who familiarize themselves with other cultures and know how to move easily between cultures; she defines "transnationals" as people who, while moving, build encapsulated cultural worlds around themselves, most typically worlds circumscribed by religious or family ties.[9] The usual assumption is that the lives of working- and lower-middle-class immigrants are quite similar to the lives they would have led in their homelands—that they are transnational but not cosmopolitan. Diasporic identities are often said to be increasingly "religious-ethnic," particularly those of the more ethnic, or less cosmopolitan, sectors of the immigrant community. Yet some of these transnationals might also be termed "global," in that they envision their own community writ large playing a major role on the world stage. Those Muslims who envision the international umma as an emerging reality might be considered global.

Recognition of Muslims' wide-ranging transnational or cosmopolitan networks helps counteract the popular idea in the United States that all Muslims have some kind of "diasporic orientation" to Saudi Arabia or the Middle East. V. S. Naipaul (1998, 71–72) has asserted, in a widely read book about Muslims in Indonesia and elsewhere, that "the cruelty of Islamic fundamentalism is that it allows only the one people—the Arabs—a past, and sacred places, pilgrimages and earth-relevances. . . . Converted peoples have to strip themselves of their past." This simplistic statement, made only about "fundamentalists" but predictably generalized in readers' minds to all Muslims, is quite wrong, and never more so than for Muslims in the United States.

In the United States, indigenous Muslims and new immigrants now greatly outnumber the early Arabic-speaking groups. The global cosmopolitan and transnational networks and affiliations of American Muslims today are extremely diverse. Michael Fischer and Mehdi Abedi (1990), tracking diasporic Iranians from the homeland to Kansas, Texas, and elsewhere, illuminate the multiple worlds of these transnational and cosmopolitan exiles and immigrants. American Muslim women are working with Malaysian Muslim women; some Sufi orders in the United States also reach to Southeast (and South) Asia;[10] and some African American Muslims are reaching out to African Muslims. Especially after September 11, 2001, international politics has brought the divisions and conflicts in the Muslim world into American living rooms, disrupting stereotypical Orientalist notions of a monolithic and specifically Middle Eastern Islamic world.

It is true that Mecca, the pilgrimage destination for all Muslims, and other holy places are in Saudi Arabia and the Middle East. This sacred geography orients Muslims around the world to the holy sites, and going on hajj has been a transformative experience for many—most notably perhaps, among American converts, Malcolm X, who wrote: "We were all participating in the same ritual, displaying a spirit of unity and brotherhood that my experience in America had led me to believe never could exist between the white and the non-white" (Malcolm X and Haley 1966, 340).

The orientation to Mecca can also cause conflicts. Thus, among Shi'a, the maraji' taqlid sometimes differ on exactly where Mecca is with respect to the worshiper. While Ayatollah Khui said that adherents in the United States should face southeast when praying, followers of Fadlallah and the Dawa movement disagreed, and being rationalistic, scientific people, they decided to face northeast (Walbridge 1999, 60). An ongoing problem for Muslims in the United States has been the setting of the dates for the beginning and ending of the Ids (festivals, one marking the end of the Ramadan month of fasting and the other the last day of the pilgrimage to Mecca): many Arab Muslims continue to observe the dates proclaimed in Saudi Arabia by moon sightings there, while South Asians, Africans, and others rely on sightings in the United States or projected scientific calculations. The same general split between Arabs and South Asians and Africans occurs with respect to the Prophet's birthday: the former do not observe it, and the latter two generally do so with great enthusiasm. Finally, there is significant opposition among American Muslims to the current Saudi government and its policies with respect to Islam and the Islamic holy places (Abou El Fadl 2002).

It is true that in earlier decades some Muslims in the United States accepted Middle Eastern patronage and assistance. Today the political costs of accepting foreign assistance have become too high, but that was not the case in the past. In the Arab world most mosques are controlled and funded by governments, so the extension of foreign support to early mosques in the United States, where government funding was not available, seemed natural. The recruitment of imams and to a limited extent their financing in the United States often had overseas help, from Egypt's Al-Azhar University in the 1960s and then from the Muslim World League (Haddad 1983, 73), founded and sponsored by Saudi Arabia in 1962 and strongly committed to da'wa. Saudi Arabia has given Qur'ans to many mosques in the United States and funded many building projects (Poston 1992, 30, 39). Other American Muslims accepted funds and gifts too, including the Nation of Islam.

It could be argued that the Gulf states saw the African American Nation of Islam as a kind of special "returning diaspora" in the 1970s and 1980s. In 1978 the Gulf states of Saudi Arabia, Abu Dhabi, and Qatar named W. D. Mohammed their official receiver of funds for conversion efforts in the United States (Poston 1991, 134). Given Mohammed's turn to mainstream Islam, it made sense for him to accept this position. But a Saudi Arabian Muslim looking at the Nation of Islam then, Z. I. Ansari (1981, 148), found that "references to the Holy Prophet in the writings of Elijah Muhammad are scarce, are couched in a highly matter-of-fact phraseology, and lack the love and devotion which characterize a Muslim's attitude towards him." After 1975, when W. D. Mohammed acceded to leadership, this seemed to be changing. Ansari continued to see the Nation of Islam as heretical, but he also saw it as unique because it arose in a non-Muslim milieu and its spread took place not at the expense of Islam but at the expense of black Christianity. That circumstance and the changes initiated by W. D. Mohammed led Ansari (1981, 174–76) to write that "the observers of the movement have watched in wonder and excitement the skill and boldness with which the new leader has proceeded with the task of doctrinal re-orientation" (see also Ansari 1985).

Immigrant Muslims often relate to both their new and old countries, seeing themselves with dual political and cultural roles to play in the global community. These dual roles can create tensions, especially when American foreign policy goes against immigrant Muslim commitments to homeland issues or to issues they see linked to the international Muslim community. The religious affiliations may take second place to political issues and cultural loyalties, as with the early Arabic-speaking immigrants and the Iranians in the United States today.

Sometimes dual roles are imposed on immigrant Muslims. Since the mid-1990s the U.S. government and public has been "more disposed to hear certain concerns of ethnic Americans who endeavor to influence American diplomacy toward their country of origin, *if and when* their governments can be presented as 'democratic.' " The downside is that Arab and Muslim Americans are held, however unfairly, somewhat accountable for the "repudiation" of American culture and values in their homelands (Shain 1994, 85, 105).

Attempts to retain cultural ties despite political alienation from the home country can also lead to tensions, producing creative identities in the diasporic settings. Iran and Iranian Muslim immigrants are a case in point. Hamid Naficy (1993b, 173) argues that Iranian Muslims, predominantly secular and opposed to the Iranian Revolution, nevertheless have come to view the azan (call to prayer) as an emblem of Iranian nationality and "national culture," and that this view is shared by non-Muslim Iranians as well. Another study focuses on the children displaced by the Iranian Revolution who have been affected by both American and Iranian politics. In the words of Fereydoun Safizadeh (1996, 124, 128, 142), they have become "the focal points of diverse and often contradictory identity claims, and their minds have become the terrain for adult battles." Safizadeh interviewed Iranian-origin women undergraduates at the University of California at Berkeley, looking for some sense of a national culture, a state political system, and territoriality. He expected to find evidence of transnational identities and membership in a cosmopolitan international culture, and the students' mixed use of Persian and English, their accents, and their nonverbal communication reflected that, he thought. While the students saw being caught between two cultures as a problem, Safizadeh noted that it was also clearly a source of personal agency or power.

Not only do Muslim immigrants have dual roles, they may be members of diasporic communities that bridge more than two sites in the world today. That too can create tension. Comparing Muslim and Jewish Iranians in Los Angeles, Arlene Dallalfar (1996a, 95) found that the Jewish networks were more concentrated in that city, while the Muslim women were more frustrated, lonely, and disoriented because extended kin were located in Iran, Europe, Canada, Australia, and elsewhere in the United States. The scattering of their relatives around the globe caused anxiety and emotional instability in Muslim households, as it did among the Palestinian women in Chicago studied by Louise Cainkar (1996) (see chapter 4).

In the global arena we see two very different kinds of American Muslims: those who consider themselves members of a developing international Islamic community, or universal umma, and those whose smaller, particular communities are already globalized, in either a transnational or a cosmopolitan way. News about the imagined community of the umma is given regularly in almost all the Muslim newspapers, journals, and media in North America. Some American Muslim political actions are directed toward that ideal community (see Findley 1989). Garbi Schmidt's (forthcoming a) case study of Muslim social activism in Chicago includes a transnational analysis of the influence of young Islamic activists in the United States on Scandinavia and Europe in general, through the Internet and burgeoning English-language publications and dialogue. Schmidt argues that these young Muslims are taking directions very different from those of their immigrant elders (for example, their discourse on gender), directions strongly marked by their socialization in the United States.

This kind of diasporic or international Islamic politics also goes both ways: Muslims abroad develop an enhanced consciousness of their cobelievers in the United States. For example, the Los Angeles-based

Minaret broke the story in April 1997 that the U.S. Supreme Court chambers had an image of the Prophet. Figural images, and certainly representations of the Prophet, are generally prohibited in Islam (Denny 1984), and after the story broke, the Baluchistan provincial assembly in southwestern Pakistan demanded that the image be removed. This unexpected demand from far-off Baluchistan reminds us that we should question whether modernization in the West is truly secular. When we look for Christian discourses and practices in the United States, we find them—or as Talal Asad (1986, 5) put it, we find "the detailed workings of disciplinary power in Christian history." Similarly, Charles Taylor (1999, 157) discusses "the possibility that Western modernity might be sustained by its own original spiritual vision . . . what we used to call Christendom," and Nikki Keddie (1997, 24–25, 39), in an extended discussion of secularism and modernity, emphasizes the strong public presence of Christian and other religious influences in the United States.

At first glance, the Shi'a Nizari Isma'ili community seems to qualify as some kind of global or transnational political-religious entity, perhaps a stateless nation without a desire for territory, a multiracial and multilingual diaspora "that does not rely on the Qur'an and is headed by a monarch" (Kassam-Remtulla 1999, 89). The community does have a constitution, promulgated in 1986 by Aga Khan IV, and also an official flag. The Aga Khan has a seal and a personal standard, and he awards titles to meritorious community members. Boundaries are marked and are not really open; the few converts are typically spouses or adoptees. The three holiest Isma'ili celebrations, all held in the jamatkhanas and thus for members only, are Navroz (Persian New Year, the strongest remaining sign of the movement's earlier homeland), the birthday of Aga Khan IV, and the day Aga Khan IV gained the Imamate. The same uniqueness that allows the Nizari Isma'ilis to adapt—their reliance on the spiritual authority of their leader—keeps them apart from other Muslims, so that even in the diaspora setting of the United States they identify most closely with each other rather than with other Muslims (Kassam-Remtulla 1999, 82–83).

But as Ali Asani (1994, 24) points out, the nation-states in which members live and their legal systems determine major aspects of Nizari Isma'ili life. In India and East Africa, where many members formerly resided, the judicial systems granted legal sanction to the imams as legislators within the Isma'ili community, and the sweeping reforms of the Aga Khans proceeded rapidly. In Pakistan the "Islamic" law of the land is applicable to all Muslim citizens, and reforms have not been introduced that are as far-reaching as elsewhere. Yet the Isma'ilis in Pakistan, nontraditional in their beliefs in ways similar to the Ahmadis, have not been treated like the Ahmadis (declared non-Muslims) because of their wealth and the Aga Khan IV's outstanding contributions to the nation: a private medical school, numerous health centers, and schools (Kassam-Remtulla 1999, 86). There is also the fact that the Nizari Isma'ilis have compromised with Sunni Islam in Pakistan, following Hanafi Sunni laws and marriage and burial practices in the Punjab and Northwest Frontier areas where their numbers are small (Asani 2001, 162). In the United States, the state offers constitutional protection to "functional" religions without taking a position on issues of belief (Moore 1991, 136–37), yet the Nizari Isma'ilis are being treated like the Ahmadis by some of their fellow American Muslims.

The case of the Nizari Isma'ilis shows the continuing importance of state contexts and policies in shaping the identities of transnational and cosmopolitan communities over time and space. The instances of tension among Isma'ili teachings, state laws, and other Muslim communities lead us nicely to a detailed consideration of Islamic law, its sources and agents of authority, and debates about its application in the U.S. context.

=== Chapter 6 ===

Islamic Discourses and Practices

I SLAM is likely to continue, in some profound sense, as the core of many of the Muslim identities and affiliations being developed in the United States as Muslim Americans seek a moral imperative for their lives. This chapter reviews the literature on Islamic or religious law and sources and agents of authority among American Muslims, discussing discourses and practices in tension with each other and primarily within the Muslim community.

Scholars who have been working with Muslims in the United States over the last few decades have seen a rise of Islamic consciousness (Haddad and Smith 1993, 21; Haddad and Lummis 1987). It may reflect the impact of recent immigrants from more conservative homelands or of changing American values—that is, a perceived "lowering" of moral and ethical standards with the countercultural, sexual revolution, feminist, and gay movements. One must also keep in mind the rise in religious or spiritual consciousness in the United States since the 1970s, especially the development of alternative religious movements. Steven Tipton (1982) describes these movements as conservative Christian, neo-Oriental, and psychotherapeutic. Thomas Tweed and Stephen Prothero (1999) review Asian religions and their American transformations. Robert Wuthnow (1988) looks at changing patterns of primarily Christian denominationalism, the rise of special-purpose religious groups, the growing polarization between conservative and liberal Christians, and the changing public dimensions of religious culture in the United States. Islam and Muslims are barely mentioned—or not mentioned at all—in most scholarly work on broad changes in American religion in the late twentieth century (including the three books just mentioned). It is an obvious yet challenging task to relate Islam and Muslims to this mainstream literature.[1]

The role of the nation-state as the source of social recognition and arbiter of rights differs across countries and has important consequences for the conceptualization and management of differences among Muslims and other religious and ethno-racial groups. American Muslims are not living in an Islamic state, or even in a state dominated by Muslims. Their political spokespeople and specialists in Islamic law must work within the framework of American civil and criminal law,[2] and they are often in conflict with each other as they attempt to define the nature of Islamic authority and determine its force in the United States.[3] I first review broad issues of state and religion involving Muslims and their relationship to other Americans and then move to narrower issues of Islamic law, jurisprudence, and cultural transmission involving primarily members of Muslim communities. Even those identities grounded in religion are diverse: specialized rituals and everyday practices thought to be Islamic vary across regional and national boundaries (those having to do with gender being good examples).

State and Religion

How do we contextualize Islamic law? As Talal Asad has stated (1980, 465): "It is the way in which 'the word of God' is reproduced, and the [political] situation to which it is addressed, which together determine its force, and not the lexical and syntactic forms of the sacred text considered in isolation." Islamic law itself has long been characterized by pluralism. There are four major Sunni schools of law: the Maliki, found today in north and sub-Saharan Africa; the Shafi'i, in Egypt and Southeast Asia; the Hanafi, found in the Middle East and South Asia; and the Hanbali, found in Saudi Arabia. The leading Shi'a school, the Ja'fari, is based in Yemen. For most Shi'a Muslim communities, authority vested in a hidden imam focuses attention on ijtihad, the interpretations by his representatives in the world, the maraji' taqlid (or in the case of the Nizari Isma'ilis, the living Aga Khan). If these interpretations are context-specific or flexible, adaptation may be very easy indeed. The Aga Khan III stated that while the Qur'an remains the same, "every generation, every century, every period must have a new and different interpretation to that of the past, otherwise Islam will die" (cited by Asani 1994, 24).

The problems associated with the understanding and practice of shari'a and fiqh in the United States derive partly from the scarcity of specialists in Islamic law in this country and partly from the emergence of the new spokespeople, who are not well schooled in Islamic civilization and law but well credentialed in modern professions (see chapter 2). As the new spokespeople sought to mobilize Muslims, they confronted issues rooted in Islamic law. The first issue was whether the United States was dar al-Islam (the abode of Islam) or dar al-harb (the place of war). If the latter, did Muslims have to migrate from the United States (Masud 1990)? If they remained, were they bound by the laws of the non-Muslim host state or not? As recently as 1986, national Muslim leaders advocated residing only temporarily in dar al-kufr, or the place of unbelievers (the United States). But by the end of that same year, ISNA had taken a position favoring citizenship and participation in mainstream politics in the United States (Poston 1992, 32).[4]

Muslims taking an active role in modern American politics have encouraged legal designations for the United States such as dar al-aman (place of order), dar al-da'wa (place of outreach), and dar al-'ahd or dar al-sulh (place of alliance or treaty), terms reflecting usages in South Asia and the new South Asian American leadership. Mohommed A. Muqtedar Khan (1998b, 115, 118–19), an Indian American, has concluded that most American Muslims believe the United States to be dar al-aman. Since there is no explicit declaration of war against Islam, the United States cannot be dar al-harb, and since there are no specific treaties with resident Muslims, it cannot be dar al-sulh. (India is categorized as dar al-aman by Muslims there.)

The obligation of Muslims everywhere to undertake da'wa—to invite others to hear the message of Islam—can be interpreted as calling others but without compulsion to convert them. It can also be interpreted as "correcting the distortions" of Judaism and Christianity and emphasizing conversion (Poston 1992, 5–6).[5] Some Muslims in the United States have entertained hopes that the country will turn to Islam. They see American society as immoral and decadent and feel a strong sense of mission. Two early Arab intellectual leaders spoke strongly in this vein. Isma'il Al-Faruqi (1983, 269), a Palestinian immigrant and professor of religion at Temple University in Philadelphia, said:[6]

> The Islamic vision provides the immigrant with the criterion with which to understand, judge, and seek to transform the unfortunate realities of North America. Here is a whole continent giving itself to alcohol and drugs, to sexual promiscuity and exploitation, to family destruction and individualism, to cynicism and pessimism, to racism and discrimination, to the pursuit of Mammon at the cost of morality and justice, to the rape of Mother Nature, to political and economic imperialism against the rest of humanity.

The other early leader, Muhammad Abdul-Rauf (1983, 278), imam of the Washington, D.C., Islamic center, saw Islam as an equal, not dominant, partner in building American society:

> This writer enthusiastically envisages [the Islamic community] as developing into an organic element of the multi-cultural American social fabric, dovetailing the major values expressed in the American constitution and the Declaration of Independence with our fundamental Islamic val-

ues to contribute toward a viable 21st century American society that can truly live under the divine protection of the One Mighty God, Allah, in Whom we trust.

Members of minorities within Islam have looked to the United States as a pluralist, democratic country in which variations of Islam can flourish. In an eloquent essay written after September 11, 2001, Ali Asani (2002), a Nizari Isma'ili scholar of Islam, addresses pluralism, intolerance, and the Qur'an, speaking as a pluralist Muslim and an American against antipluralist, or exclusivist, interpretations of the Qur'an in the contemporary Muslim world.

American Muslim discourse now includes discussions of the compatibility of Islam and democracy and Islam and human rights. For example, the new Center for the Study of Islam and Democracy (CSID), a membership-based nonprofit organization in Washington, D.C., was formed in 2000.[7] Proponents of democracy argue that the selection of the caliph (the political head of the umma, abolished by Turkey's Ataturk in 1924) was not based on hereditary principles, and they promote the institution of the shura, or "mutual consultation" council, as analogous to democratic institutions in the West. There are both national and regional experiments with shuras, which often focus initially on practices. Shuras typically try to set common dates for all mosques and Islamic centers, for example, for the offering of the Id prayers ending the Ramadan month of fasting (a matter on which, as mentioned earlier, Arabs and South Asians often differ).

Shari'a and Fiqh in the United States

Leading scholars of Islamic jurisprudence in the United States, like Khaled Abou El Fadl, professor of Islamic law at UCLA, and Taha Alalwani, president of the Fiqh Council of North America and head of the Graduate School of Islamic and Social Sciences, urge that the context should strongly shape decisions about Muslim practices in the United States.[8] Speaking of the Qur'an and hadith, the sources of Islamic law, Abou El Fadl (1996a, 23) has said: "My books, in this context—you are so foreign, so marginal. . . . Here, in this time and place, you are fossilized showpieces. . . . Yet, I know that you are eternal and immutable because you speak forever. But you are contextual because it is the people that read you who must speak to the age . . . our new age and new place."

Both Abou El Fadl and Alalwani disapprove of the application of Islamic legal decisions made elsewhere to the contemporary American context and encourage fiqh scholarship in the United States. Alalwani rebutted opinions that it is unlawful for Muslims to hold citizenship in non-Muslim states and that Muslims can disobey U.S. laws and regulations, arguing that wherever Muslims find the freedom to practice Islam is dar al-Islam and dar al-da'wa (place of outreach) and a place where the laws must be obeyed and the message of Islam should be spread (Hadhrami 2000, 488–53). Abou El Fadl (2000, 41–42) wrote despairingly of the pronouncements of the Shari'a Scholars Association of North America, fiqh specialists who met for three days in Detroit in November 1999. Although "half of the thirty-eight or so scholars have never lived in the U.S., the vast majority have never stepped foot in an American court room, and at least half live under corrupt and oppressive governments," these men issued a double-spaced thirteen-page set of opinions on major issues facing Muslims in North America.

Yet, while fiqh and shari'a have historically played central roles in defining Muslims and Islamic communities, some see them as losing importance in the United States. It is the new spokespeople (who far outnumber scholars of Islamic law in the United States) who have been speaking out, authoritatively and publicly, on issues ranging from citizenship and voting to marriage and family law. "In the United States the field of shari'a is flooded with self-declared experts who inundate our discourses with self-indulgent babble and gibberish . . . those who are unable to differentiate . . . the fundamentals of Islam from its particulars" (Abou El Fadl 1998b, 41).

There have been national-level efforts to establish a fiqh council for North America, an Islamic shura or representative council to issue opinions, or fatawa (plural of fatwa)—interpretive and nonbinding rulings on questions brought to it.[9] A fiqh council was begun in the 1970s as a committee of the Muslim Students' Association (MSA) but was limited in scope, dealing chiefly with setting the dates for starting and ending the month of fasting. In 1988 the ISNA Fiqh Council reorganized to become the Fiqh Council of North America (DeLorenzo 1998, 68–69). Its presidency rotates annually between the heads of ISNA and ICNA and two African American leaders (W. D. Mohammed of Chicago and Imam Jamil Al-Amin, the former H. Rap Brown, of Atlanta).[10] However, it is "overwhelmingly composed of naturalized Muslims," men who know little about U.S. family law and inheritance rights, according to Aminah Beverly McCloud (1995, 126–27), an African American Muslim scholar. This council and similar regional or local shuras are in any case seldom accepted as authoritative, not even by all immigrant Muslim scholars.

The Fiqh Council recognizes all schools of Islamic law equally and several Islamic ways of life—DeLorenzo (1998, 71, 69) stressing the plurals, "schools" and "ways"—but it has been presented with questions never considered by traditional scholars. For example, does having a credit card qualify one as having the means to undertake the hajj even if one does not have the requisite amount in cash? Can Muslim marriages be terminated only Islamically in the United States, or must they be terminated through the state court system? What are properly Islamic dress and haircuts, and can a Muslim youth wear dreadlocks? Other cases specifically address the circumstance of being a minority in a non-Muslim society (see also Abou El Fadl 1998b).

According to Abou El Fadl and others, the puritanical Wahhabi strand of Islam so strongly associated with Saudi Arabia today and promoted elsewhere erases reliance on these classical schools of law—not least in the United States, with its dearth of Islamic legal scholars and traditions. In one sense, the new spokespeople and new kinds of media have reinvigorated Islamic discourse, developing a wider role and mainstream audience for Islam, but in another sense they have standardized and simplified the discourse and weakened the commitment to pluralism. As Muhammad Khalid Masud put it (1990, 45–46), speaking generally about Western-educated intellectuals and their calls for the propagation of Islam:

> For the simple reason that they are not hindered by the complexities of traditional legal thought, [these intellectuals] have the freedom of selecting more eclectically from tradition and justifying their views directly from the Qur'an and hadith. They often earn instant popularity because of reference to the "sources," but, since their interpretations do not form a continuity with tradition, their impact is often partial and ephemeral. The new intellectuals are therefore continually compelled to search for dramatic, and often extremist, solutions.

These confident new spokespeople have produced, according to many scholars of Islam and Islamic law, a landscape devoid of respect for the schools and methods of Islamic legal scholarship and for pluralism (Asani 2002; Abou El Fadl 2001a, 1–42). In the 2000 national survey of mosques (Bagby, Perl, and Froehle 2001, 28), the respondents—imams and presidents and members of governing boards—placed the traditional schools of law at the very bottom of the list in terms of "sources of authority in the worship and teaching" of their mosques. Fifty-two percent felt that the teachings of a particular madhhab, or school of law, were of little or no importance, 25 percent found them somewhat important, 18 percent said they were very important, and only 5 percent deemed them absolutely foundational.[11] The other recent social science survey of American Muslims, by Project MAPS in 2001 (Project MAPS 2002), did not even ask about sectarian affiliations or views of sources of religious authority.

Islamic legal traditions persist in the United States, however, and some scholars have been called upon by the media since September 11,

2001, to clarify Islamic teachings about terrorism and jihad (struggle or warfare). The legal traditions support pluralism within the religion and legitimate debates among Islamic legal scholars established in the United States. Reportedly, members of the American Society of Muslims are thinking about constituting a new and separate legal school based on the views of Imam W. D. Mohammed (Bagby 2001–2002, 211), and feminist Muslim scholars are also carefully categorizing and debating texts and teachings related to gender.

Important Distinctions: Usul and Furu', Culture and Religion

In Islamic law an important distinction is that between usul al-fiqh, the basics or fundamentals of jurisprudence upon which disagreement is not tolerated, and furu', the branches or subdivisions in which disagreements and new and original problems and cases are permitted. In the long history of disputation, debate, and disagreement among Muslim jurists since the classical period of Islam, there has been disagreement about what is usul and what is furu'. The historical debate has always been about the use, authority, and interpretation of different sources of knowledge (human reason or a textual source and, if the latter, the various levels of authenticity). Then there was debate about the phrase "every mujtahid (interpreter) is correct," with its implication that every sincere seeker of the Divine Will reaches a truthful understanding of it, and whether this phrase should be applied only to furu' or to both usul and furu'. In the United States today the trend among the new spokespeople is to assign positive commandments of the law (ahkam) to one or the other category (usul or furu') definitively, but they tend to assign more and more laws to usul and to disallow disagreement about usul, thus limiting the scope for legitimate disagreement and discussion. Abou El Fadl (2001a, 173, 162, 28–30), on whom I rely here, sees these efforts at simplification and standardization as authoritarian rather than authoritative, and as limiting the search for the truth that lies at the heart of Islamic jurisprudence.

I use this scholarly legal distinction here to introduce another distinction more commonly made by ordinary Muslims—nonspecialists in fiqh. That is the distinction between culture and religion, one frequently invoked as Muslims debate beliefs and practices that are allowed or disallowed in Islam. Lay Muslims argue about which beliefs and practices are fundamental to the religion and which have accrued to it because of "culture" in one or another place or country. This is an issue also raised by others, non-Muslims and non-Americans, who see culture as having usurped the function of religion, so that religious difference now signifies primarily cultural difference for many in the Western democracies (see, for example, Viswanathan 1998).

Encounters between religion and culture occur in all American Muslim arenas. Robert Dannin (1996a, 169, 168–69) says: "In terms of Islamic identity, America has now become an arena for competing self-images where religious authority and cultural preferences are often conflated if not altogether displaced and de-territorialized." He illustrates this by quoting a young imam at the First Cleveland Mosque about the Tablighi Jamat, a nonpolitical missionary movement originating in South Asia that sends missionaries to Muslim communities in North America and elsewhere (see Metcalf 1996). Looking at a young African American who had spent time in Pakistan and come back with a Tablighi Jamat group, the imam said: "They're just spreading Pakistani culture. They've even got brothers eating on the floor with their fingers and telling them that using toilet paper is 'against the Prophet's tradition.' "

Converts are especially likely to notice whether religious practices are based on core texts or on allegedly religious customs that clearly differ among Muslims according to national or ethnic origin. Sometimes linguistic competence is confused with religious affiliation: an American convert found that her Pakistani American niece expected her to learn Urdu so that she could "really" be a Muslim (Ron Kelley 1994, 142). African American and Euro-American converts share certain dissatisfactions with the stances taken by many immigrant Muslims (McCloud 1995; Lang 1994). McCloud argues eloquently that immigrant Muslims are trying to impose ethnic customs derived from their homelands on American Muslims, particularly gender-related customs (McCloud 1995, 145, 157–58, 163–73).

Just as some scholars have asserted about the conflict over usul and furu', the conflict over religion and culture in the United States often centers on issues involving women (Abou El Fadl 2001a, 17–18; Asani 2002). In determining gender roles among Iranians in Los Angeles, Nayereh Tohidi (1993, 175, 177–78) argues, shared culture is more important than religious or ethnic diversity, even among these educated middle- and upper-class immigrants. Migration has heightened conflicts between parents and children and between women and men, producing a rising rate of divorce, and changes in traditional conceptions of women's roles are taking place faster in women than in men. Nevertheless, Tohidi attributes these changes to trends well under way in Iran itself before emigration.[12] Distinguishing between the religious and cultural values that affect Lebanese young women involved in mut'a (temporary) marriages in Dearborn, Michigan, Linda Walbridge (1997, 186–87) asserts that virginity is much prized in Lebanese culture but not in Islam. Therefore, these young women were taking a risk only if the mut'a marriage was a first marriage, since loss of their virginity would make it difficult to contract a permanent marriage.

Women: The Focal Point

The grand narratives of religion in the Islamic Old World heartland, like those of religion in the United States, have focused on men. In the United States those men have been Anglo-Saxon, mainline Protestants from the Northeast. "Retellings" of American religious history seek to broaden the scope and acknowledge other influences on the narrative and other voices in the conversations about religion in the national culture (Tweed 1997, 3–6). Women in the United States have constituted the majority of participants in Christian religious activities and institutions, Ann Braude (1997) argues, and women have increasingly exercised moral authority in both religious and civic institutions (see also Wuthnow 1988, 225–35).

Women are also assuming increasingly influential (if contested, as in Judaism and Christianity) roles in Islam. In 1975 in Mexico City, during the International Women's Year Tribunal, I attended a small but interesting session called by Muslim women and led informally by women lawyers from Egypt and Turkey. Two Muslim men, of Pakistani origin but from Chicago, also attended and insistently voiced their views; at the end they volunteered to write up the minutes and coordinate future activities. A lawyer from Turkey politely but firmly refused their offer, saying, "We women also have the right of ijtihad." Now we are seeing that meeting writ large, with Muslim women around the world putting forward their interpretations of Islam. Like those of men, these interpretations are not uniform, and the efforts of women scholars to establish themselves in the field of fiqh range from tentative to impressive.

A good introduction to the work of American Muslim women scholar-activists is Gisela Webb's (2000) edited volume (for background, see Rippin 1990–1993, 115–26). Amina Wadud (2000, 20), an African American Muslim and an Islamic studies professor at Virginia Commonwealth University, calls for a radical and continual rethinking of the Qur'an and hadith.[13] Asserting that much now considered divine and immutable shari'a is the result of a long, male-dominated intellectual process, she says: "The attempts to address the question of Muslim women's autonomous agency and authentic Islamic identity in the context of Islam and modernity can only be successful when a complete reexamination of the primary sources of Islamic thought, praxis, and worldview is made that intentionally includes female perspectives on these sources and that validates female experiences."

Wadud's book *Qur'an and Woman* (1999, x, xii–xiii, xviii–xix, 81) is a leading contribution to what she and others term the "gender jihad." It was first published in Malaysia in 1992, where Wadud has been active, and then translated and published in Indonesian (1994) and Turkish (1997), evidencing the global reach of the gender jihad. Hers is a hermeneutic analysis: she assesses what the Qur'an says, how it says it, what is said about it and by whom, and what is left unsaid. The book has been very widely read, generating reactions from "more conservative Muslims." Wadud writes: "As a woman, of African origin, and an American convert to Islam, I was not supposed to seek beyond what others hand down to me. . . . I used to think that 'Islam' and 'Muslim' were one and the same [but] situations may arise where one might be forced to choose between the two." She believes that Islam requires struggle for justice. Wadud asserts that Islam *as practiced* today is patriarchal, but *true* Islam is not.

In support of such views, Amira El-Azhary Sonbol (2000, 144), Egyptian-born and now a professor of Islamic history at Georgetown University's Center for Muslim-Christian Understanding, argues that "through legal codes based literally on fiqh texts selected and interpreted by a modern patriarchal order," state power has been added to male biological power to extend men's control over women. Sonbol also argues that the actual lives of Muslim women in premodern societies were freer than religious texts would suggest, because fiqh was being constantly reinterpreted (Abugideiri 2000, 95).[14] Sonbol is lauded, along with Wadud, as one of three models of Islamic leadership for American Muslim women, the third being Sharifa Alkhateeb. Born in Philadelphia to a Yemeni father and Czech mother, Alkhateeb took degrees in literature and religion and has led in numerous ways. She was founding president of the National American Council for Muslim Women (NACMW) in 1983, a council urging Muslim women to acquire and use Islamic knowledge to gain control over their lives. It was the first national Muslim organization to make domestic violence and violence against children topics of discussion at a national conference, and it conducted a survey about violence against women in 1993 (Abugideiri 2000, 97–99).

Sufis have their own perspectives on women's position in Islam. Recognizing that Islam, at the time of its birth, improved the condition of women in Arabia but that women's position under Islam has deteriorated over time, the noted scholar of Sufism Annemarie Schimmel (1997, 14–15, 180) argues that "there is one area in which the woman does enjoy full equal rights, and that is in the realm of mysticism, even if the perfect woman is still referred to as a 'man of God.' " As the male principle dominates in "all religions and cultures," she says, so in Islam "much suffering has fallen to the lot of women because simple Qur'anic precepts have been interpreted more and more narrowly over the course of time." Yet "women in the mystical tradition in general can be looked upon as the most attractive, pleasantly fragrant manifestations of the One." Similarly, Laleh Bakhtiar (1996) asserts women's equality in the spiritual journey of Sufism as she profiles seven American women of diverse backgrounds in the Naqshbandi Order.[15] (One of them is the wife of Shaykh Muhammad Hisham Kabbani.) Marcia Hermansen (forthcoming b) comments on Lois Banner's (1998) autobiographical account of a friend's journey to Islam through Sufism and Sufism's resonances with American feminism.

The Webb volume (2000) contains another fine article that weaves together many of these strands. The African American Muslim Gwendolyn Zoharah Simmons (2000) is a Sunni and a Sufi, and she came to Islam after participating in the civil rights and black power movements. She began identifying as a feminist while in Mississippi working for black civil rights. Learning that religion and culture "have been used historically to convince women of their inferiority and their second-class status just as it had been used to convince African Americans of the same," she had "no desire to reoppress myself as a woman in the name of religion" (Webb 2000, 200–1, 205). She identifies with the growing number of Muslim women scholars and activists "seeking to separate Islam, the religion, from culture, tradition, and social mores . . . at times bringing to the foreground the interpretations of earlier sects or groups in Islam who were labeled heterodox and their views dismissed."

Simmons also talks about American—and specifically African American—problems: issues of modesty and chastity, children born out of wedlock, and teenage and sometimes polygynous marriages as antidotes to sexual activity. Her closing paragraph deserves to be quoted in full (Webb 2000, 225):

> Rigid gender segregation, hierarchical gender relations, relegation of women to primarily domestic roles, marginalization of women's theological/ religious participation in the interpretation of Islam, and advocacy of unmodified patriarchy are not what is needed to produce a full flowering of Islam in America. I long to see the promotion of an egalitarian, compassionate, merciful, and peaceful Islam where male and female believers grow in the three thousand gracious qualities and ninety-nine attributes of the living God. I hope to engage in whatever work I can do to promote a universalist, egalitarian, and pluralistic Islam.

Some of the issues concerning Muslim women in the United States are explicitly discussed in debates that often turn on distinctions between usul and furu', or between religion and culture. Muslim women's clothing and the ways in which women should interact with men are sources of anxiety to many American Muslims, and the debate seems to emphasize women's status as symbols of sexual temptation. The necessity of wearing a hijab (head scarf) or the jilbab or chador (full cloaks) is a key issue, and it turns on whether the injunction to do so is usul or furu' and also on whether the reason for covering is because of fitna (seduction or sexual arousal, caused by women) or because of 'awra (the private parts a person must cover for modesty, depending on one's gender and a woman's status as free or slave). Abou El Fadl (2001a, 79, 121–38) provides a fascinating and very detailed discussion of these issues.

Many imams and new spokespeople in the United States routinely advocate donning the hijab, and Islamic organizations may take sides, inviting women to events but requiring them to wear "Islamic attire," usually defined as the hijab. Yet this can be a barrier to conversion (Lang 1998, 112 passim). At one mosque one woman was reluctant to become a Muslim when the members' consensus was that, if she wanted to take the shahada (submission to Allah), she had to wear the hijab or declare her intention to adopt it. But, writes Abou El Fadl (1996b, 43):

> [H]ijab does not involve a pillar of Islam or a hadd crime. . . . [It] was not decreed till the very end of the Medina period [in a verse specifying its purpose was to prevent harm]. If harm is the operative cause of the law of hijab what greater harm is there than to desire the Shahada and be denied it? . . . Whatever causes hardship and misery cannot be a part of Sharia even if people believe it to be so . . . [but] perhaps there is no greater hardship for the Muslim umma today than the calamity of women not being properly covered.

The wearing of the hijab can also occasion generational struggle, and in the contemporary United States it is usually daughters who want to wear it. In one case, a mother insisted that her daughter accept an arranged marriage and, as a first step, that she remove her hijab, asserting that obedience to parents took priority over modesty. The point, again made by Abou El Fadl (1997c, 43) was that,

> if parents have the power to uncover their children's bodies, they also have the power to decide who these bodies enter into conjugal relations with. . . . [But] respect and blind obedience are not synonymous and the authoritative and authoritarian are not the same. First and foremost the worth and dignity of a human being must be demonstrated and taught in the parent-child relationship. Even parents may not replace the Will of God with the authoritarianism of human will.

Some Muslim male scholars and laymen are what I would call feminists. Abou El Fadl, as one can tell from these quotes, is one of them.[16] Commenting on legal decisions concerning Muslim women's rights in marriage, El Fadl (1999, 41) wrote that, [despite] endless rhetoric about the rights of women in Islam . . . I fear that the seclusion of women has taught [Muslim men] that what is secluded is to be possessed and owned . . . and used. . . . The fact is that those who ache to regulate women are those who invariably violate them, and those who are obsessed with defining the limits for women are the ones who observe no limits with women.

Another important thinker on women in Islam is the late Sudanese Muslim reformer Mahmoud Mohamed Taha, whose writings have been influential in American Muslim circles.[17] The young American Muslim political philosopher Mohommed A. Muqtedar Khan (2002, 90–94) also urges greater inclusion of women in Muslim public life and in ijtehad (interpretation) of Islamic law.

Opposition to state "interference" in domestic affairs is another aspect of the reinforcement of patriarchy, and Muslim women's recourse to American laws and services intended to assist women and/or children is often problematic. Many Muslims oppose the intervention of state agencies to prevent abuse of women and children or to remove children, for any reason, from their parents' custody. Cries of outrage result when Muslim children are put into Christian foster homes, but in one highly publicized case in Texas in the 1990s there were no Muslim foster parents on social service rosters with whom children from an Albanian American family could be placed. NISWA, a southern California Muslim women's organization, has begun to find and list Muslim foster parents and to work with government agencies to avoid such outcomes.

Domestic abuse in Muslim families is a problem of unknown but significant proportions. Muslim women in the United States find that government-sponsored programs like shelters for battered women, support groups, legal services and the like are not well-oriented to Muslim clients' needs, but when they do try to use them, they face opposition from their religious and cultural institutions (Ayyub 2000, 239). At a major Islamic conference in Los Angeles in 1996, an African American Muslim woman observed that Muslim women should not be afraid to turn to mainstream institutions for help with domestic abuse, since the "brothers" could not be counted on. She mentioned a recent instance in which a Muslim brother was honored in the mosque although everyone knew he had recently beaten his wife senseless.

Sexual abuse and incest are almost never discussed in relation to Muslim families. After counseling a Muslim woman whose father had repeatedly molested her sexually, Abou El Fadl (1997b) wrote: "I open the books . . . and I find no mention of her or her suffering. The jurists were very reluctant to hold parents liable for offenses committed against their children. . . . The only place I can find a discourse about her is in the writings of non-Muslim authors. . . . Unfortunately, my sister, you have not yet entered our consciousness." In this instance, he counseled that mainstream discourse and institutions seemed to be the woman's only recourse.

To avoid mainstream institutions, however, some imams have advocated setting up Islamic arbitration committees to deal with disputes over domestic abuse, sexual abuse, and divorce. Yet when women turn to their mosques, they are not sure of a welcome. Women's access to mosques for meetings of their own is regulated by the imams, men who in immigrant mosques are usually trained outside the United States and are not necessarily sympathetic to meetings about domestic abuse. In New York State, for example, of 158 Islamic centers recently surveyed, only a handful provided any services for women (Ayyub 1998, cited in Ayyub 2000, 242).

Ingrid Mattson (1999), a Canadian-origin professor of Islamic studies and Christian-Muslim relations at Hartford Seminary who has been in the United States for over a decade, spoke out in 1999 about Muslim women's exclusion from having any public or authoritative presence within their own Muslim communities. Shortly afterward she became ISNA's first woman officer, a vice president of the society, and she has served on its shura council.[18] The situation she decried in 1999 appears to be changing with scholars, activists, and, as we will see, younger Muslims leading the way.

= Chapter 7 =

Becoming American

A MERICAN Muslims understand and practice Islam in ways inevitably and strongly shaped by the American context. I return here to the range of Muslim identities being developed in the United States and consider the extent to which they resist or reflect accommodation with or integration into American society.[1] I explore this by examining work on political organizations and institutions, "American" mosques and religious patterns, the Islamic education and knowledge industry in the United States, Muslim expressive culture (artistic expressions related to Islam or carried out by Muslims in the United States), and the activities of young American Muslims.

There are Muslims in the United States who oppose accommodations with Western, and particularly American, society and are seeking alternative Islamic "constructions of modernity." While I cannot do justice here to the debate between modernizers and their opponents in Islamic scholarly circles in the United States, let me briefly indicate its parameters. Leading scholars among the (in some respects) antimodernists lament the rising popularity of the new spokespeople for Islam in the United States, many of whose interpretations betray a lack of classical or traditional Islamic training. Thus, Seyyed Hossein Nasr (1987, 299, 301–2) writes about the "intrusion of modernism into dar al-Islam":

> The Muslim modernists . . . place value and some degree of trust in one aspect or another of that post-medieval development in the West which is called modernism; and also . . . they have tried and continue to try to interpret Islam, or some of its features, according to the ideas, values and norms drawn from the modern outlook, with its own wide range of diversity. The modernist schools range from those which wish to reinterpret Islam in the light of the humanistic and rationalistic trends of Western thought . . . to those which are drawn to the Marxist world-view.

Similarly, William Chittick (1994, 163–64) believes that these conspicuous modernist movements represent "an intensified destruction of Islamic

100

values. The Islamic concept of human perfection has been banished from the stage, to be replaced by various types of outwardly orientated human endeavor borrowed from contemporary ideologies."

On the other hand, Islamic modernizers, men like Fazlur Rahman, who was professor of Islamic studies at the University of Chicago, envision a rethinking of Islam best accomplished in the West and work to contextualize Islam and reinterpret it as part of Western civilization and science.[2] To such scholars, and to Muslim postmoderns like Professors Ebrahim Moosa at Duke University, Ferid Esadi at Virginia Institute, and others writing in Omid Safi's *Progressive Muslims* volume (forthcoming), the centrality of the United States in an evolving international umma might parallel that of the Haramayn (Mecca and Medina) in the eighteenth century (Voll 1980). A major difference might be the shift of orientation from purely scholarly to scholarly and political work on the hadith traditions and neo-Sufism (along lines suggested by women in the gender jihad).

Political Organizations and Institutions

The study of the American Muslim politics now developing among indigenous and immigrant Muslims is just beginning. Early African American Muslim groups stood against participation in American politics, and so did early immigrant Muslims—that is, as Muslims: they began mobilizing politically as Arabs. But now American Muslims are being urged by national leaders and organizations to participate in politics at all levels, and "all levels" reflects a great many organizational resources, as Gary David and Kenneth Ayouby's (2002, 130–31) list of metropolitan Detroit Middle Eastern organizations well illustrates. Agha Saeed (2002), himself a national political leader (of AMA and AMPCC), skillfully sets American Muslim politics in context, reviewing domestic and foreign policy issues and outlining Muslim hopes and responses to them in the United States.

Some idea of the grassroots support for Muslim political efforts comes from, again, the recent national surveys of American mosques and Muslims. The 2001 Project MAPS poll was an explicitly political effort, and it asked many questions about political views and voting behavior. A major finding was that 79 percent of Muslims were registered to vote. (African Americans and women were the high groups.) Among those registered (and answering the question), 40 percent were Democrat, 23 percent Republican, and 28 percent independents or small-party members. African Americans were more likely to be Democrats, Pakistanis to be Republicans, and the Arabs were almost evenly divided among the three categories. Although over 90 percent of the respondents favored big government solutions to issues like health care and poverty, respondents were very conservative on social issues.[3] U.S. foreign policy concerns were clear: 84 percent wanted the United States to support a Palestinian state, 70 percent wanted the United States to reduce financial aid to Israel, and 61 percent wanted the United States to reduce support of undemocratic regimes in the Muslim world. Fifty-seven percent thought mosques should express views on questions of the day, while 37 percent thought they should not (again, with African Americans and women the high groups). Finally, a healthy percentage of the African Americans, 39 percent, were raised as Muslims ("born Muslims," as opposed to "new Muslims"), while 98 and 95 percent of the Arabs and South Asians were raised as Muslims.

The surveys of mosque representatives in 1994 and 2000 did not ask for views about participation in politics, but they did ask about affiliation to the major national Muslim organizations. These national organizations and the coalitions among them are based on religious affiliation— on being Muslim (as they define it). Their inspiration comes partly from the example set by American Jews and their successful political coalition-building and partly from the visions and ambitions of the American Muslim leaders. The results of the two surveys show that about half of the mosques are currently affiliated with one of the national organizations, but there have been important shifts. In 1994, 39 percent were with ISNA, 19 percent with W. D. Mohammed, 4 percent with ICNA, 5 percent with the Tablighi Jamat, 2 percent with Imam Jamil Al-Amin, and 7 percent with "others." Twenty-four percent of mosques in 1994 were unaffiliated. In 2000 these percentages had changed to 27 percent with ISNA, 19 percent with W. D. Mohammed, 5 percent with ICNA, 3 percent with Tablighi Jamat, and 6 percent with "others"; an almost-doubled 45 percent were unaffiliated (Bagby, Perl, and Froehle 2001, 57).[4] These results, coupled with the emergence of the new African American "historically Sunni" group (MANA) splitting off from yet bridging both indigenous and immigrant groups (Bagby 2001–2002), suggest that dramatic changes are under way.

Current American Muslim politics needs close study, and the four leading journals (Nyang 1998) provide plenty of material. *Islamic Horizons* is published by ISNA, the *Muslim Journal* is published by the Ministry of Imam W. D. Mohammed of the American Society of Muslims, *Message International* is published by ICNA (which also maintains a popular website, SoundVision), and *The Minaret* is published by the Islamic Center of Southern California. *The Minaret*, which has been analyzed by Juan Campo (1996), represents one of the most successful inter-ethnic Islamic congregations in the United States, makes a very self-conscious effort to formulate and represent an American Islam, and is probably an exceptional case. We need more studies of American Muslim discourse and politics in these journals, where one first sees the changing political stances and alliances. For example, the desire to put forward strong Muslim men as leaders in the United States arguably contributes to the immigrant Muslim eagerness, evident in *Islamic Horizons* and *The Minaret*, to embrace African American Muslim charismatic leaders and personalities like Mohammad Ali, Kareem Abdul-Jabbar, Louis Farrakhan, and Mike Tyson, despite their sometimes questionable Islamic credentials.[5]

Support for "family values," also a major theme in the leading journals, has led Muslim organizations to support extremely conservative candidates and causes in the American political context. Muslim magazines have occasionally recognized a kinship with fundamentalist Christians, running sympathetic articles, for example, when the Southern Baptists reemphasized patriarchal family values in an amended statement of belief passed in 1999. The Mormon Church has also been held up as an example for Islamic community-building in the United States. Muslim periodicals admire its family values, cooperative governing structures, tithing system, and, apparently, its opposition to the Equal Rights Amendment and influential role in "foreign policy and domestic intelligence."[6]

The Internet provides many new sources for the study of American Muslim politics, and utilizing these are two forthcoming studies by Garbi Schmidt—on Sufi charisma on the Internet (Schmidt, forthcoming b) and on young Muslim reactions in Denmark and the United States after September 11, 2001 (Schmidt 2002b). Some of the material produced by Muslim youth—for example, some of the homosexual support group information mentioned later in the chapter—is probably available only on the Internet.

Political participation by American Muslims need not be based on religion. Tayyab Mahmud (forthcoming) argues that opting to participate in American politics under the banner of Islam rests on flawed assumptions of a unified Muslim identity, cohesive Muslim political interests, and the role of religion in American political processes. He proposes that alliances with others in the United States along the lines of race, gender, and class would be a more effective way to contribute to the universal Islamic goals of equality and social justice. Jamillah Karim (forthcoming a) focuses on the American Society of Muslims and its leader, W. D. Mohammed, and examines the African American relationship with immigrant Muslims; she sees differences of race, ethnicity, class, and, ultimately, "God-consciousness." Such issues undoubtedly played into MANA's split-off, and the conversions to Islam occurring in U.S. prisons among African American men are another reminder that race remains a key issue in American politics and by extension in American Muslim politics (although convicted felons may not vote).

Gender issues have political potential, since national organizations like ISNA and ICNA have restricted their leadership positions to men. (This changed for ISNA when Ingrid Mattson was elected a vice president in 2000.) Some, including ICNA, seat women separately at meetings and in the rear during prayers, practices debated in the American Muslim press.[7] MAPS, holding a leadership conference in May 2002, noticed afterward that the only woman participant had come as staff to two of the men. The National American Council of Muslim Women (NACMW) and a new "indigenous Muslim" group, MANA, also see gender issues as very important.

Politics in Arab (not just Muslim) Detroit has been studied (Rignall 2000; Howell 2000b), and several political studies spearheaded by Ann Chih Lin follow up gender, class, generational, and religious variables among Arab Americans in the Detroit area. The studies rest on in-depth, qualitative interviews between 1997 and 2000 with fifty-three to ninety-two Arab immigrants, half male and half female, who had been in the United States for between five and fifty years. Twenty-five percent of the interviewees were Christian (Orthodox and Catholic), and the remaining 75 percent were Muslim (Sunni, Shi'a, and Druze); they came from seven nations (Palestine, Syria, Lebanon, Iraq, Jordan, Algeria, and Egypt). Sixty-seven percent were U.S. citizens, and almost all of the rest were permanent residents. The broadest study explores identity construction and finds three major types of community: a group of immigrants for whom cultural and religious observances are seen as indistinguishable; a group of immigrants for whom pan-ethnic Arab identity is most important; and a group of immigrants for whom being Muslim is more important than being Arab (Lin and Jamal, forthcoming). Another study, by Ann Chih Lin and Amaney Jamal (2000), focuses on gender, relating citizens' involvement in the political system to their gender-differentiated social networks and perceptions of state authority. (The men and women responded to questions about street repair, police harassment, and domestic violence.) Another study (Jamal, Lin, and Stewart, forthcoming) examines "patriarchal connectivity" and individualism, again giving gender a key explanatory role in the analysis. A fourth study (Lin, Hackshaw, and Jamal 2001) explores Arab immigrants' ideas about discrimination and tries to relate them to the agendas of advocacy groups and political organizations.

The fifth of these nuanced studies, models of careful research and analysis, is the only one to focus exclusively on Muslim Arabs (Jamal 2002). It looks specifically at the effects of engagement in religious institutions on engagement in civic life and finds that those Muslim Arabs affiliated with mosques (and sharing "common-fate perceptions") differ from unaffiliated Muslims in their responses to concerns about police harassment. All respondents expected the state to uphold the law fairly and equally, but the majority of the "mosqued" Muslims would file complaints against the officer while the majority of the "unmosqued" would blame the speeding Arab motorist.

Some very special-purpose groups of American Muslims are entering the political arena. Decades ago, financial matters like usury, loans, and interest presented problems in Islamic law to Muslim immigrants (Haddad and Lummis 1987, 98–102), and in some respects continue to do so (Smith 1999, 134–37). Maurer (forthcoming) describes how that has changed: some Muslim financiers now persuasively link Islamic and American ideas of community and see themselves as fully American and the United States as an enabling environment for Islam. He outlines the developing compatibility of the Islamic and American legal concepts that govern banking, investment, and profit-sharing enterprises. To these financiers, Islamic banking exemplifies American populism. Maurer reports that Muslim bankers say that only in America do they have the freedom to do what they do, and they hope to export their techniques back to the Muslim countries from which they emigrated. Interestingly, these Muslim bankers find Californian Muslims more open to different ideas, particularly ideas about home financing. A leading Islamic finance house, American Finance House-LARIBA (Los Angeles Reliable Investment Bankers Associates), started calling its business "faith-based financing" after September 11, 2001, appealing to President Bush's faith-based initiatives. Freddie Mac, the U.S. mortgage underwriter, has signed a contract with this group to underwrite "Islamic mortgages" (Bill Maurer, personal communication, February 14, 2002).

The Muslim financial special-purpose firms, and perhaps many American Muslim political groups, can be analyzed along the lines proposed by Robert Wuthnow (1988) for American "mainstream" religions. Looking at trends among Christians in the United States, Wuthnow found that denominationalism, understood as adherence to the particular denomination of Christianity into which one was born, has declined as people change church memberships and marry across denominational lines. Rising levels of higher education have made both Protestant and Catholic denominations more homogeneous as well as liberalized Christian thinking on social issues. Yet as denominational boundaries have become less rigid, special-purpose groups—voluntary associations formed to oppose or support issues based on particular religious convictions (such as anti-abortion or anti-gay groups)—have increased in numbers and public activity. All these developments have fueled a growing polarization in the United States between conservative and liberal Christians, and the public dimensions of religious culture have also grown in tandem with the power of the nation-state. Wuthnow discusses the Judeo-Christian civil religion of the United States and the ways in which Christianity, capitalism, liberty and justice, and a possible special role for America in the world are entangled in conservative and liberal religious thinking.

These mainstream religious developments have obvious relevance for American Muslim politics as well. Mohommed A. Muqtedar Khan (2002, 27–35, 4–6, 75–78) is concerned about the polarization between what he calls "Muslim Democrats," who focus on American democracy, and "Muslim Isolationists," who focus on American foreign policy. These groups take very different views of the U.S. role in the world, American social issues, and issues of freedom and pluralism or multiculturalism. Himself a political scientist and a liberal Muslim (Muslim Democrat), Khan believes that the destiny of American Muslims is to play the role of mujaddid, or reviver and reformer of Islam. He discusses the transformative power of what Muslims themselves are now calling an American Muslim perspective. Arguably, this and other expressions of American Muslim aspirations to leadership of the transglobal umma are partially based on the freedoms and strengths derived from residence and citizenship in the United States and on the U.S. vision of itself as leader of the world.

American Mosques and American Islam

It used to be thought that, as people became modern, religions would decline in significance in their lives, but this has not happened. The "secularization paradigm" is dead, as scholarship in disciplines ranging from sociology to religious studies shows, and research on distinctively American forms of religious belief and practice has become a fruitful area (Warner and Wittner 1998; Yang and Ebaugh 2001). Many argue that religion in the United States is a private concern rather than a public concern, more so than in the past or in other parts of the world. Whether this is true will be hard to assess for American Muslims, since we have so little data on "unmosqued" American Muslims; qualitative, ethnographic work is in order.

There are other characteristics attributed to religion in the United States. Social scientists hypothesize (or think they have established) that religious institutions and practices become "congregational" in the United States; that religious specialists take on a "pastoral" role that spans a wide—not a narrowly religious—range of functions; that religious practices help maintain cultural—particularly linguistic—identities for immigrants and thus are a form of social capital that both challenges adaptations to the United States and strengthens immigrant self-confidence; that the political potential for mobilization along religious lines is enhanced by location in the modern United States; and that immigrants' diasporic religious interactions with home countries have strong ("Americanizing"?) influences back home (Stepick, forthcoming; Vasquez, forthcoming; Leonard, Stepick, and Vasquez, forthcoming).

Many of the authors cited (particularly Lincoln 1997 [1983] and Mamiya 2001–2002) have already made the case for African American Muslim roots in the religious movements of the late nineteenth and early twentieth centuries. The mosque survey of 2000 points to distinctively African American Muslim structural features, such as imam-headed, English-using congregations based in urban and inner-city communities (Bagby, Perl, and Froehle 2001). Less clear is the extent to which the beliefs and practices of immigrant Muslims reflect accommodations with or adaptations to American society.

For immigrant Muslims, Abdo Elkholy (1966, 131, 94–95) actually anticipated today's "being religious is a way of becoming American" line of analysis. He tried to assess assimilation, using the switch from Friday to Sunday activities as one measure, and his major finding was that the more religious Muslim community in Toledo, Ohio, was more integrated or assimilated than the Muslim community in Detroit.[8] Elkholy went on to relate Arab nationalism inversely to religious orientation, showing that Arab nationalism was stronger in Detroit and weaker in Toledo. This anticipates later assertions that, in effect, Arab and Muslim votes cancel each other out (Jamal 2002; Curtiss 2000), assertions that American Muslim political leaders are now trying to disprove. Elkholy (1966, 124–27) called Toledo (and the emphasis is his) a "*Moslem-American* community" in which Islam encompassed more than Arabs. Toledo's religious leader was a Yugoslav graduate of Cairo's famous Al-Azhar University, the mosque accepted Indians, and the second and third generations knew little about Sunni and Shi'a differences. "They are all just Moslems— American Moslems," he stated.

Since Elkholy's 1966 study, descriptive material has abounded on "congregationalism" at immigrant Muslim mosques and the functions performed by imams. Congregationalism is generally understood as a religious organization having a formal decisionmaking structure, a defined membership, hired clergy, and regularly scheduled activities. These indices may put the cart before the horse, however, since the initial and key issue seems to be that of legal incorporation to qualify as a tax-exempt religious organization and build up a dues-paying membership. This step involves new concepts of membership and of dues-paying for most immigrant Muslims. The idea of affiliating with a particular mosque or Islamic center and paying dues goes against Old World Islamic traditions that every Muslim is automatically a member of any Muslim mosque or Islamic center.[9] The experience of having to write a constitution for a new mosque or Islamic center almost inevitably produces conflict over board membership and leadership, takeovers, removals, and splits in congregations (Lahaj 1994, 305–7).

I discuss later the important issue of where imams are trained and what they teach. Here I will point out that Linda Walbridge (1997) is one of the few whose work is relevant to Alex Stepick's (forthcoming) argument that religion and language are forms of social capital, keys to the maintenance and transmission of secure identities. She analyzes imams' use of the forms of Arabic and the contents of their speeches and describes how both of these fit with past discursive traditions and the present expectations of the congregations among the Shi'a in Dearborn. The work on African American Muslims by Yusuf Nuruddin (1994) and Susan Palmer and Steven Luxton (1997) is also relevant here, with its emphasis on street talk and charismatic speech as elements of identity and group solidarity.

The Druze experience exemplifies a long and gradual process of change (not necessarily typical, as we shall see). The Albakourat al-Durzeyat (later the American Druze Society) was formed at a national convention in 1914; it changed its written and spoken language over the years from Arabic to English and finally rewrote its constitution in 1971 to become a tax-exempt charitable and religious organization (Haddad and Smith 1993, 34–36, 47). Members were divided into 'uqqal and juhhal, the former being an elite group of male and female initiates into the esoteric beliefs and practices of the faith and the latter being "ignorant." Then congregational worship practices were introduced, including instrumental music and leadership by a non-'uqqal member. There was controversy, because the community had not worshiped together, music had never been used, and the tradition was that only the initiated members could lead in worship. (Other displacements suffered by the elite because of changes in education are discussed later in the chapter.) Yet Druze Society annual conventions now feature a congregational, devotional service. In contrast, the Nizari Isma'ilis, a similarly small and bounded Muslim community, had practiced congregational worship long before migrating to the United States, so this form was not produced by residence in this country. And for neither the Druze nor the Isma'ilis was dues-paying new; these and similar Muslim communities had been tithing to support their Shi'a leaders for centuries.

Study after study comments on "American" or "Christian" influences on mosques as they add social, educational, and political functions to spiritual ones.[10] Congregational prayers at many mosques are better attended on Sundays than on the traditional Fridays, and imams spend time counseling married couples and taking on other aspects of a pastoral role. They may also find themselves holding or convening informal sessions on law and social services. Imams newly arrived from abroad find, depending on location, that they are expected to hold weddings in mosque premises, work with women on boards or in Islamic school positions, and allow men and women to sit without a curtain separating them in the prayer room. Mary Lahaj (1994, 308–9), Yvonne Haddad and Adair Lummis (1987), Linda Walbridge (1997), Larry Poston (1992, 95), Nabeel Abraham (2000), and Rogaia Mustafa Abusharaf (1998) all testify to these changes.

Abusharaf's (1998) work appears in an influential volume that proposes that congregational worship is a sign of Americanization for many religions brought to the United States by immigrants. She introduces another significant trend in the Brooklyn mosque she studied, however, and puts it ahead of congregationalism. Calling it "ethnicization," she describes the change from an earlier, more cosmopolitan membership to an almost exclusively Yemeni one. Not only did the Brooklyn mosque change from multi-ethnic to ethnic membership, but women's participation, once significant, completely ceased. These sorts of changes (though not to so great an extent) have also occurred in mosques in the Detroit-Dearborn area as new immigrant groups and/or new imams have fought the trend to "Americanize" and reintroduced orthodox religious or cultural practices.[11] But even the Brooklyn mosque studied by Abusharaf has a governing structure, enjoys nonprofit status, employs a professional imam, and sponsors Sunday events.

Evelyn Shakir (1997, 115), a third-generation Arab American, beautifully captures such changes in this description of what is probably the more typical pattern for long-established communities and mosques:

> Sometimes the very impulse to build a mosque was a response to persistent queries from American-born children who wanted to know why they alone, among their friends, didn't have a "church" to go to. In that case, the mosque was a step toward acculturation, the American thing to do. . . . American mosques inevitably borrowed heavily from American churches, using them as models. . . . Soon the mosque became the scene of weddings and funerals, of cake sales and dinners. Sunday Schools were established and the habit of community prayer on Sunday took hold (drawing more participants than the traditional but inconvenient Friday prayers). In the last two decades, revivalists from abroad have moved to root out those innovations that seem to them egregiously out of keeping with their faith and to restore the mosque as a place devoted exclusively to prayer, preaching, and Koranic exegesis. Thus, in some places, Friday prayers have been reinvested with new life, beer is no longer sold at mosque picnics, and teenage dances on mosque premises have been eliminated, as have political meetings and rallies. . . . Raffles and other forms of gambling have been banned as have bank loans and mortgages. . . . Sometimes, too,

as in a major Detroit mosque, the reformers have ousted American-born imams, replacing them with religious leaders from overseas whose views coincide with their own.

In looking at the attitudes of Muslim Americans toward American holidays and religious observances, we see another revisiting of issues dealt with by earlier immigrants in the apparent contrast between past and present understandings of how religious beliefs fit with American society. Elkholy (1966, 35) discussed early Arab attitudes toward major American holidays and religious observances. "When the new Moslem generations in America share with the prevailing Christian population the celebration of Christmas, they feel it is analogous with the Prophet's sharing with the Jews of Medina the fasting of Yawm 'ashuraa,' " he says, maintaining that the flexible tenets of Islam are the very substance of its capacity to function within any social structure and that "rigidity in religion was very much disliked by the Prophet." But today, whether or not Muslims should observe American holidays, from Halloween and Thanksgiving to Christmas, is hotly debated in the American Muslim press and by fiqh specialists, both the traditionally trained and the new spokespeople (Smith 1999, 139–42).

As for defining American Islam, or "Islams," there are questions of process or practice and questions of content that must be addressed. Lin and Jamal (forthcoming) see their informants who chose a Muslim religious identity over a (continuing and indistinguishable) cultural-religious identity or an Arab ethnic identity as making a choice; by choosing rather than inheriting their religion they are understanding it in new ways. Lin and Jamal consider this a distinctively American practice. Similarly, feminist Muslims tend to affirm an American version or versions of Islam. In helping to shape this new version of Islam, they sometimes emphasize difficulties within the Muslim community (see, for example, Abugideiri 2000, 101, 103, n. 5), and sometimes they emphasize the negative aspects of the North American context, noting racist and sexist stereotyping and marginalization by the larger community (see, for example, Khan 2000). But both positions emphasize struggle, and generally the American setting is viewed as an enabling one, a secular site for the shedding of cultural baggage and a political site that allows freer creation of "new" religious practices and institutions (Mazrui 1996).

Some scholars argue that both the process and the content of Islam in the United States reflect its setting.[12] Thus, Juan Campo (1996, 299) sees mosques and Islamic publications in the United States engaged in processes of appropriation as they learn and use a modern discourse of democracy, civil society, pluralism, human rights, freedom of thought, and individualism. Campo illustrates this by analyzing the Los Angeles

Islamic Center and its publication, *The Minaret*. He does note that little room is given in *The Minaret* to radical Islamic ideologies or to Shi'a and Sufi ideas, however.

Despite Campo's optimism, his vision is also one of struggle. Others speak from positions of closer engagement with such a struggle. Abou El Fadl (2001a, 11–14) describes his disillusionment with the kinds of Islam flourishing in the United States, and some who are Sufis or non-Sunnis also speak from personal positions of struggle (Asani 2001; Hermansen, forthcoming d; Khan 2002). They assert that their movements, which reinforce pluralism, democracy, and individualism (notably through esoteric spiritualism), are central to Islam, and especially to American Islam. These and other scholars speak and work against the narrowing and standardization of definitions of Islam in the United States.

A young second-generation American Muslim feminist who is not a scholar but has written a popular book exemplifies multiple appropriations of American culture. Asma Gull Hasan (2000, 130, 132, 180) entitled one of her chapters "Growing Up in America: Creating New World Islam" and argues that Muslims must distinguish culture from religion and let go of ethnic cultures. While saying that new approaches to the Qur'an are needed, Hasan thinks that reforms of Islam are not needed since it can be practiced without difficulty in the United States (privately?). She does think separate schools and social arenas for Muslims would be good to encourage marriages among Muslims (religious endogamy). In her final pages, Hasan is confident that American society will benefit from adding Muslims to the dialogue because Islam is part of the religious foundation of Western culture, and tolerance, democracy, and compassion are basically Qur'anic ideas. To achieve the goal of unity, she says, Muslim communities must accept cultural Muslims, "Eid Muslims" (those who go to mosque only on Id), and even those who are less observant. She ends with a statement against religious authoritarianism: "It is not the place of a Muslim to tell another that he or she has sinned against God; Muslims believe that only God can make such a pronouncement."

Education and Knowledge

Islam is taught and transmitted in the United States in several arenas. First, there is the teaching of Arabic and the founding texts to children, in both family and institutional settings. The number of Islamic schools in the United States is increasing: there are now several hundred elementary and secondary schools, the majority attached to mosques. At least two institutions of higher education have been established, and Muslim students are increasingly visible on college and university campuses across the country. An entire Islamic knowledge industry has sprung up to produce and distribute comic books, books, audio- and videocassettes, CDs, and films; software programs are also available to help with Arabic, Qur'anic exegesis, and many other Islamic ventures. Very little research has been published on any of these areas (for overviews, see Smith 1999; Lotfi 2002; Nimer 2002b).

An essential responsibility for American Muslims is that of teaching their children, both female and male, to read Arabic and recite the Qur'an. Looking for an Islamic "discursive tradition that includes and relates itself to the founding texts of the Qur'an and the Hadith," as Talal Asad (1986, 14–15) enjoins, orthodox doctrine denotes the correct process of teaching as well as the content of what is to be learned. Thus, the way in which a child in the United States is taught the Qur'an, by reading and memorization under the guidance of a particular teacher, is very much like the way described for Old World Islamic settings. Discussing Muslim literate culture in the Middle East, Brinkley Messick (1997, 388, 392, 395) stresses the centrality of a recitational form of "reading" and instruction and the personal rather than institutional nature of the student-teacher relationship. He also stresses the social and public dimensions of "reading"—as opposed to the individual and private—and the importance of "hearing" the text read aloud to a group of listeners. These remarks resonate with how the child's first reading of the Qur'an is often celebrated in the United States: it is not unusual for American Muslims to invite non-Muslims to attend this ceremony. This broadening of the audience speaks, I think, to an attempt to overcome a generalized American "doubt, indifference or lack of understanding" with respect to Islam. It is an attempt to recover power in the new setting and use reason to overcome resistance, much as Talal Asad (1986, 15–16) has theorized: it pulls Americans into encounters with Islam, compelling them to recognize the emphasis Islam gives to education and learning.

Since African American and immigrant Muslims tend to live in different residential areas, they have developed separate educational institutions (McCloud 1995, 120–21). The first Islamic schools in the United States were established by African American Muslims, and indeed, it was more often the African American Muslims in the early years who wanted Islamic schools (Haddad and Smith 1994, xxviii). In the Hudson River Valley, for example, two separate mosques serve the immigrant and indigenous Muslims and only the latter group founded and supported a school for its children (Kolars 1994). The role of education in the Nation of Islam and the American Society of Muslims has been important, although we have the fullest details only about the structure and content of lessons from the early period (Essien-Udom 1962). I have cited work earlier on the role of education in producing class divisions and organizational schisms within the Nation. Robert Dannin (2002a,

238–50) discusses the development of Islamic pedagogy in the United States and looks at both a national effort by indigenous and immigrant Muslims to design a national curriculum[13] and a local effort in Cleveland to reconstruct an inner-city community morally. Gregory Starrett (1999) focuses on instructional content and methods in one setting—an American Society of Muslims congregation combining resources and constructing a mosque-based identity. Garbi Schmidt (1998) discusses similar work among immigrant Muslims in a Chicago mosque.

Immigrants are beginning to invest funds and energy in Islamic schools. They share with indigenous Muslims a major concern about sex and violence in American schools; many object strongly to sex education programs and the encouragement of coeducational socializing in the public school system. Many Muslims see the establishment of Islamic schools in multi-ethnic America as a step in bringing the international umma into being, although Hoda Badr (2000, 208–9) discusses conflicts between Arabs and South Asians in Houston arising over schools. The same immigrants who send their children to Islamic schools, however, may also want their children to benefit from excellent American educational institutions. Highly educated themselves, they want their children to succeed, and they see the personal networks that can be formed in high school and in leading colleges and universities as key links to the wider society. Some mosques that sponsor elementary and secondary schools resist parental pressures to add higher levels of schooling for this reason. Studies of second-generation mobility will have policy applications here for Islamic educational institutions. Issues of gender in the burgeoning Islamic education industry also need investigation, since most teachers are women, it may be that more students today are female, and young women in Islamic schools may be marrying earlier than those in mainstream institutions.[14]

Another difference between the educational programs of indigenous and immigrant Muslims is that work with prison populations is emphasized more among African American Muslims. After prisoners are released, African American mosques may provide rehabilitative programs, sometimes in conjunction with social service programs run by city or county governments (see, for example, Kolars 1994, 494–97). Muslim college and university students, primarily young Muslims of immigrant background, are also getting involved in prison work, but I know of no research on this.

Of special concern to Muslims in the United States is Islamic education, which involves the building of institutions, the teaching of languages and culture, and the training of religious specialists and educators in North America. One article has assessed the Islamic educational industry in Chicago (Husain and Vogelaar 1994, 247), but the situation has since changed, and both national and international studies are needed. Muslim leaders and educators based in Islamic institutions are often highly qualified and knowledgeable about their religion, yet they publish material pitched at a very general level, presumably to educate non-Muslims. A recent guide to teaching about Islam and Muslims in the public school system produced by the California-based Council on Islamic Education (1998) is perhaps typical (but one does not really know). This is a good basic introduction, although it is, of course, a Sunni view, with minimal information on divisions within Islam.[15]

In a book intended for American teenagers, Richard Wormser (1994, 54, 57, 117, 121) interviewed Muslim teenagers to present positive facts about their lives and views. According to him, there were 165 full-time Muslim schools in the United States at that time (many going only through eighth grade), so one of ten Muslim children in the United States attended a Muslim school (but this estimate cannot be right). Those interviewees who were in Islamic schools felt secure in their religious beliefs and said they faced no problems like pregnancy, birth control, abortion, diseases, or drugs and alcohol. In contrast to the Council on Islamic Education (1998) guide, Wormser gave a positive image of the Nation of Islam, and his overall message stressed unity and tolerance and having an American Muslim, rather than an ethnic, identity. Jeffrey Lang (1998) is also concerned about Muslim children growing up in the United States, although his stance is more critical and more self-consciously American.

The new teaching materials reflect their American context: they usually rely on English as the medium of instruction and, when using Arabic, sometimes translate familiar (and quite outdated) American texts. Thus, *See Spot Run* and similar children's textbooks serve as beginners' texts in Arabic. Some of the material reflects the class position of the post-1965 Muslim immigrants. For example, a textbook for Islamic education produced in Orange County, California, for Muslim youngsters explains zakat (charity): "Some have a lot and some have none. We live in America, the richest country in the world. We live in big houses, drive good cars, wear good clothes and play with the best toys. . . . We should also look at the other people here or in other countries who have nothing" (Ali 1991, 67).

Focused studies of education among American Muslims are very much needed. For example, we have enough information on the Druze (thanks to those pioneers in so many areas covered in this book, Yvonne Yazbeck Haddad and Jane Smith) to see the tremendous changes produced through education in the new setting. The necessary education of the second and later generations in English has led to a divulgence of details of the faith formerly kept secret from all but an elite group of initiates and the Shaykhs (the 'uqqal; the juhhal were the uninitiated or ignorant). Oral transmission from elders was not deemed sufficient by the young people, who wanted something definitive and standardized, in writing. (Oral transmissions varied tremendously.) The written and standardized texts produced have led to attempts to eliminate the category of juhhal, since no one has reason anymore to be ignorant of the basic teachings (Haddad and Smith 1993, 29, 35–38, 47).

In higher education there have been two attempts to establish Islamic colleges and universities. The first institution, the American Islamic College, was founded in Chicago in 1983 (Husain and Vogelaar 1994, 245–46). Approved by the Illinois Board of Higher Education to offer bachelor's degrees in Islamic studies and Arabic studies and two-year associate's degrees in various disciplines, it survived many difficulties but came to an end in 2001.[16] It was entirely run by Muslims, with a board of trustees and a board of directors. Leaders of the Muslim community sent their children elsewhere for higher education, however, even as the college attempted a number of innovative outreach and cooperative programs (Schmidt 1998).

The Graduate School of Islamic and Social Sciences (SSIS) is an ambitious effort to integrate "Islamic" science and "modern" science.[17] Very much the personal project of Dr. Isma'il Al-Faruqi and others, this project had transnational plans and does have a campus in Kuala Lumpur. Christopher Furlow (1999) has begun a study of this institution,[18] which was first established as the International Institute of Islamic Thought (IIIT) in 1981 in Washington, D.C. In 1996 it moved to Herndon, West Virginia, and was reshaped as SISS with a small home campus in Leesburg, Virginia. It offers master's degrees in Islamic studies (an American-style graduate program) and in Imamate studies (religious training for imams). It trains imams for the U.S. armed forces and has offered to train imams for Louis Farrakhan's Nation of Islam.

Other efforts have been made to establish Islamic higher educational institutions in the United States. The (Shi'a) Imam Ali Seminary in Medina, New York, reportedly admits both men and women, but I know of no research on this. Jane Idleman Smith (1999, 157–59) reviews the scene with respect to imams and chaplains in educational institutions, prisons, and the U.S. military, pulling together materials from journals and newspapers. The National Association of Muslim Chaplains, which focuses on prisons, was founded in 1979, but little is known about it.

Finally, although Muslim Student Association groups on campuses were crucial in mobilizing and directing early Muslim political efforts in the United States, no study of the MSA has been completed (ISNA is undertaking one), and studies of Muslim students on campuses are just beginning. Curriculum is one issue that merits study. While affirmative action programs in American universities have not set quotas but goals, are meant to be transitional, and do not usually include Arab or Asian Americans in the goal-setting at either the student or the faculty level, these programs have had an undeniable effect in encouraging curricular and structural focuses on Asian American, African American, Chicano and Latino, Native American, and women's studies programs. Muslims, like Jews, do not fit easily into these boxes. Religious studies, rising in popularity among students, provides one avenue for adding classes on Islam and Muslims to campus curriculums.

A few studies of Muslim student interactions with others in campus settings are emerging, almost always highlighting gender and hybrid identity issues (Safizadeh 1996; Schmidt 1998; Chaudhry 1997, 1999; Naber, forthcoming; Ali, forthcoming a). Lubna Nazir-Chaudhry (forthcoming) gives us a vivid portrait of a young Pakistani woman immigrant, using the young woman's own words and full accounts of her own interactions with her to explore multi-hyphenated identities. Nazir-Chaudhry's broader concern is with Muslim women's experience of the American educational process.

A wealth of material on Muslim youth is available in the Muslim American press, and the range of topics addressed by that material moves us into the next two sections.

Expressive Culture

Muslim American aesthetic and artistic activities reflect the tensions that arise from continuing allegiance to an ancestral culture, integration into the dominant culture, and the creation of cross-over or fusion cultural products, the latter often transnational or cosmopolitan in nature. These activities include the visual arts, music, literature, drama, dance, and the media (as well as architecture and the use of domestic space, as discussed in chapter 5). Most research published on these activities illustrates the difficulties of separating religious beliefs and associated cultural and artistic practices when their carriers transplant them to new contexts. Not only do they attract new audiences, but they stimulate processes of change and adaptation in their new contexts as well.

For African American Muslims, researchers have usually focused on music, but most work has been either brief (Bayoumi 2001) or part of— often incidental to—longer projects (Gardell 1996; Dannin 2002a). Many jazz musicians in the 1950s were African American Ahmadis—men and women who had turned to Islam partly because they thought it put them in a different racial category. In his autobiography, Dizzy Gillespie quotes a typical convert: "If you join the Muslim faith, you ain't colored no more, you'll be white. . . . I don't have to go under the rule of colored because my name is Mustafa Dalil" (quoted in Dannin 2002a, 59). Moustafa Bayoumi (2001, 261) asserts that these musicians arrived at Islam through a particular "aesthetics of living." Melani McAlister (2001) reviews the black arts movement of the 1960s and shows that Islam had become a cultural symbol for many cultural nationalists who were not converts. She analyzes the 1965 play *A Black Mass* by LeRoi Jones (now known as Amiri Baraka) as an exemplification of the cross-fertilization and appropriation that linked Islam and black cultural production.

Young African American Muslims today are producing rap and hip-hop music that is strongly marked by Nation of Islam teachings and is often part of Nation observances like Savior's Day. Louis Farrakhan's own roots as a musician play a part in this connection. The hip-hop movement has spread knowledge of black militant Islam well beyond its primary audience of black and Hispanic urban youth (Gardell 1996, 293–300). Aidi (forthcoming) and Swedenborg (2002) write about "Islamic hip-hop," and there is also "Muslim rap" (Ted Swedenborg 1996; Lorraine Sakata, personal communication, 1999), a hybrid music closely connected to urban black politics and probably incomprehensible to immigrant Muslims. When young African American rappers include references to Islam in their lyrics and perform in ways that older Muslim immigrants might find inappropriate or even shocking, the clash is not only between generations but between national cultural traditions.

Turning to Arab immigrants, Sally Howell (2000c) shows the movement from "Arab immigrant cultures" to "ethnic American cultures" (Abraham and Shryock 2000, 484–85) in Detroit by looking at first-generation "traditional" artists (flute players and other musicians, doll-makers, needleworkers, calligraphers). Given the variety of origins and arrival times of the immigrants, Howell sorts out the complex picture by looking at performers, audiences, and performance occasions such as baptisms, weddings, engagements, graduation parties, and ethnic or more broadly public functions. Some of the artists are expressing Palestinian nationalism, while others are working on everyday useful objects. (A Muslim calligrapher, for instance, makes decorative champagne glasses.) In another piece that emphasizes the marginalized Arab American transnational political and aesthetic concerns and their repackaging to create a new and explicitly Arab American ethnic identity, Howell (2000d) shows how hybrid aesthetic representational strategies led to participation in mainstream Detroit institutions and coalition politics.

Howell (forthcoming) again evokes the Arab expressive culture of Detroit in her explicit analysis of the interplay of Arab and Islamic elements among that culture's producers, patrons, and clients. Despite clear attempts to separate the ethnic and religious components of music, painting, and other arts, she sees the hegemonic influence of Islam on

Arabic cultures still pervading the increasingly secular expressions of Arab art in the United States. Pioneering work on Muslim and ethnic identity is also being done by Munir Jiwa (2002) in his examination of the works and lives of visual artists in New York City.

Returning to the prevalent focus in Detroit on Arabs rather than Muslims, Anne Rasmussen (2000, 552, 567) looks at musicians and music patronage in that city's Arab American community as musicians, singers, and dancers (often cherished and stigmatized at the same time, she says) have moved from amateur to professional status. Lebanese musical styles have dominated, but Iraqi Chaldean and Yemeni styles are part of the musical landscape. Rasmussen sees parallels between the work of musicians and that of immigrant women: both serve as "ritual specialists" and "cultural caterers" and work to maintain rather than to adapt cultural traditions.

Long-standing immigrant communities like the Arab Americans have produced works of English-language fiction and autobiography in English, a literature expertly and elegantly discussed by Lisa Majaj (1996, 267, 271; see also Rahimieh 1990). These works rely strategically, she notes, on "essentialized depictions of ethnic identity," which are characterized by "the difficulty of achieving panethnic group articulation, the uneasy political relationship between Arabs and Americans, and the general delegitimation of Arab culture within mainstream American contexts." Majaj likens her analysis to that of Lisa Lowe (1991) on Asian American ethnicity. Both writers ignore or minimize religion as they focus on national, gendered, and generational nuances within their chosen categories.

Hamid Naficy's work on newspapers, films, videos, and television programs is similar to that of Majaj on Arab American literature—that is, he writes deftly and elegantly about Iranian Americans rather than about religious subgroups. He delineates the processes of signification, acculturation, and social relations that link this displaced community to its homeland. Given the diasporic and postmodern characteristics of the cultural products he analyzes, Naficy's work ranges from Los Angeles (1993a, 1993b, 1998) to the global media culture (1999, 2001), dispensing either concentrated or fragmentary information about Iranian Americans in the process. Most relevant here are the articles about Los Angeles, where the production and distribution of music videos is centered. Naficy's review of the content and impact of these videos links pop culture to identity politics. He traces changes from the early postrevolutionary "death videos" to the more recent "tough guy" and other genres that reflect increasing syncretism with the dominant American culture.

Immigrant Muslims have a wide range of performance traditions. Most feature music and poetry rather than dance, although comments on the dabka, the popular Arab line dance, feature in the work of Howell

(2000b, 2000c, 2000d, forthcoming) and Rasmussen (2000). We know from Abdo Elkholy (1966, 33–34) that, in earlier decades in Detroit, the dabka could be danced in the mosque, while in Toledo, the mosque loudspeaker broadcast not only recorded Qur'anic verses before Friday prayers (for the first generation) but also waltzes (for the second generation) and rock and roll music (for the third generation) for dancing parties. Arab music was recently mainstreamed by inclusion in the mainstream television Grammy Awards in 2000. (The Algerian singer Cheb Mami, with Simon Shaheen, led an all-Arab violin group, Jihad Racy and Ensemble, which played with Sting.)

Sometimes the same music and dance that flourishes in North America as an evocation of the homeland has been declared un-Islamic and become endangered in the homeland itself. This was the case with Afghan arts, and is still true for Iranians. Aspects of Iranian music and dance are being preserved as a secular heritage in Los Angeles by the Avaz International Dance Theater.[19]

The Sufi traditions in Islam encourage music and dance, but there are still no performance sites, such as Sufi shrines and dargahs (tombs), in North America (Naim 1995, 4). The tomb of Samuel Lewis in New Mexico may be the first Sufi shrine in the United States (Hermansen 1997, 162). Performers of Sufi qawwalis (devotional music), which is played in South Asia in devotional settings, often reach out in North America to non-Muslim audiences more accustomed to rock and roll.[20] The late Nusrat Fateh Ali Khan from Pakistan is an example: his qawwali performances drew a wide range of people, and he did sound tracks for movies as diverse as *The Last Temptation of Christ* and *Dead Man Walking*. In a forthcoming paper (Sakata and Leonard, forthcoming), Hiromi Sakata and I look at South Asian Muslim music and poetry in the United States, tracing the transnational bases of production and performance and their reception by sometimes religious, sometimes ethnic, and sometimes fusion audiences in the United States. Like Iranian film, qawwali has been appreciated and in some ways appropriated by entirely new audiences who probably do not relate to the Islamic resonances in the performances.

In the domain of the arts, generational, gender, and identity issues are at the forefront of most analyses. Additional issues are language (members of the second and subsequent generations lose competence in the languages of the homelands) and integration into the dominant American culture as fusion or cross-over cultures emerge. The use of both public and private space is heavily influenced by dominant culture practices, and immigrant Muslim women are often more visible in artistic performances than in their homelands (Leonard 1993). In Los Angeles I saw a young Muslim woman from India celebrate her debut as an Indian bharatnatyam (classical) dancer, a tradition strongly linked to

Hindu temples and themes in the homeland, and other young South Asian Muslim girls from Pakistan as well as India are studying this dance tradition as part of their "ethnic heritage." Edward Curtis IV (personal communication, 2002) tells me this is also happening in St. Louis, Missouri, and San Antonio, Texas, and often as part of the Indian festival of Diwali celebrations in high schools and colleges.

Work needs to be done on the material culture of Muslim Americans. Community performances and rituals, such as weddings and funerals, and graveyard tombstone art deserve ethnographic study. (For a model study of ethnic and regional graveyards, see Jordan 1982.) The circulation of objects like the Eid stamp could be analyzed. Released in 2001, this U.S. Postal Service commemorative stamp with Arabic calligraphy seemed in danger of not being reissued after September 11, 2001, but, to the relief of American Muslims, it has been reissued. Work could also be done on public displays (museum exhibitions of Islamic art, Middle Eastern and Muslim decorative arts, and ethnic histories) and other depictions of Muslims and Muslim life.[21] Edward Said (1997) reviews press coverage of public displays and depictions of Muslims, Laurence Michalak (1989) and Jack Shaheen (2001) review film treatments of Arabs and Muslims, and Asma Gull Hasan (2000, 98–106) gives her reactions to more recent films featuring "movie Muslims."

Young American Muslims

The differences and similarities among American Muslims reported by researchers have been considered in various ways, but we need to consider more fully the new generation of Muslims growing up in the United States. This generation's path already seems quite different from that of earlier cohorts, and it is not just a matter of generational differences, of familial conflict between the first generation and later generations of immigrants. Lisa Lowe (1991, 26 passim) cautions against interpreting Asian American culture in terms of master narratives of generational conflict and filial relations, thus displacing and privatizing class, gender, and national diversities into familial oppositions. I hope I have made the case against that as well by drawing attention to forces beyond families that have a powerful influence on the lives of young American Muslims. Just as compelling political events and experiences marked earlier indigenous and immigrant Muslim histories, formative social and political experiences are crucially shaping Muslim youth, rooting them in the histories, cultures, and languages of North America. The ways in which they think about themselves and form political coalitions are new and different, and their religious and political markings are colored by the ways in which they are creating a new generational memory and "claiming America."

In the religious arena, the centrality and future dominance in the Muslim umma of the second generation (thus termed by the post-1965 new spokespeople, reflecting their immigrant perspective on the national Muslim landscape) has been predicted by many. When these younger people will take over the leadership of American Muslim institutions and organizations, however, is not clear, since many of the first generation new spokespeople who control the leadership positions may not be ready to turn them over to younger, American-born or American-raised Muslims (see Badr 2000, 224). Also, there has been a continuing influx of older new immigrants, men who can replace the earlier first-generation leaders and imams in the mosques, although this may have slowed after September 11, 2001.

In earlier decades it was foreign university students who founded the MSA (and eventually ISNA), but today American-born Muslims dominate the MSAs across the country. The national MSA leaders have spoken out more strongly as Muslims than their elders since September 11, 2001, insisting on their right to continue protesting American foreign policy and taking advantage of the national focus on Islam to expand educational outreach activities. They have made new political coalitions and gained unexpected allies—the homosexual organization Just Act was one of the first to come forward in support of Muslims after the attacks. The MSA leaders also used the Internet very aggressively to rally support and maintain self-confidence, and it was this network that helped make Shaykh Hamza Yusuf such a central figure after the terrorist attacks (Schmidt 2002b). Work by younger Muslim academics reflects this self-confidence and claiming of political rights (see, for example, Khan 2002).

Some post-1965 immigrant Muslims had hoped to avoid an "Americanization" of Islam, which they saw occurring among earlier Muslim immigrants and among some of their contemporaries.[22] It was probably a relaxation or liberalization of beliefs and practices brought from the homelands that they worried about. Yet younger Muslims born or almost wholly raised in the United States can be more Islamically orthodox than their parents. Looking more closely, however, perhaps we should say that these young people are choosing a Muslim identity and using Islam in ways that change family and community cultural dynamics. Thus, young women putting on the hijab or young people insisting on the freedom to select their own marriage partners are exercising individual choice, confounding their parents in unanticipated ways.

Many young American Muslims are on what might be called an "Islamic roots" trip, one framed by a strategic politics of race and gender in urban America. Nadine Naber (forthcoming) reproduces and analyzes the compelling voices of young second-generation Arab men and women in San Francisco who see themselves as Muslim first and Arab second. Most of Naber's interviewees see Islam as empowering to women. Young women invoke it to argue for higher education or to support a marriage of choice with another Muslim rather than an arranged marriage within a certain ethnic group. Denise Al-Johar (forthcoming) found that three sorts of marriages were being made by young Muslims at a Houston mosque: arranged, "self-initiated," and "self-achieved." All three were Islamic marriages, but the first emphasized an ethnic identity, the second an Islamic identity, and the third an American identity. The self-achieved marriage involved dating and often marrying outside national origin, ethnic, or religious boundaries, although non-Muslim spouses usually converted to Islam. Of the twenty-seven marriages Al-Johar surveyed, all twelve arranged marriages were endogamous, while the seven self-initiated and eight self-achieved ones were all exogamous with respect to national origin or ethnicity. Intermarriage, a traditional measure of assimilation, needs to be studied.[23] It also needs to be studied comparatively across America's many Muslim communities.

This "Islamic roots" or "Islam first" identity assertion (see Hermansen, forthcoming c) has led some young women to put on the hijab even though their mothers and grandmothers may not have worn it. This comes from a self-assertion of Muslim identity and a reliance on texts and nonspecialist interpretations of them. The hijab is a powerful marker of identity for Muslim women in America's public spaces. The decision of second-generation Muslim women to put on the hijab is partly an individual one and partly a reflection of larger changes in American society, and the trend is increasing, as Syed Ali (forthcoming a) shows for primarily South Asian immigrant youth. Ali's work reinforces Naber's (forthcoming) conclusions about the sense of empowerment provided by religious identity, as is well illustrated in Ali's report about a popular T-shirt being sold to young Muslims at a recent national ISNA conference. The T-shirt featured the head of a young woman in hijab with the slogan, "It's good in the hood"; the link with urban American youth culture is the unexpected twist.

These creative and oppositional forms of acculturation are occurring among privileged Arab and South Asian youth—those who seem most adapted or assimilated—and not just among black youth in the inner city, where most would expect to find such acculturation. Naber (forthcoming), Al-Johar (forthcoming), and Ali (forthcoming a) could be said to be researching the fully assimilated who are "turning back" to—or more accurately, creating anew—conservative religious roots of identity. These Muslim youth could be seen as undergoing deliberate "de-acculturation" but turning the process to highly individualistic ends (Andrew Shryock, personal communication, 2002).

Young Muslim voices are speaking out against wearing the hijab as well. The other trend among young American Muslim women is to view the hijab as a cultural rather than religious marker and to reject it emphatically. Traditionally, wearing the hijab is more strongly associated with Arab, Iranian, and Turkish Muslims than with South Asian ones, although its use depends partially on class and sectarian affiliations in the homelands. Some African American groups have taken up the hijab or other styles of modest attire for women, and some have not. The Muslim feminist argument is that the hijab has been forced on women in some Islamic cultures because of men's failure to control their sexuality. Thus, "Will men ever learn to control themselves?" is the subtitle of the chapter on the hijab by the second-generation writer Asma Gull Hasan (2000, 35–36); she believes that "modesty comes from the inside-out."

Young women's voices are louder than young men's when it comes to personal experiences and subversive reinterpretations or even rejections of parts of their Muslim heritage. These expressions are ways of beginning a dialogue with family and community, as Sabah Aafreen's (1999, 57) brief, almost playful voice and the many Arab American voices in Evelyn Shakir's (1997) book testify. Naheed Hasnat (1998, 38–40) bases her identity in Islam, but in a feminist Islam that conveys legitimate rights to her with the help of the American government: "America has given me the freedom to practice the rights given to me by Islam and curtailed by South Asian cultural practices." Lubna Chaudhry's (1998) young Pakistani American women interviewees draw on both Pakistani and Muslim identities to resist the power that their own parents and non-Muslims attempt to exercise over them.

American Muslim youth are taking many paths. Some will be lost to Islam, and some will "return" to "orthodox" Islam through study of the Qur'an and the hadith. Their formulations of Islam are likely to be their own, not necessarily the ones represented by ISNA, the MSA, or other organizations. Islam is taught to young people in the United States primarily through texts, not context. On the one hand, this can result in greater standardization and "orthodoxy," yet many of the texts are new ones—books, audio- and videocassettes, and Internet materials produced in the United States. Open to the global flows of Islamic information, interpretation, and activity, these young American Muslims are nonetheless firmly grounded in the United States, not in the diverse homelands that motivate much transnational activism among the older immigrant Muslims (Werbner 1998; Leonard 2000).

Young American Muslims rely heavily on Islamic messages and mediums not necessarily prepared or accessed by their elders. Islamic doctrine and discourse is being presented by very popular speakers like Shaykh Hamza Yusuf and Siraj Wahaj, a Euro-American convert and

African American convert based in San Francisco and New York, respectively. These men are treated like rock stars, their talks avidly attended, recorded, and widely distributed on cassettes. They and others like them are distinguished by their use of new technologies and new media to define themselves and their religion. Just as skilled speakers elsewhere in the Islamic world relate Islamic texts to the daily lives of their audiences, these relatively young speakers reach American Muslim youth and college students through many media. Hamza Yusuf frequently cites texts used in academic contexts like those by Marshall Hodgson and Michel Foucault. Then there is "Muslim rap," a hybrid music that is integral to the politics of young African American Muslims but is reaching well beyond that audience, and Sufi qawwali, which is also reaching a wider audience.

Everyday life experiences, including dating and sexuality, concern young Muslims, and the Muslim American press is filled with material on this. Some of the young people compete with the older fiqh specialists and advice columnists. As noted by one young American Muslim (quoted in Wax 1999), who came as a student from India: "The Internet has made everyone a mufti [legal adviser] . . . [opening up] a variety of opinion . . . [it is] the globalization of the mufti."[24] This young man and others like him offer advice on the Internet, but the National Fiqh Council refused telephone calls and insisted on written letters until 2000 (when it began to accept e-mail), and many fiqh scholars ridicule the new trends.

Despite the divisions among the immigrant and African American older generations, many scholars see an American Muslim identity emerging among the younger people. (It looks to me that the turning point between old and young is somewhere around the age of forty.) While Fred Halliday (1996, 115) has argued that "Muslim" cannot be used as a meaningful term of ethnic identity, and I would argue that it certainly does not stand for a "total way of life" (a phrase often applied inaccurately to many other religions as well), I have argued that an American Muslim identity is being constructed. Just as their parents have made choices about political coalitions, religious sites, and social networks, young American Muslims have choices to make as well.

Campus settings seem particularly important sites for making these choices. On campuses, Muslim students can choose to join an MSA, a South Asian or Middle Eastern group, an Asian American coalition, a People of Color coalition, a feminist group, or a very specific national-origin or Muslim sectarian group (and there are others). David Hollinger (1995, 2–3) has proposed the term "postethnic" to describe the multicultural perspective that "favors voluntary over involuntary affiliations, balances an appreciation for communities of descent with a determination to make room for new communities, and promotes solidarities of wide scope that incorporate people with different ethnic and racial backgrounds." This perspective emphasizes the cosmopolitan rather than the pluralist element in America's multiculturalist movement, and it also emphasizes contextualized, changing, and multiple identities or affiliations. Muslim students and their choices to affiliate with one or more campus groups often exemplify postethnicity rather than whatever ethno-racial groups they are affiliated with by descent.

It is on campuses, or on the Internet, that young Muslims most often encounter gay and lesbian groups as well. The voices of young gay and lesbian Muslims in North America are beginning to be heard. At least one national group for gay Muslims has been founded: Al-Fatiha (The Opening), based in Washington, D.C. This international organization for Muslims who self-identify as gay, lesbian, bisexual, or transgendered, or who are questioning their sexual orientation or gender identity, has seven local branches and more than three hundred members (Wax 2000). Queer Jihad offers a website that is run by Sulayman X. Then there is Trikone, the South Asian support group for queer people. This group is especially strong in California, and young Muslims participate in San Francisco's annual Gay Pride parade.[25]

A few young Muslims have produced articles or books about being gay and lesbian. Surina Khan (1998) and Naheed Islam (1998) talk about being lesbians and "exiles" from family, community, and religion, and in his autobiography (Khan 1997), Badruddin Khan (a pseudonym) traces his journey from Pakistan to North America and his discovery and claiming of a gay identity. The feature article of a recent *Gay and Lesbian Times* (a southern California publication) gives personal information about some of the young Muslims leading the move for acceptance (Silvay 2002).

So many possibilities, so many research projects—as Ron Kelley (1994, 165) put it, an American Muslim identity is being formed on playgrounds, at schools and colleges, and in front of TV sets. It seems to me that the American Muslim identities being formed by young American Muslims are as likely to be cosmopolitan as pluralist (following the distinction made by Hollinger 1995). All of the topics discussed in this chapter reflect creative tensions among the asabiyya or ethno-racial identities of the diverse indigenous and immigrant communities in the United States, a "Muslim identity" ascribed to members of a single, universal umma by outsiders and members alike, and various American identities subscribed to by younger American Muslims.

═ PART III ═

FURTHER RESEARCH

= Chapter 8 =

Contemporary
Research Agendas

A LTHOUGH I have been suggesting all along the scholarly work that needs to be done, this chapter attempts a more general and theoretical overview of research agendas that will further knowledge about Muslims in the United States. I do this comparatively, first and very broadly by contrasting the state of research on Muslims in Europe and the United States. Then I advocate more inclusive and comparative work on Muslim groups in the United States. Following a consideration of the ways in which Islamic studies and religious studies scholars are moving closer together, I return to the impact of September 11, 2001, on American Muslim activists and their writings and on scholarly research on American Muslims. In conclusion, I discuss the importance of Islam and Muslims for American religious and political history in the twenty-first century and ways of relating the work on Muslims to that on more general patterns of changing religious affiliation and practice, ethno-racial affiliation, and cosmopolitanism and pluralism in the United States.

The State of Research on Muslims in Europe and the United States

Scholarship on Islam and Muslims in the United States is said to be less developed than scholarship on Islam and Muslims in Europe, but I am not so sure. This perception seems to be the result of looking only at immigrant Muslims in both places. The balance shifts markedly and acquires greater historical depth when we take into account African American Muslims and the long, rich tradition of scholarship on them.

Certainly there are limitations to U.S. scholarship on Islam and Muslims and differences from what is being done in Europe. Muslims are among the most-studied contemporary immigrants in Europe, and culture, especially religion, is a major focus of scholarly attention in immigration and ethnic studies there. The North American academic scene was configured differently, but it is now changing. In the United States before the 1990s, Muslims were divided into two categories, African American and immigrant, and studies of them were seldom connected. Studies of African American Muslims stressed black nationalism and racial issues, and studies of immigrants focused on ethnic identity, ethnic entrepreneurship, and gender and generational issues. There was very little, if any, scholarly dialogue across these boundaries.

Prior to the 1990s, scholarly divisions of labor often overlooked Muslims in the United States altogether. Although scholars of the Muslim world were established in North America, most were area specialists who seldom looked at Islam in the United States. Scholars who were writing about Muslims in this country tended to be not only very specialized but descriptive and atheoretical; as a result, their studies neither crossed disciplines nor reached a wide audience. Scholars of a variety of Muslim subjects were based in American universities, but except for African American Muslims, noticeably few of those writing and speaking on significant American Muslim issues were themselves Muslim. Scholars and funding institutions began transcending these limitations in the 1990s, and the radical Islamist terrorist attacks on the United States of September 11, 2001, confirmed the importance of comparative and theoretical work. Leading research and funding institutions are setting new priorities today.

In contrast to the European research agenda, the American research agenda has four special features. First, the United States is home to significant, indigenous, largely African American Muslim communities, whose importance in both numbers and challenges to Old World concepts of Islam I have established. African American Muslims present immigrant Muslims with an opportunity to realize Islam's potential to overcome ethno-racial divisions, and together the two Muslim communities present the United States with a challenge and an opportunity to realize its potential as a postethnic society and nation-state.

Second, a strong case can be made for the "Americanization" of Islam in the United States. Following Talal Asad's (1996) suggestion that core assumptions that guide conceptions and practices can be termed "Islamic" in origin, and looking at the new versions of Islam being constituted from American ways of being Muslim, we can try to see what is "Islamic" and what is contextual about American Muslim discourses and practices. "Islamic" themes include: self-placement in the West and as one of three "religions of the book"; Qur'anic reading and recitation practices that emphasize the transmission of knowledge through oral instruction and links to specific teachers and texts; efforts to get close to the state or political power; a strong commitment to egalitarianism and to erasure of race and class; a strong emphasis on patriarchy and fear of its loss in family and community; a critique of the United States and defense of Islamic or Muslim history and identity; and finally, aspirations to leadership of a transglobal umma. All of these themes can be seen as coming from Islamic pasts, yet all have been changed by their rooting and development in the United States. The American components in Muslim American experience might emerge even more clearly upon closer examination, much as Werner Sollors (1986) suggests for ethnic literary history and discourse. As I have already suggested, the American Muslim aspirations to leadership of a transglobal umma are almost certainly reinforced by America's own current aspirations to world leadership (not that the relationship between the two sets of aspirations is an easy one).

Third, I think that immigration studies and religious studies in the United States, particularly the former, are actually further along than in Europe. The two fields were not well connected before 1990—and often not connected at all—but that began changing in the 1990s. Some comparisons of Muslims with Jews and Catholics in the United States have been made (for example, Walbridge 1997), and some forthcoming work will offer further comparisons between Christians and others in the United States (Casanova and Zolberg, forthcoming; Raboteau and Alba, forthcoming; Leonard, Stepick, and Vasquez, forthcoming; the Pew Gateway city projects on immigrant religions and societal integration).[1] African American religious movements, Asian American religious movements, Chicano or Latino religious movements, and Native American religious movements are finding room in the mainstream religious studies narratives as the United States reconceptualizes the symbolic boundaries and public dimensions of its religious culture. These groupings follow Hollinger's (1995, 19–50) ethno-racial pentagon, with Euro-Americans as the unmarked, taken-for-granted fifth category.

Fourth, because of America's long experience with immigrants becoming citizens and political actors, American Muslim ambitions and achievements are ahead of European ones. There are already histories of Muslim integration into regional political systems, notably in metropolitan Detroit. Further movement into mainstream politics and society is promised by the higher socioeconomic position of Muslims overall in the United States compared to Europe, the aspirations of well-educated professionals, and the intellectual talents of Muslim scholars who are increasingly well placed in American universities. Muslims in the United States are writing their own histories as they make them and are active participants in the research endeavor.

In addition to these four special features of the American research agenda, at least three centralizing forces are working to standardize and bring together versions of Islam and groups of Muslims in the United States. The same processes may well be going on in Europe, but within many national arenas, not just one large one, and the scale if not the intensity or speed of these forces is assuredly different. First is the force of the law, which sets standards for citizenship and political participation, for community and mosque definition and governance, and for domestic practices of marriage, inheritance, divorce, and other family matters. American civil and criminal law erases distinctions among Muslims that were maintained by state legal systems in many former homelands and also brings them into conformity with all other Americans.

The second force is the hard work of the Muslim national religious and political organizations in the United States to bring together many different kinds of Muslims by blending Islamic and democratic ideals. Despite differences and even conflicts among groups, mobilization is clearly proceeding and winning recognition from non-Muslim individuals and constituencies in the process.[2]

The third centralizing force would have to be the young American Muslims, striking out and defining their identities, building organizations (particularly on campuses), and increasingly marrying spouses of their own choice, usually within the Muslim community but beyond the boundaries set by their parents. Creative appropriations and reconfigurations of both "Islamic" and American cultures by those Muslims born or largely raised in the United States seem to be diminishing differences within a broadly defined national Muslim community, although consciousness of other differences in the national arena may be increasing.

Toward More Inclusive Narratives

In writing this book, I have hoped to stimulate scholarly projects and dialogues not only in the areas discussed but in those I have been unable to discuss. There are many indigenous and immigrant groups of Muslims in the United States, some of which stand organizationally and doctrinally outside mainstream Sunni Islam. Their stories could become part of the main narrative. Indeed, some of their stories could transform the main narrative. At the very least, African American religious movements and Muslim immigrant movements could be better related to each other, and study of them needs to be better integrated into American religious studies and history.

We have seen not only boundaries but silences in the literature. We need more work on African American Muslim groups—for example, the Atlanta community previously led by Jamil Al-Amin (the former

H. Rap Brown) and now led by new people. We need more work on the
interactions between African American Muslims and contemporary
Afrocentric movements (for the potential in this area, see Allen 1998;
Nuruddin 1998). Changing constructions of race for all Muslims clearly
need to be retheorized and taken into account by scholars in many fields
implicated in this book, from immigration studies to religious studies to
international studies.[3] Work on Sufism touches on but does not fully
explore the political and religious conflicts over the place of Sufis and
their leaders in the American Muslim landscape; here too, indigenous
and immigrant groups interact tentatively and intermittently. There is
no detailed work on the extremist or fundamentalist Islamist movements, like the Hizb-ul-Tahrir (Liberation Party), which opposes democracy and advocates reconstitution of the Caliphate and a wholly Islamic
system of government. We have glimpses of the growing importance of
Islamic materials on the Internet, but this area, we well as the burgeoning Islamic knowledge industry in the United States, needs much fuller
exploration. Finally, the lives and experiences of secular, or cultural,
Muslims have not been adequately explored, yet this is surely a significant and growing group if the American history of other religious groups
is any guide.

The contextualized development of fiqh in North America is an excit-
ing area for further research. The intersections of American and Islamic
law in the lives of American Muslims concern first and later generations
of immigrants, and African American Muslims also draw upon both
Islamic and American law with respect to marriage, divorce, and inheritance practices. Issues of gender and law need to be investigated sys-
tematically in terms of both American and Islamic law and practice.
Some scholars are discussing the reformulation of shari'a, particularly
with respect to gender issues (Abou El Fadl 2001b; An-Na'im 1991;
Bayyah 2001).

Then there is the emerging consensus in law in the United States and
many European countries that homosexuality is founded in nature and
that homosexuals deserve legal rights and protections. This movement
presents a major challenge to Islamic, as well as Jewish and Christian,
traditional doctrine and practice. Peter Gomes (1996) has examined contemporary and controversial Christian religious beliefs and practices
in the United States, creatively finding a way not to condemn loving,
monogamous, and faithful homosexuals. Will this be done by an American Muslim for Islam?

Gender and sexuality issues often inform identity issues for both
immigrants and converts. Here we need sectarian and regional comparisons in the United States. For example, women's roles in the Ahmadi
community have been explored (Ahmed-Ghosh, forthcoming), but not

compared to women's roles in other Muslim groups. Another example can be found in the contrast between young northern California Arabs, who are putting Islam first and their Arab heritage second (Naber, forthcoming), and young people in Detroit, the early and still-leading center for American Arabs of both Muslim and Christian background. We get glimpses of Muslim students on campuses as they wrestle with hybrid identities (Nazir-Chaudhry, forthcoming; Naber, forthcoming; Schmidt 1998), but fuller views of Muslim student groups and of what is being taught about Islam and Muslims in America's higher educational institutions would provide important insights into the next generation of American Muslims.

Expressions of Muslim identities in art and popular culture go far beyond the research published so far. We have no full treatments of African American Muslim jazz musicians or contemporary "Islamic hip-hop" and "Muslim rap"—vital ingredients of American popular culture. African American Muslim athletes in many sports, from basketball to boxing, deserve attention: figures like Muhammad Ali and Kareem Abdul-Jabbar loom large in American sports history and public life. Many aesthetic traditions brought by post-1965 Muslim immigrants have not yet entered the multicultural arena but are likely to do so.

Islamic Studies and Religious Studies

The relationship between Islamic studies and religious studies is changing: once seen as widely separated (Martin 1985), the two disciplines are drawing closer together (Brodeur 2002), and this is very relevant to considerations of Islam and Muslims in the United States. The historical study of religions contrasts with the largely ahistorical self-view held by adherents, and the comparative study of religions contrasts again with the study of any specific religion by being aware of developments across religions in the general history of religions (Waardenburg 1997, 184). Scholars of Islam have studied that religion largely within the context of Islamic civilization and culture, without comparative breadth; they have stressed internal religious developments and defended the uniqueness of Islam.[4] Also, there has been a sharp distinction between "normative" Islam and "actual" Islam, between the prescriptions, norms, and values generally recognized as divine guidance and the many forms and movements, practices and ideas, that have in fact existed (Waardenburg 1997, 199). Scholars of immigrants in the United States are contributing to religious studies by emphasizing the material and ritual practices that contribute to the lived experience of Muslims and others, and this new emphasis (Vasquez, forthcoming) will invigorate Islamic studies as well.

Islamic studies scholars have embraced new ways of thinking. The new work reflects an encouraging trend: scholars and methods in the field are becoming increasingly cosmopolitan, partly owing to the migration of European scholars to the Americas and also to the migration of Muslim world scholars to both Europe and the United States (Nanji 1997, xix). Muhsin Mahdi (1997, 154) points out that one cannot easily break contemporary scholarship into "Western" and "Muslim"; these two groups of modern scholars are close, but both are far from traditional Muslim scholars' ways of understanding and teaching Islam.

Azim Nanji (1997, xviii, xix) has remarked on the need to rethink the ways in which the Muslim world has been mapped geographically and intellectually. Concepts of dar al-Islam and dar al-harb are now irrelevant, he says, as is European scholarship that sees the center of Islamic studies as the Near or Middle East, thus marginalizing large groups of Muslims. He calls for vibrant humanistic scholarship that will be more diverse and encompassing than before and will include considerations of the increasing public participation by women and the new interactions among Muslims living in the West. Nanji also wants to resist "present-mindedness"—a focus on "fundamentalist" expressions of Islam, which he does not see as the primary expressions of Muslim identity in the modern world. Mohammed Arkoun (1997, 220) speaks of the need to "encourage and initiate audacious, free, productive thinking on Islam today," but again, he would have this thinking focus not on the "revivalism" that has monopolized the discourse but on the Islam of true believers. He calls for Muslim thinkers and intellectuals to insert their critical approach into the social and cultural space presently dominated by militant ideologies.

Clearly, we do need to look closely at those militant and fundamentalist expressions of Islam rather than ignore them. That is one of the lessons of the Islamist terrorist attacks on the United States of September 11, 2001, although it is not the only one.

The Impact of September 11, 2001, on Research Agendas

Fawaz Gerges (1999, 39–58, 110) writes about American foreign policy in a way that helps set the scene for an exploration of the impact of September 11, 2001, on scholarly work. Discussing U.S. relations with Muslim states and societies, he remarks that the United States has been less constrained by colonial, historical, and cultural factors than were European powers in dealing with the Near East or other Muslim countries. "In contrast to the Europeans, Americans do not appear to be concerned about the presence of a large immigrant Muslim community in their midst," he says, and goes on to assess American policies toward Islamist resurgences with respect to security and strategic interests rather than clashes of culture and ideology. In Gerges's view, the Clinton administration was increasingly opposed to political or militant Islam and reached out to moderate Muslims, and moderate American Muslim groups were themselves building up and reaching out at the same time. The American Muslim political aspirations just before September 11, 2001, were realistic, despite problems between the United States and Iran and the difficulties plaguing the Arab-Israeli peace process.

Then came 9/11. I see three important trajectories in the responses of American Muslims. First, although media commentators and government officials continue to draw on a wider range of Muslim spokespeople (drawn from beyond national organizational boundaries) and there have been political realignments among Muslims, Muslim organizations have rallied and declared themselves even more fervently American, democratic, and supportive of civil liberties. Viewed in the context of the polarization suggested by Robert Wuthnow (1988) between conservative and liberal Christians in the United States, this is an interesting change of emphasis from a politics many saw guided chiefly by conservative social values and foreign policy concerns.

Now, despite evidence of increased prejudice against Muslims in the United States, we hear the increasingly confident voices of American Muslims in the public sphere, joining in calls for adherence to the Constitution and civil rights.[5] Hate crimes against people perceived to be Muslim have soared, and especially, owing to general ignorance on the part of the American public, against South Asian Americans.[6] Although national Muslim political organizations, notably CAIR and MPAC, regularly issue news bulletins highlighting hate crimes and other anti-Muslim incidents, they also issue statements of loyalty to the United States. They have called upon President Bush and the Republican Party to respond better to the fears and desires of Muslim citizens.[7] The large national religious organizations, ISNA and ICNA, held their annual conventions in the summer of 2002, the former in Washington, D.C., with many themes and presentations stressing that Muslims are part of America and "a blessing" to it. Mansoor Ijaz, a leading Pakistani American media commentator, argued in a *Washington Post* article called "Citizenship Before Civil Rights" (April 4, 2002) that America's Arabs and Muslims should willingly stand up to greater scrutiny and assist U.S. authorities as law enforcement agencies try to prevent terrorist activities in the country. James Zogby, president of the Arab American Institute and an eminent pollster, wrote in the *Arab News* (Saudi Arabia's first English daily) on September 4, 2002, that, in the year since September 11, 2001, Arab American rights had been adequately defended by the Department of Justice and the FBI.

The second trajectory may be greater openness about conflicts among Muslims and perhaps a higher level of comfort with this pluralism. Despite the brave show of unity and support for the nation by the national Muslim political organizations, there are signs that divisions among various African Americans, other converts, and immigrant Muslim groups may be widening. I am thinking here, first, of W. D. Mohammed renaming his group the American Society of Muslims (an immigrant group had begun using the group's former name, the Muslim American Society) and the formation of the Muslim Alliance of North America (MANA) in particular. Immigrant Muslims have expressed resentment at the attention given to the views of Euro-American converts like Shaykh Hamza Yusuf, and Jesse Jackson has been quoted as saying: "Before September 11, you people thought you were white and thought you're the elite, but now you too are black like us" (Niaz 2002, 32). Yet American Muslim media and organizations have become more open about divisions among Muslims and more comfortable with their own diversity and pluralism. *The Minaret,* a leading American Muslim periodical, ran a special feature story (Alibhai 2002) praising Sufi thought and W. D. Mohammed's African American Muslim community and advocating modern training for imams, including the training of women imams. (Sufis and African American Muslims are seldom featured or praised in mainstream immigrant Muslim publications.) MPAC has reached out to Japanese Americans (who were among the first to reach out to Muslims after September 11, recalling their World War II experience being incarcerated in camps shortly after the Japanese attacks on Pearl Harbor).[8] Other new connections are being made between American Muslim and non-Muslim groups and organizations in local contexts.

In the third trajectory, voices from within the American Muslim community are speaking out against militant Islamist ideologies and for serious rethinking and reforms of Muslim discourse and practice in the United States. Public distancing from violent or extremist Islamist expressions has increased, and moderate or modernizing Muslims are speaking up more. This is not so much a change as a continuation of views voiced in the 1990s by some American Muslims, particularly scholars of Islamic jurisprudence and history.[9] Mainstream media attention, however, has helped give the ideas of some of these scholars wider circulation among Muslims as well as non-Muslims.

This brings us to scholarly responses to 9/11. While an overview like that by Daniel Pipes and Khalid Duran (2002) overstates the Islamist threat, liberal and moderate Muslims in America have been confronting their conservative cobelievers more since September 11, 2001, as a close reading of the contemporary press and Internet sites shows. An Islamic website article (Caldwell 2001) talks about activists embracing modern scientific and social changes. They are arguing for greater equality be-tween men and women, interfaith dialogue, an emphasis on the arts, an end to anti-Jewish rhetoric, a less literal reading of the Qur'an, and full acceptance of American ideals of freedom and tolerance. Ali Asani (2002) published a passionate plea for tolerance of Islamic pluralism, and Abou El Fadl (2001d, forthcoming) proposes the name "Salafabism" for the Wahhabi co-optation of Salafism, which has proponents in the United States and sees Islam as being at odds with the West.

Since September 11, there has been a predictable outpouring of schol-arly work on Islam, Muslims, and Muslims in the United States, ranging from very good to very bad. Among the worst are books by Steven Emer-son (2002) and Martin Kramer (2001). Emerson has an appendix called "The Terrorists' Support Networks: The Sea in Which the Fish Swim" in which he slanders most of the national organizations and leaders dis-cussed in this book (CAIR, AMC, ICNA, MPAC, AMA, ISNA).[10] Kramer, like Samuel Huntington (1993) before him, seems to equate Islamic fun-damentalism with Islam in general. In indicting the entire Middle Eastern Studies Association (founded in 1966, MESA has some 2,600 members, most of them academics) for not understanding or explaining Middle Eastern politics adequately to the American government and people, he ignores the many differences and conflicts within the association.

More balanced responses, like John Esposito's (2002), seek to counter-act the newly invigorated "clash of civilizations" thesis (proposed by Huntington in 1993), which sees Islam and the West as long-standing ene-mies (for other critiques of this thesis, see Denny 1994; Lawrence 1998; McAlister 2001). Liisa Malkki (2003) traces the impact of Huntington's analysis on the U.S. Department of Defense, where it has produced a dis-tinctive and aggressive "new culturalism" in security studies, led by "defense intellectuals." Pnina Werbner (2002, 29), writing that September 11 precipitated in Britain, as in the United States, a widespread "moral panic about Islam, multiculturalism, and the toleration of difference," noted that "the danger is that diaspora Muslims in the West will increas-ingly withdraw from positive engagement with their . . . neighbors, and lose faith in the capacity of their country of settlement to recognize what they perceive to be their deepest moral commitments and aspirations." Placing the terrorists' attack in the context of the history of terrorism, David Rapoport (2001) shows that terrorism has become deeply rooted in mod-ern culture in the last two centuries, and that September 11 was part of the fourth of successive, overlapping waves of terror. This fourth wave began in 1979 with the Iranian Revolution and included the 1989 defeat of the Soviets in Afghanistan. It has been characterized by religious justification, and not only from Muslims; in this vein, Rapoport discusses Sikhs in India, Jews in Israel, Buddhists in Japan, and Christians in the United States.

Much new research since September 11, 2001, is being done by and about Muslims in the United States. The few studies published so far show a range of political responses from both Muslims and the mainstream. Hoda Badr (2002) reports that Muslim women in Houston are keeping the hijab and continuing to veil in a spirit of defiance despite a climate she characterizes as Islamophobic. In a recent article, Leonard (2002b), I reported significant shifts in who is representing the "Muslim community" and how it is being defined since September 11, shifts determined largely by the American media and mainstream political leaders, including the president. Garbi Schmidt (2002b) has outlined changes in vocabulary, changes in strategies because of increased visibility, and increased use of the Internet to regain self-confidence among young Muslims in the United States and Denmark. Lori Peek (2002) finds that a highly religious group of Muslim university students in New York has been generally satisfied with the reactions of professors, counselors, administrators, and other students on their campuses; they feel that their own parents and elders have been overly concerned about their welfare. Kathleen Moore (2002a) finds changing attitudes among Americans toward the immigration and presence of Muslim and Arab Americans. Heather Lindkvist (2002) finds that the lives of Somali Muslims in Maine have been disrupted by the post-9/11 closure of hawalas (money transfer services) and the suspicion cast on Somalia, difficulties intensified by the release of the film *Black Hawk Down*. Gregory Starrett (2002) finds increasing debate among African Americans about whether to present themselves as Muslims or as African Americans, a more complex set of frames of identity and perception. Andrew Shryock (2002) has found similarly shifting identities and perceptions among outsiders and Arabs in Detroit, with the media displacing Detroit's previously acculturated "Arab American face" and seeing its alien or "Arab Muslim face."

The good news is that more research on Muslims in the United States is being funded and published. The bad news may be that an overemphasis on "the impact of 9/11" will obscure the continuities in American Muslim histories, highlighting only the more sensational developments and neglecting or distorting other important aspects of American Muslim experience.

American Muslims in the Twenty-First Century

There is much about Muslim experiences in and of America, and about America's experiences of Muslims, that requires a broader and definitively national research agenda. Despite the setback 9/11 undoubtedly represents for Muslims, it has drawn those in the United States more closely into the culture and politics of the nation-state than ever before. Events flowing from the terrorist attacks raise problems and prospects central to the identities of most Muslims in the United States, challenging them to define, defend, and perhaps rethink their self-concepts and affiliations. The same is true for non-Muslim Americans, who are also called upon to define, defend, and perhaps rethink their concepts of civil religion, justice, and individual freedoms. American Muslim national organizations have spoken out strongly for constitutional safeguards of civil liberties, embracing American domestic freedoms in ways that can only be empowering for them and other citizens.

Review of the literature on Muslims and very minimal review of the literature on religious trends in recent U.S. history have shown that Muslims in the United States share in many of the trends observable among America's dominant, Christian religious groups (Wuthnow 1988). Higher education has produced greater homogeneity across denominational lines and moved many Christians to more liberal interpretations of religious texts. Both religious conservatives and religious liberals have formed special-purpose groups that cross traditional denominational boundaries. The role of the state and the public dimensions of religious culture in the United States have both expanded, raising the stakes for inclusion in the national civil religion and pushing it beyond its Judeo-Christian base. American Muslims are already passionately involved in debates about all the issues discussed here, and they are well equipped, by education, interest, and inclination, to participate in them.

Wuthnow (1988, 242) writes of the content of American public discourse and also of a deeper level of understanding, "a level of implicit and explicit claims about the character of the nation itself, the propriety of its actions, and the nature of its place in history and in the world." David Hollinger (1995) argues that the nation-state is still important, and that the U.S. civic (not ethnic) character is important. Cosmopolitan postethnicity, not the pluralist version of multiculturalism, is the more promising way to ensure that civic character. He sees three threats to a civic national culture. The first comes from a transnational or global capitalist American business elite, and the second from numerous diasporic or transnational affiliations, both forces that look beyond the United States and downplay the significance of America's civic character. The third threat comes, he thinks, from forces of political conservatism and/or evangelical Christianity; these forces diminish the importance of the state but claim the nation as their own. Wuthnow (1988, 244–50, 316–17) also notes the rising importance of business interests and conservative Christians and their mutual reinforcement.

Hollinger (1995, 120, 124) states that American multiculturalist debates have rarely addressed religion. He sees religious affiliations as often inherited from parents but also understands them as ultimately private and voluntary, and Wuthnow and other writers on American religion tend to confirm this view. With religions brought into the multicultural arena, Hollinger speculates, they could be treated as some ethno-racial groups have been—as entitlement-seeking units based on enduring identities. (However, rising rates of intermarriage increase people's choices of identity and affiliations.)

What Hollinger (1995, 21, 122–24) advocates, in fact, is the opposite: treating ethno-racial groups like religious ones, that is, extending this view of private and voluntary affiliation, of exit rights, to ethno-racial groups. But this understanding might be harder for newer immigrant Muslims and the long-standing ethno-racial groups already represented by most indigenous Muslims to accept and implement. For example, the ambitious new *North American Muslim Resource Guide* (Nimer 2002b) proposes that American Muslims satisfy the demands of citizenship but maintain their ethnic and religious identities; it stresses maintaining both cultural and religious practices. Much of the research discussed here relates directly to these major issues in national public discourse of how religious, ethno-racial, and national identities and affiliations relate to each other in the United States.

When Wuthnow (1988, 268–82) wrote in the 1980s about national religious trends, he felt that America's confidence in its ability to shape the world was waning, that a sense of pessimism and doubt about American capitalism, governmental supremacy, and central legitimating beliefs prevailed. He saw the United States as reluctant to assume the mantle of world leadership and to exercise its power globally. But in 2003 things look very different. American multinationals and global capitalism play important roles in the contemporary picture, and U.S. culture is heavily influencing many other societies. Moreover, President George W. Bush seems ready to exercise American political and military power in many parts of the world unilaterally. The nations most frequently named as targets of political or military action are Muslim ones, despite the protestations of U.S. leaders that the enemy is not Islam and their affirmations of religious pluralism in the United States.

There is a conservative Christian edge to the present national agenda as well. One indication of this is the rhetoric that government officials and others employ to rally support for the national cause; another is the federal funding of faith-based social initiatives. While some American Muslims welcome the chance to obtain federal resources for faith-based service organizations, others see greater resources flowing to the far more numerous, established, and often evangelical Christian organizations.

They worry about the anti-Muslim sentiments and perhaps proselytization likely to be engendered by support to such organizations (Khan 2002, 43–45).

Finally, I believe that struggles over pluralism should be put high on the research agenda. Most immediately, attention should be given to the struggles within the broader Muslim community in the United States to reestablish respect for the many movements that identify themselves as Islamic. A narrowing of definitions of Islam and Muslims had occurred among immigrants in the United States before September 11, 2001, but struggles before and after 9/11 may be broadening the boundaries of Islam or making "denominational" lines less important. These struggles will continue among Muslims, although the views of outsiders, including researchers, may play some role.

But the larger struggle is over pluralism in the American context, and here Muslims and other Americans must think hard about the kind of nation the United States is becoming and about its role in the world. Researchers must be sure not to analyze Muslims in the United States stereotypically as members of bounded, enduring units based on descent rather than voluntary affiliation, but as citizens with multiple identities and affiliations working to develop a national civic culture that will be more democratic, inclusive, and cosmopolitan.

$=$ Appendix 1 $=$

Appendix 1.A1   Overview of Major Divisions in the Islamic Old World

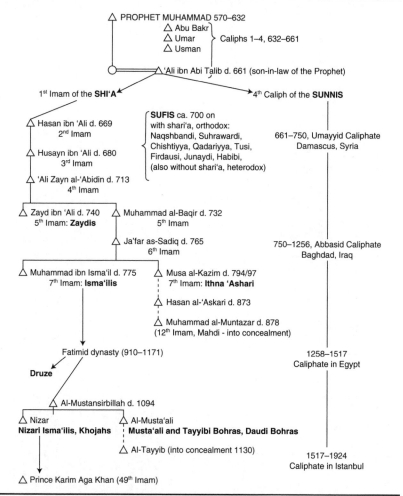

Source: Author's configuration.

Note: This figure is a very rough guide to the divisions within heartland or old world Islam over time in the main lines of transmission. Intended only to assist those who like to refer to names, dates, and descent time lines, it is admittedly incomplete and drawn from numerous sources that sometimes differ slightly with respect to dates and spellings.

Appendix 2.A1   Major Muslim American Organizations

Name	Founding Date	Founder(s)	Initial Location
African American Muslim organizations			
Moorish Science Temple	1913, 1920s	Noble Drew Ali	East Coast, Midwest
Nation of Islam[a]	1930	W. D. Fard, Elijah Muhammad	Detroit, Chicago
Ahmadiyyas	1920	Missionaries from Indian (later Pakistani) sect	East Coast
American Islamic organizations			
Federation of Islamic Associations (FIA)	1953	Lebanese immigrants	Midwest, Canada
Muslim Students' Association (MSA)	1963	Arabic-speaking foreign students in the United States	Plainfield, Indiana
Islamic Society of North America (ISNA)	1982	Grew out of MSA	
Islamic Circle of North America (ICNA)	1971	Pakistani Jamati Islami party ties	New York
American Muslim political organizations			
American Muslim Alliance (AMA)	1989	South Asian leaders	Fremont, California
American Muslim Council (AMC)	1990	Arab leaders	Washington, D.C.
Muslim Public Affairs Council (MPAC)	1988	Multi-ethnic leaders	Los Angeles, California
Council on American-Islamic Relations (CAIR)	1994	Arab leaders	Washington, D.C.
American Muslim Political Coordinating Council (AMPCC)	1999	AMA, AMC, MPAC, and AMPCC	Youngstown, Ohio

Source: Author's compilation.

Note: This appendix is intended to assist readers who are unfamiliar with the major Muslim organizations in the United States and the many abbreviations used for them in the text. This list necessarily omits many other organizations.

[a] Warith Deen Mohammed, son of Elijah Muhammad, assumed leadership in 1975 and renamed the group World Community of Al-Islam in the West, then Muslim American Mission, then Muslim American Society, then American Society of Muslims (as of 2003). Louis Farrakhan split off and resurrected NOI in 1978; in 2000 Farrakhan began to reconcile with W. D. Mohammed.

Appendix 3

U.S. Local and Regional Studies of Muslims in America

A T LEAST one publication by each of these authors can be found in the bibliography. See also "America" in the critical survey and bibliography in Haddad, Voll, and Esposito (1991).

Boston, Massachusetts

Diana Eck

Chicago, Illinois

Karen Ahmed, Louise Cainkar, E. U. Essien-Udom, Asad Husain and Harold Vogelaar, Craig Joseph, Lowell Livezey, Paul Numrich, Garbi Schmidt, Raymond Brady Williams

Cleveland, Ohio

Robert Dannin

Delano, California

Jonathan Friedlander

Detroit-Dearborn, Michigan

Nabeel Abraham, Barbara Aswad, Barbara Bilge, Gary David and Kenneth Ayouby, Charlene Eisenlohr, Abdo Elkholy, Amaney Jamal, Sally Howell, Anahid Kulwicki and Penny Cass, Ann Chih Lin, William Lockwood and Yvonne Lockwood, Alixa Naff, Anne Rasmussen, Jen'nan Ghazal Read, Karen Rignall, Kim Schopmeyer, May Seikaly, Andrew Shryock, Michael Suleiman, Frances Trix, Linda Walbridge

Durham, North Carolina

Elise Goldwasser

Dutchess County, New York

Christine Kolars

Houston, Texas

Denise Al-Johar, Hoda Badr, Michael Fischer and Mehdi Abedi, Raymond Brady Williams

Indianapolis, Indiana

Steve Johnson

Los Angeles, California

Mehdi Bozorgmehr, Kambiz GhaneaBassiri, Shideh Hanassah, Ron Kelley, Prema Kurien, Hamid Naficy, Georges Sabagh, Nayereh Tohidi, Barbara Weightman

New York, New York

Zain Abdullah, Rogaia Abusharaf, Syed Ali, Ruksana Ayyub, Rosemary Coombe and Paul Stoller, R. M. Mukhtar Curtis, Robert Dannin, Joann D'Alisera, Mamadou Diouf, Victoria Ebin, Marc Ferris, Khalid Griggs, Munir Jiwa, Aminah Mohammad-Arif, Yusuf Nuruddin, Susan Palmer and Steve Luxton, Donna Perry, Usha Sanyal, Susan Slyomovics, Gisela Webb, Barbara Weightman

Quincy, Massachusetts

Mary Lahaj

Rochester, New York

Tamara Sonn

San Diego, California

Huma Ahmed-Ghosh, Marcia Hermansen

San Francisco, California

Lubna Nazir-Chaudhry, Mary Elaine Hegland, Nadine Naber

St. Louis, Missouri

Edward Curtis

Seattle, Washington

Miriam Adeney and Kathryn DeMaster

Toledo, Ohio

Abdo Elkholy

=== Notes ===

Chapter 1

1. In October 2001, two new studies put the number of Muslims in the United States at 2.8 million or less. In the first study, the American Jewish Committee commissioned Tom W. Smith of Chicago's National Opinion Research Center to analyze twenty-four existing population estimates of the Muslim population, and he concluded that Muslims numbered between 1.4 million and 2.8 million. In the second study, a random telephone survey of 50,000 households conducted by the City University of New York, researchers arrived at a figure of 1.1 million adults and 650,000 children. Muslim organizations dispute these studies and usually cite figures of 7 million or 8 million.

2. Julie Dash effectively used the figure of an African Muslim slave in her fine 1993 film *Daughters of the Dust*, but otherwise the image is rarely invoked.

3. The only Muslim speaker at the Parliament of Religions, however, was the white convert Muhammed Alexander Russell Webb (Smith 1999, 189–90; Eck 2001, 234).

4. In addition, a Pakistani began the Hanafi Madhhab movement (Kareem Abdul-Jabbar is a Hanafi member), and the Darul Islam, once the largest black Muslim Sunni group in the United States, was transformed into a Sufi movement in the 1970s by its leader's devotion to a South Asian shaykh of the Qadariyya Order (McCloud 1995, 18–21, 24–26, 57–58; Smith 1999, 97–98; Curtis 1994).

5. Whether the Ahmadis consider their founder a prophet or not is contested, and there are differences among Ahmadis as well (Friedmann 1989). They were declared non-Muslims in 1974 in Pakistan after the third of three court cases, but the earlier decisions, based on the same body of textual material as the third, did not find them unorthodox; the third decision was reached only under extreme political pressure (Mahmud 1995).

6. Edward Curtis (2002a) argues against identifying Farrakhan with separatism.

7. A Puerto Rican immigrant woman began PIEDAD (Propagacion Islamica para la Educacion y Devocion de Ala' el Divino) in New York in 1987, inspired by increased interest among Latina women married to Muslims and young Latino men in prison (Ferris 1994, 223).

8. Abdo Elkholy's (1966, 73–76) view of Arab Muslims in Detroit and Toledo was that the Shi'a saw mosques as Sunni institutions and favored national social clubs; his survey found sectarian differences to be more pronounced in Detroit, with fewer intermarriages and distinct institutions. Elkholy also thought Shi'a in Detroit were more educated and active than Sunnis, whom he perceived as more "nationalistic" Arabs (133).

9. Iranian Muslims, a much smaller group, are also highly educated but overwhelmingly secular. Most of these Iranians fled because of the 1979 Iranian Revolution; also, they are Shi'a, the minority sect within Islam and within American Islam.

Chapter 2

1. There are many smaller organizations, such as the African American Five Percenters; the Muslim Students' Association-Persian Speaking Group (MSA-PSG), formed by Iranian Shi'a after 1979; and the Hizb-ul-Tahrir, which publishes the journal *Khalifornia* and rejects participation in kafir (unbeliever) American politics.

2. The ISNA has many affiliated organizations and institutions besides the MSA, including the Islamic Medical Association (IMA), American Muslim Engineers and Scientists (AMSE, founded in 1969), and American Muslim Social Scientists (AMSS, founded in 1972). See Nyang (1998, 7–38), Smith (1999, 167–71), and Ahmed (1991, 11–24).

3. "Landmark Meeting of Arab and Muslim American Organizations," *Pakistan Link,* February 5, 1999, 39. The Muslim groups were the AMA, AMC, CAIR, MPAC, and CFGG (Coalition for Good Government), and the Arab ones were the ADC (American-Arab Anti-Discrimination Committee), AAI (Arab American Institute), AAUG (Arab American University Graduates, which ended in 2001), and NAAA (National Association of Arab Americans, which merged into the ADC by 2001).

4. The survey was part of a national project involving forty denominations, and the Muslim component was sponsored by four organizations—CAIR, ISNA, the Islamic Circle of North America (ICNA), and the Ministry of Imam W. D. Mohammed—indicating a major coalition effort by Arab, South Asian, and African American Muslim leaders. It is discussed later again and again.

5. C. Eric Lincoln (1961, 221), among the first to publish authoritative work on America's black Muslims, found that, in 1960, "the Ahmadiyah were generally accepted as a legitimate sect of Islam"; omitting them from the national survey erased an important link between immigrant and African American Muslims.

6. The questionnaire and interview results are available at *www.projectmaps.com/ PMReport.htm*. The method was to create a phone list by matching the zip codes of three hundred randomly selected Islamic centers (excluding Nation of Islam and Ahmadi mosques) against local telephone exchanges, then

identifying people with common Muslim surnames from the local telephone books and calling them. If the person answering identified himself or herself as Muslim, the interview proceeded.

7. In the speech Kabbani had alleged that "many Muslim organizations . . . are not moderate, but extremist"; that Muslim organizations were set up to collect money and send it to "extremists outside the United States"; that most Muslim leaders and most mosque boards of trustees were "being run by the extremist ideology, but not acting as a militant movement"; and that "this extremist ideology is spreading into universities through national organizations, associations and clubs." Roundly condemned for these overstatements, he had been boycotted by all major American Muslim groups. Sulayman Nyang, a professor of African and Islamic studies at Howard University, attributed Kabbani's new visibility to "that competition for attention from American leadership." Interviewed by Laurie Goldstein in the *New York Times*, he said on October 28, 2001, "America is a big magnifying mirror, and they compete for access to it, because it projects you internationally and makes you look big" (Goodstein, Laurie. 2001."Muslim Leader Who Was Once Labeled an Alarmist Is Suddenly a Sage." *The New York Times*, October 28, 2001, p. B5.)

8. Khan's views aroused great controversy among American Muslims, since he argued, among other things, that "Israel treats its one million Arab citizens with greater respect and dignity than most Arab nations did . . . their citizens."

9. "Some people for example said that America is evil. . . . We can say that American foreign policy is wrong, but America is not evil, and even when we say 'American foreign policy' we should specify which issue," said a spokesperson for the Islamic center of southern California and AMPCC. See Goodstein, Laurie. "Influential American Muslims Temper Their Tone." *The New York Times*, October 19, 2001, B1, B8.

Chapter 3

1. Essien-Udom (1962, ix) achieved good rapport for interviews but failed in administering a questionnaire.

2. See Walbridge (1999) for a discussion of past and present figures. In 1976 the leading marja' in Iran, Abul Qasim Khui, sent a representative to the United States to guide followers. (In 1987 he sent another to the United Kingdom.) The Alawi Foundation from Iran and the Khoja Shi'a Ithna 'Ashari from the United Kingdom have also expanded to the United States.

3. In contrast to Sunni Islam, "where the rulers were theoretically subject to the 'ulama (jurisconsults) as guardians of the legal tradition, Isma'ili doctrine gave the Imam absolute right to interpret or reinterpret the faith as he saw fit"; see Ruthven (1997, 371).

4. Entered into by contract for a specified time, a mut'a marriage basically legitimizes sexual intercourse between a man and a woman. This is justi-

fied as a way for poor or widowed women to gain support and protection or a way for men to achieve sexual satisfaction when traveling away from home, studying abroad, or going on long business trips or pilgrimages. As will be discussed later, it occurs in the United States.

5. For all these changes and followers' reactions to them, see Kassam-Remtulla (1999).

6. The U.S. council reported to the Supreme Council in Nairobi and to the international secretariat at Aiglemont, France (Williams 1988, 211–21).

7. The authors of the handbook include the Harvard scholar of religions Ali Asani, the nonpolitical spokesman featured after 9/11, and Annemarie Schimmel, a noted scholar of Sufism, who helped design the logo.

8. The Baha'i movement is somewhat similar but began only in the nineteenth century. Initiated by an Ithna 'Ashari Shi'a leader in Iran, it was begun in the United States in 1894; it has a center in Illinois (Haddad and Smith 1993, 20).

9. The British succeeded the Sikhs in the Punjab, and the Ahmadi movement was notably pro-British from its origin; it sent missionaries to many parts of the British Empire. In 1914, after Ghulam Ahmad's death, the movement split into the Qadiani and Lahori factions, based in Qadian and Lahore, respectively. (The Lahoris say Ahmad was a mujaddid or renewer; the Qadianis say he was a Prophet but one obedient to Muhammad and bringing no new laws.) After the partition of India in 1947, many Qadianis moved to Pakistan, where Rabwah is their headquarters. The khalifa (head of the community) is in Rabwah, and there is a national amir (head) in Washington, D.C. The Lahoris are also represented in the United States (Haddad and Smith 1993, 52–54).

10. I know of only one study of an early Sufi group of immigrants: Frances Trix (1994) studied Albanians in Dearborn and Detroit, Michigan.

11. Most Sufis and Sufi influences in the United States probably fall into Hermansen's "perennial" category (1997, 169; see also Barboza 1994), but hybrid groups are growing, and there are some artistic crossovers. South Asian qawwali music popularized by Pakistan's late singer, Nusrat Fateh Ali Khan, has won a place for at least one "old world" Sufi performance tradition in the emerging category of world music (this will be discussed later).

12. The French spellings, "Mourides" and "Tidianes," are used by Perry (Senegal was a French colony). See Diouf (2000) for background on the Murids.

13. However, participants in mixed marriages and the children of such marriages were often leaders in Islamic religious activities. Elkholy (1966, 124) found that, in 1959, the most religiously active members in the Toledo community had married outside the faith; further, that the "Islamic organizations in America, including the Federation of Islamic Associations in the United States and Canada, are the product of the mixed-marriage children."

14. The total population figure of which this is a percentage is itself controversial, as noted earlier.

15. The story calls the poll a representative sample of the American Muslim
population, but the percentage of African American respondents was
weighted at 20 percent. (Additional samples of such respondents were
taken because the telephone survey missed those with Anglo-American or
non-Muslim surnames and was therefore low on African American Muslims.) This throws off the other figures for ethnic composition: South
Asians, 32 percent; Arabs, 26 percent; African, 7 percent; other, 14 percent;
not available, 1 percent. See also *www.projectmaps.com/PMReport.htm*.

16. This survey could profitably be replicated, since many attitudes have
changed.

17. A study of Iranian immigrant women in the Los Angeles ethnic economy
does not specify the religion of the ten informants; one is described as
Muslim, but without discussion (Dallalfar 1996b, 119). The study argues
that Iranian women are active entrepreneurs but are rendered invisible by
gender-neutral social science terms.

Chapter 4

1. The Nizari Isma'ilis have no common mother tongue, yet the Aga Khans III
and IV have proclaimed English the secular language of the community. All
firmans and speeches are in English and are read in prayer services (Kassam-
Remtulla 1999, 83–84). One might note that these congregational services
have long characterized the community and were brought to the United
States rather than developed upon arrival as a sign of Americanization.

2. Recently, Lawrence Mamiya (2001–2002, 27) has taken a harsher stance
toward the early African American Islamic movements than in his earlier
work, referring to them as "Black nationalist groups that relied on Islam as
a cover." See also Ernest Allen Jr. (1997).

3. After that, Mohammed again changed his community's name, first to
World Community of Al-Islam in the West, then to the American Muslim
Mission, then to the Muslim American Society (putting nothing before the
word Muslim). The present-day name is the American Society of Muslims.

4. Thanks to Amardeep Singh, who passed out this document as he gave
his paper at the conference of the Asian Pacific Americans and Religion
Research Initiative, Berkeley, California, August 3, 2002.

5. Segal (2002) argues that Brodkin (1998) is talking about social mobility and
class interests, not this shifting constellation of religious and civilizational
identities.

6. I have already commented on the survey biases. Earlier surveys also had
problems. Fareed Nu'man (1992, 12–13) relied on immigration figures and
based the percentage of Muslims among national-origin populations in the

United States on the percentages in the homeland populations; for indigenous and convert Muslims, he computed conversion rates combined with group mortality and fertility rates. Ilyas Ba-Yunus and Moin Siddiqui (1999) review previous attempts to survey or estimate the American Muslim population and describe their own mosque-based method of obtaining a random sample of 1,042 households in 1994. (They found somewhat higher levels of both education and income than the two surveys discussed earlier, with 49.4 percent of their respondents being engineers or computer science professionals [34].)

7.   McAlister (2001, 96–97) places Nation of Islam doctrines on gender relations in historical context, but the exclusion of this movement from much current survey and other research activity hinders our knowledge. McCloud (1995, 55 passim) points to polygyny among members of the Darul Islam and their strong enforcement of gendered norms, which are also enforced by the Five Percenters, some branches of the Nation of Islam, and the Ansaaru Allah (Haddad and Smith 1993, 127–31).

8.   Muslims working in the liquor business compartmentalized their occupational and religious lives. Michael Harris (1995) points out that young Bangladeshi men working in convenience stores selling liquor must do the same thing today. He reports that they often see their American customers, both men and women, as morally suspect.

9.   Once a young American Muslim woman trying to bring her betrothed over from Pakistan asked me to write a letter stating that Islamic law prohibited a man and woman from meeting before their marriage. The Prophet is on record, however, as encouraging a man and woman contemplating marriage to meet each other first.

10. Having converted long ago from Hinduism, the group had continued the high-caste prohibition on widow remarriage, whereas other Muslims routinely practice widow marriage.

11. In fact, these are the five subject areas considered comparatively by Christian Green and Paul Numrich (2001) in their guide to religious perspectives on sexuality. The "faith traditions" covered in the guide are conservative Protestantism, moderate and liberal Protestantism, Roman Catholicism, Judaism, Islam, Buddhism, and Hinduism. The guide is oriented to the Cairo Program of Action formulated at the United Nations International Conference on Population and Development held in Cairo in 1994.

12. Michael Wolfe (1998, 8–9), a convert and public figure, writes that Islam's frank appreciation of sexuality attracted him.

Chapter 5

1.   Numrich tells me that of the mosques he describes as "Indian and Indo-Pakistani mosques," one is entirely Gujarati Indian Muslims and the others have mixed congregations. He notes (2000a, 266, n. 3) that the INS has

counted Indians and Pakistanis separately since 1973 but that ethnic studies often employ the single category "Indo-Pakistani." In California we use "South Asian," a regional difference. Earlier studies of religious landscapes in Chicago and Houston by Raymond Brady Williams (1988) also mapped the populations.

2. Lowell Livezey and Paul Numrich are part of the Religion in Urban America Program, a Lilly Endowment study conducted at the University of Illinois at Chicago.

3. There has been resistance to the building of other non-Christian institutions. My favorite case involves the Hindu temple in Norwalk, California, which was forced to change its Hindu architectural style to Spanish Mission. As a letter-writer protested, confusing religions, "Who wants a Taj Mahal in one's backyard?"

4. For the Muslim part of the survey, mosque representatives (an imam, board president, or board member) were interviewed by telephone. I have already pointed out that Nation of Islam, Ahmadi, and Nizari Isma'ili mosques or jamatkhanas were not included in the total of 1,209 mosques identified; 631 mosques were approached for the survey.

5. The average number of converts per mosque was 16.3 (Bagby, Perl, and Froehle 2001, 22), or nearly 20,000 converts, of whom 13,000 were men, 7,000 were women, and 14,000 were African American (and remember that prison mosques were omitted from this survey). Lawrence Mamiya (2001–2002, 31) cites a speech by Ihsan Bagby in which he estimates an annual growth of 100,000 American Muslims, 60,000 of them arriving immigrants and 40,000 of them African American converts.

6. Mamiya (2001–2002, 39), comparing black churches and African American masjids, notes that while 70 to 80 percent of participants in Friday mosque prayers are male, in black churches 70 to 80 percent of participants are female. He relates these statistics to the national rate of black single-parent families (60 percent) and black women's explorations of Islam, suggesting that they are also seeking husbands and stable families.

7. The mosques designated by Bagby (2001–2002) as HSAAM seem to be integrating immigrant and indigenous Islamic traditions in an American Islam. Bagby, a chief designer and implementer of both the 2000 mosque survey and an earlier 1994 pilot study, is a member of MANA, whose elected leader is Siraj Wahaj, imam of Brooklyn's Masjid al-Tawqa. MANA participates in national coalition efforts, such as a MAPS leadership conference held in May 2002.

8. The UISA grew out of a dues-paying membership plan of 1938 to start a rural agricultural venture to feed the urban communities during the depression. This Muslim Ten-Year Plan was led by El-Hajj Wali Akram and created for the benefit of formerly Ahmadi converts in the Ohio River Valley region.

9. Werbner (1999) draws on definitions proposed by Ulf Hannerz and Jonathan Friedman. Hannerz (1992, 252) defines "cosmopolitans" as "willing to engage with the Other" and "transnationals" as frequent travelers

who carry with them meanings embedded in social networks. Friedman (1997, 84–85) shows the encapsulation of cosmopolitans as well. These categories might usefully distinguish between the Kurdish Shi'a and the Nizari Isma'ilis—representing the transnational and cosmopolitan, respectively—or distinguish, in Dearborn, between new and older Shi'a immigrant and refugee populations.

10. Shaykh Muhammad Hissam Kabbani of the Naqshbandi Order mentioned earlier founded the As-Sunnah Foundation of America, the organization that (along with the American Muslim Assistance Relief Organization) promoted and funded the International Islamic Unity Conference in Los Angeles in 1996. The conference received no donations from any government, but it drew on the global Naqshbandi Order's connections with royals from Malaysia, the president of Chechnya, the sultan of Brunei, and the grand muftis of Lebanon and Cyprus.

Chapter 6

1. Diana Eck (2001) simply adds Muslims and other non-Christians to the salad bowl, in good pluralist fashion.

2. This is generally true for Muslim minorities in Western countries, unlike those living in India, for example, where Muslim personal law is privileged and has not been changed or standardized, as Hindu law has been.

3. The Sikh community in North America, much smaller and less internally diverse, has comparable issues; see Dusenbery (1995) and Barrier (2001).

4. Larry Poston (1992) cited Siddiqi (1986). By 1999–2000, Dr. Siddiqi's views had changed, and he was president of ISNA. For ISNA's initiative, see Johnson (1991, 111).

5. Poston (1992, 31) categorizes Muslims in the West as either "defensive-pacifist" or "offensive-activist," distinguishing those who are concerned with retaining their religion from those who want to change the societies in which they reside in a more Islamic direction. He sees this distinction as a simplification of Haddad and Lummis's (1987) threefold distinction: liberals, "born-again evangelicals" who emphasize personal piety, and highly organized international promoters of an Islamic vision of a religious and just government.

6. Smith (1999, 191–93) reviews Al-Faruqi's life. He and his wife, Lois Lamya, were important mentors for many Muslim students and key participants in building institutions of Islamic higher education and in interfaith activities. Both were murdered in their home in 1986.

7. See www.islam-democracy.org. The center's chair, Ali Mazrui, is also the director of the Institute of Global Cultural Studies at New York's Binghamton University, and the center's vice chair, John Esposito, is director of the Center of Muslim-Christian Understanding at Georgetown University (along with Yvonne Haddad).

8. Abou El Fadl is from Kuwait but was educated in Egypt and the United States. He is the Omar and Azmeralda Alfi Distinguished Fellow at UCLA's Law School and a regular columnist in *The Minaret*. Alalwani, of Iraqi origin, has headed the Fiqh Council since 1986, when ISNA upgraded and expanded its thirty-year-old Fiqh Council. He is also president of the School of Islamic and Social Sciences (SISS).

9. A fiqh "councillor," or mufti, differs from a qadi (judge) in that his interpretation is usually not legally binding; in North America the word might better be "counselor," DeLorenzo (1998, 65–66) suggests, since local imams, respected elders, or directors of Islamic centers are often called upon for interpretations.

10. Thought to include 65 percent of all mosques in North America, the arrangement has been jeopardized by Al-Amin's arrest for murder in 2000 and recent conviction and W. D. Mohammed's reported withdrawal from the shura in 2000.

11. Their preferred sources of authority (absolutely foundational) were the Qur'an (95 percent), Sunnah of the Prophet (90 percent), the teachings of the righteous salaf (predecessors) (16 percent), the teachings of great scholars of the past (10 percent), human reasoning and understanding (10 percent), and the teachings of certain recent Muslim leaders and scholars (7 percent).

12. Like others, Tohidi (1993, 195, 213) sees Iranian Muslims as more secular than the other Iranian groups in Los Angeles, but she mentions a sufreh, a religious meeting, that was attended by a wide range of women and clearly served emotional as well as religious needs.

13. Wadud taught in Kuala Lumpur's International Islamic University for three years and participated in the influential "Sisters in Islam" group; for a brief biography, see Smith (1999, 201–2).

14. The same kind of argument is made by Leila Ahmed (2000, 87–88), who contrasts oral culture in the Gulf with the Arabic literate culture that "Arab governments are zealously imposing on their populations through schools and universities." Ahmed is beginning to work on Muslim women in the United States.

15. Bakhtiar, trained in philosophy and psychology, writes on Islamic psychology, ethics, and morality as components of mental health; see Smith (1999, 199–200) for a brief biography.

16. Many of Abou El Fadl's columns in *The Minaret*, including those cited in this book, are in *Conference of the Books: The Search for Beauty in Islam* (El Fadl 2001b). His book *Speaking in God's Name: Islamic Law, Authority, and Women* (El Fadl 2001c) is a very full discussion of Islamic law followed by case studies of "determinations demeaning to women," most of them decisions issued by Saudi Arabia's official Permanent Council for Scientific Research and Legal Opinions (CRLO).

17. See the introduction by the Sudanese scholar Abdullahi Ahmed An-Na'im to Mahmud Muhammad Taha's book (1987). An-Na'im translated the book and is now at Emory Law School in Atlanta.

18. See the current members at *www.fiqhcouncil.org*.

Chapter 7

1. "Assimilation" is coming back into use among sociologists, but I resist the term.

2. Rahman was forced out of his native Pakistan in the late 1960s. He was the first Muslim appointed to Chicago's Divinity School, where he died in 1988. See Denny (1991, 96–108) for a brief biography.

3. By percentages ranging from 57 to 71 percent, respondents supported the death penalty and making abortions more difficult to obtain and opposed gay marriages, the sale and display of pornography, and physician-assisted suicide. By percentages of 53 and 59 percent, they supported prayer and display of the Ten Commandments in public schools. See Bukhari (2002) for a more complete report of the findings.

4. They explain the total of over 100 percent in 2000 by noting that some mosques have multiple affiliations.

5. See Smith (1999, 193–94, 197–98) for brief biographies of Ali and Abdul-Jabbar, and Barboza (1994) for interviews with Ali, Abdul-Jabbar, and Farrakhan. Farrakhan's Million Man March on Washington, D.C., in 1995 was lauded in the Muslim American press as a triumph for Islam, and his (partial) reconciliation in 2000 with W. D. Mohammed's (now) American Society of Muslims was enthusiastically welcomed.

6. See "Thou Shall Submit to Thy Husband," *The Minaret* (November 1999): 19–20; "A Closer Look at the Christian Coalition," *The Minaret* (June 1997): 24–29; and Aslam Abdullah (editor of *The Minaret*), "American Muslims: Problems and Challenges—II," *Pakistan Link,* May 29, 1998, p. 14.

7. In Usha Sanyal's (1999) discussion, ICNA, inspired by the Pakistani Jamati Islami, seems inclined to "Islamicize" American Muslims and perhaps also non-Muslims.

8. Elkholy's details are fascinating, but the methodology is somewhat vague, and although both populations were mostly from Lebanon, there were major differences. Also living in Detroit were Yemenis, Iraqis, Syrians, and some non-Arab Muslims, and occupational and residential patterns in the two cities differed strikingly.

9. Rogaia Mustafa Abusharaf (1998, 238–39) argues that, in Islamic tradition, communal prayer in a mosque is a congregational act that corresponds to the ideal of the umma and that most mosques, while built and maintained by governments, were attended by members of local communities. But any Muslim could worship at any mosque, and mosques had no official

memberships or professional ministers. For one look at how this tradition was adapted in the United States, see Mary Lahaj's (1994, 304) discussion of the establishment of the Islamic center of New England and the dual lists of both paid and unpaid members it had to maintain.

10. David and Ayouby (2002, 133) talk about "Presbyterian Islam" in Dearborn, Michigan, but do not spell out what they mean by that.

11. Elkholy (1966), Abraham (2000), Howell (2000a), and Walbridge (1997) bring in Sunni-Shi'a differences too.

12. Raymond Brady Williams (1991) argued for an evolving American Islam; see also Abraham (2000); the *Islamic Horizons* (March-April 1998) special issue on "Islam in America" (and note how "in America" gives the phrase a different emphasis); and Leonard (forthcoming a).

13. Ihsan Bagby supervised the work on a national curriculum for ISNA; for a brief biography, see Dannin (2002a, 239–40).

14. Students in my University of California, Irvine, class wondered about gender imbalance when their research showed a much higher proportion of girls than boys in a local Islamic school.

15. One page (Council on Islamic Education 1998, 31) presents the Twelver Shi'a, and there are two pages on Sufism as self-purification and love of God (31–32). The Nation of Islam is dismissed (46–47), but one sentence mentions that W. D. Mohammed joined the mainstream.

16. The building may be used for a religious institution being set up by Chicagoans to train young American Muslims that would be affiliated with Cairo's prestigious Al-Azhar University.

17. Although some leading figures, such as Seyyid Hossein Nasr, write about Islamic science, most of the new American Muslim spokespeople seem to believe in a universal "positivist" modern science that they do not see linked to religion.

18. Muhsin Mahdi (1997, 155) has asked questions that Furlow's work will help answer: What will Muslim institutions of higher learning in the West look like? How will the views of believing Muslims and the teachings and writings of Western students of Islam and Muslim scholars long living in the West relate to each other?

19. An Iranian American returning home for a visit was arrested and imprisoned briefly in 2002 for teaching coeducational dance in the United States.

20. Regula Qureshi's (1995 [1986]) excellent study of Sufi qawwali music in India and Pakistan cries out for replication in North America, where the music is becoming popular.

21. It should be noted that Sally Howell, Andrew Shryock, Nabeel Abraham, and others associated with the book *Arab Detroit* (Abraham and Shryock 2000) and ACCESS (Arab Community Center for Economic and Social Services) in Detroit successfully mounted an NEH project in 1994, "Creating a New Arab World: A Century in the Life of the Arab Community in Detroit."

This exhibit had a second life as part of a Smithsonian Institution photographic exhibition from 1995 to 1996. Joan Mandell, Sally Howell, and ACCESS also coproduced a film, *Tales of Arab Detroit*. All are striking visual depictions of this foundational community.

22. "There is a fear that an American version of Islam may emerge among American Muslims, especially the youth. Our hope is that this will not happen" (Athar 1994, 222; see also Afzal 1991, 11–12).

23. Mehdi Bozorgmehr (1996, 25, 29) notes that an unassimilated ethnic group would have high rates of residential concentration, in-marriage or endogamy, and use of the ethnic language. He was looking at Middle Eastern immigrants, with Iranians and Armenians scoring high on all three, Israelis scoring low, and Arabs in the middle.

24. This self-described "more liberal voice" (quoted in Wax 1999) advised readers that, while there certainly cannot be Gay Pride parades in mosques, "Clinton's 'Don't Ask, Don't Tell' was a perfectly Islamic solution." Concerning premarital sex, this mufti said: "Remember that Allah is all-forgiving, especially to those who repent sincerely (this is in case you have already been naughty)."

25. For Al-Fatiha, visit *www.al-fatiha.net*. For Queer Jihad, visit *www.well.com/user/queerjhd*.

Chapter 8

1. The Pew "gateway cities" project has awarded seven grants to researchers to study how religion can help new immigrants integrate with American society. The seven cities being studied (New York City, Los Angeles, Houston, Washington, D.C., Miami, Chicago, and San Francisco) contain half of all the foreign-born population in the United States.

2. Interfaith efforts could be mentioned here, but I have no idea how extensive or effective such efforts are.

3. See Vitalis (2002) for a revealing analysis of the early emphasis on race in the developing field of international relations in the United States.

4. Such studies are now at the stage that classical studies reached around the turn of the sixteenth century, when only the most important texts had been published and the most obvious archaeological remains had become known, according to Jacques Waardenburg (1997, 187–93), who suggests a number of comparative studies.

5. They are also beginning to voice once again strong opposition to current American Middle Eastern foreign policy, but there is disagreement about this: Mohommed A. Muqtedar Khan (2002, 24) sees an obsession with Arab issues as dysfunctional.

6. See the FBI hate crimes report available at: *www.fbi.gov/ucr/01hate.pdf*; that document shows a rise from 28 incidents in 2000 to 481 in 2001. See also the

March 2002 report of the National Asian Pacific American Legal Consortium, "Backlash? When America Turned on Its Own" (cited in *Los Angeles Times,* March 11, and *India-West,* March 15), which says that 96 percent of the 243 incidents of violence in the first three months after September 11 targeted South Asians, more than half of them Sikhs. (A Sikh and a Pakistani were killed.)

7. A September 23, 2002, MPAC press release began: "MPAC firmly supports the view that being a Muslim is fully compatible with being a loyal and patriotic American. American Muslims should find no contradiction between Islamic values and the American tradition of liberty and democracy enshrined in the Constitution." For criticisms of and calls upon the Republican Party, see MPAC's e-mail *MPACnews,* November 4, 2002, and CAIR's e-mail *ISLAM-INFONET,* April 2, 2002, reprinting Eric Boehlert's *Salon. com* piece "Betrayed by Bush," April 2, 2002.

8. The second-quarter 2002 issue of *MPAC Report* noted that three of its southern California chapters held a family picnic to honor the Japanese American community on May 19. I know of similar new connections in northern California.

9. Not only Shaykh Hamza Yusuf but the other PICS (Public Intellectual Convert Sufis, a term coined by Marcia Hermansen) with large youth and Internet followings exemplify this: see Abdal-Hakim Murad, "Recapturing Islam from the Terrorists," at: *www.themodernreligion.com/terror/wtc-murad.html;* and Shaikh Nuh Ha Mim Keller's home page at: *http://66.34.131.5/ISLAM/ nuh/main.htm.* They are also sometimes called "trophy Muslims."

10. Emerson (2002, 185–197) also mentions MAYA (the Muslim Arab Youth Association), the AIG (American Islamic Group), and the ICW (Islamic Cultural Workshop), calling the latter two "now-defunct" and "largely inactive."

References

Aafreen, Sabah. 1999. "In Search of Self." In *Emerging Voices: South Asian American Women Redefine Self, Family, and Community*, edited by Sangeeta R. Gupta. New Delhi: Sage Publications.

Abdullah, Aslam. 1998. "Expectations from American Muslim Institutions and Leadership." *Pakistan Link*, October 16, 14.

Abdullah, Omer Bin. 1995. "Eyes on the Muslim Future in America." *Pakistan Link*, August 18, 27.

Abdullah, Zain. Forthcoming. "Negotiating Muslim Space: The Incorporation of West African Muslim Immigrants in New York City." In *Religion and Immigrant Incorporation in New York*, edited by Jose Casanova and Aristide Zolberg. New York: New York University Press.

Abdul-Rauf, Muhammad. 1978. *History of the Islamic Center: From Dream to Reality.* Washington: Islamic Center.

———. 1983. "The Future of the Islamic Tradition in North America." In *The Muslim Community in North America*, edited by Earle H. Waugh, Baha Abu-Laban, and Regula B. Qureshi. Edmonton, Can.: University of Alberta Press.

Abou El Fadl, Khaled. 1996a. "Conference of Books Revived." *The Minaret* (August): 23.

———. 1996b. "The Choice: Shahada or Hijab." *The Minaret* (October): 43.

———. 1997a. *The Authoritative and Authoritarian in Islamic Discourses: A Contemporary Case Study.* 2d ed. Austin, Tex.: Dar Taiba.

———. 1997b. "The Extremities of Ugliness." *The Minaret* (January): 43.

———. 1997c. "The Rights of Human Beings." *The Minaret* (June): 43.

———. 1998a. "Setting Priorities." *The Minaret* (April): 41.

———. 1998b. "Striking a Balance: Islamic Legal Discourse on Muslim Minorities." In *Muslims on the Americanization Path?*, edited by Yvonne Yazbeck Haddad and John L. Esposito. Atlanta: Scholars Press.

———. 1999. "Colonizing Women." *The Minaret* (November): 41.

———. 2000. "The Page." *The Minaret* (January): 41–42.

———. 2001a. *And God Knows the Soldiers: The Authoritative and Authoritarian in Islamic Discourses.* 3d ed. New York: University Press of America. (2d edition published in 1997 as *The Authoritative and Authoritarian in Islamic Discourses: A Contemporary Case Study.*)

———. 2001b. *Conference of the Books: The Search for Beauty in Islam*. New York: University Press of America.

———. 2001c. *Speaking in God's Name: Islamic Law, Authority, and Women*. Oxford: Oneworld Publications.

———. 2001d. "Islam and the Theology of Power." *Middle East Report* 221(winter): 28–33.

———. 2002. "The Sites of Purity." *The Minaret* (July-August): 15–16.

———. Forthcoming. "The Orphans of Modernity and the Clash of Civilizations." *Global Dialog*.

Abraham, Nabeel. 2000. "Arab Detroit's 'American' Mosque." In *Arab Detroit: From Margin to Mainstream*, edited by Nabeel Abraham and Andrew Shryock. Detroit: Wayne State University Press.

Abraham, Nabeel, and Andrew Shryock, eds. 2000. *Arab Detroit: From Margin to Mainstream*. Detroit: Wayne State University Press.

Abraham, Sameer Y., and Nabeel Abraham, eds. 1983. *Arabs in the New World: Studies on Arab-American Communities*. Detroit: Wayne State University.

Abugideiri, Hibba. 2000. "Hagar: A Historical Model for 'Gender Jihad.' " In *Daughters of Abraham: Feminist Thought in Judaism, Christianity, and Islam*, edited by Yvonne Yazbeck Haddad and John L. Esposito. Gainesville: University Press of Florida.

Abusharaf, Rogaia Mustafa. 1998. "Structural Adaptations in an Immigrant Muslim Congregation in New York." In *Gatherings in Diaspora: Religious Communities and the New Immigration*, edited by R. Stephen Warner and Judith G. Wittner. Philadelphia: Temple University Press.

Adeney, Miriam, and Kathryn DeMaster. 1994. "Muslims of Seattle." In *Muslim Communities in North America*, edited by Yvonne Yazbeck Haddad and Jane Idleman Smith. Albany: State University of New York Press.

Afzal, Omar. 1991. "An Overview of Asian-Indian Muslims in the United States." In *Indian Muslims in North America*, edited by Omar Khalidi. Watertown, Mass.: South Asia Press.

Ahmed, Gutbi Mahdi. 1991. "Muslim Organizations in the United States." In *The Muslims of America*, edited by Yvonne Yazbeck Haddad. New York: Oxford University Press.

Ahmed, Karen Hunt. 2002. " 'Liberal Islam': What Does It Mean for American Muslims?" Paper presented to the Conference on Muslim Minorities in Western Europe and North America After September 11, Duke University, Durham, N.C. (March 23).

Ahmed, Leila. 2000. "The Women of Islam." *Transition* 9(83): 78–97.

———. 1992. *Women and Gender in Islam: Historical Roots of a Modern Debate*. New Haven: Yale University Press.

Ahmed-Ghosh, Huma. Forthcoming. "Claiming Their Space: Ahmadiyya Women in North America." In *American Muslim Identities*, edited by Karen Isaksen Leonard.

Aidi, Hisham. Forthcoming. "Jihadis in the Hood: Race, Urban Islam, and the War on Terror." In *Islam and Urban Youth Culture*, edited by Hisham Aidi and Yusuf Nuruddin.

Al-Faruqi, Isma'il R. 1983. "Islamic Ideals in North America." In *The Muslim Community in North America,* edited by Earle H. Waugh, Baha Abu-Laban, and Regula B. Qureshi. Edmonton, Can.: University of Alberta Press.

———. 1986. *Toward Islamic English.* Herndon, Va.: International Institute of Islamic Thought.

Al-Hayani, Fatima Agha. 1999. "Arabs and the American Legal System: Cultural and Political Ramifications." In *Arabs in America: Building a New Future,* edited by Michael Suleiman. Philadelphia: Temple University Press.

Ali, Faiz-u-Nisa A. 1991. *The Path of Islam: Book 3.* 3d ed. Tustin, Calif.: International Islamic Educational Institute.

Ali, Syed Faiz. Forthcoming a. "Why Here, Why Now?: Young Muslim Women Wearing Hijab." In *American Muslim Identities,* edited by Karen Isaksen Leonard.

———. Forthcoming b. "South Asian Muslims in New York City." In *Religion and Immigrant Incorporation in New York,* edited by Jose Casanova and Aristide Zolberg. New York: New York University Press.

Alibhai, Mohamed. 2002. "Islam: Faith or Religion?: The Re-education of the Modern Imam." *The Minaret* (October): 24–31.

Al-Johar, Denise. Forthcoming. "Muslim American Marriages: Reflecting New Identities?" In *American Muslim Identities,* edited by Karen Isaksen Leonard.

Allen, Ernest, Jr. 1997. "Religious Heterodoxy and Nationalist Tradition: The Continuing Evolution of the Nation of Islam." In *New Trends and Developments in the World of Islam,* edited by Peter B. Clarke. London: Luzac Oriental Press.

———. 1998. "Identity and Destiny: The Formative Views of the Moorish Science Temple and the Nation of Islam." In *Islam on the Americanization Path?,* edited by John L. Esposito and Yvonne Yazbeck Haddad. Atlanta: Scholars Press.

Allen, James P., and Eugene Turner. 1997. *The Ethnic Quilt: Population Diversity in Southern California.* Northridge: California State University.

An-Na'im, Abdullahi Ahmed. 1991. "A Kinder, Gentler Islam?" *Transition* 52: 4–16.

Ansari, Z. I. 1981. "Aspects of Black Muslim Theology." *Studia Islamica,* ex fasciculo 13: 137–76.

———. 1985. "W. D. Muhammed: The Making of a 'Black Muslim' Leader (1933–1961)." *American Journal of Islamic Social Sciences* 2(2): 245–62.

Anway, Carol L. 1995. *Daughters of Another Path: Experiences of American Women Choosing Islam.* Lee's Summit, Mo.: Yawna Publications.

Arkoun, Mohammed. 1997. "Rethinking Islam Today." In *Mapping Islamic Studies: Genealogy, Continuity, and Change,* edited by Azim Nanji. New York: Mouton de Gruyter.

Asad, Talal. 1980. "Ideology, Class, and the Origin of the Islamic State." *Economy and Society* 9(4): 450–73.

———. 1986. *The Idea of an Anthropology of Islam.* Washington, D.C.: Center for Contemporary Arab Studies.

———. 1996. "Modern Power and the Reconfiguration of Religious Traditions." *Stanford Humanities Review* 5(1): 5. See *www.stanford.edu/group/SHR/5-1/text/ asad.html.*

Asani, Ali. 1987. "The Khojahs of Indo-Pakistan: The Quest for an Islamic Identity." *Journal Institute of Muslim Minority Affairs* 8(1): 31–41.

———. 1994. "The Impact of Modernization on the Marriage Rites of the Khojah Ismai'lis of East Africa." *Journal of Turkish Studies* 18: 17–24.

———. 2001. "The Khojahs of South Asia: Defining a Space of Their Own." *Cultural Dynamics* 13(2): 155–68.

———. 2002. "On Pluralism, Intolerance, and the Quran." *American Scholar* 71(1): 52–60.

Aswad, Barbara. 1994. "Attitudes of Immigrant Women and Men in the Dearborn Area Toward Women's Employment and Welfare." In *Muslim Communities in North America,* edited by Yvonne Yazbeck Haddad and Jane Idleman Smith. Albany: State University of New York Press.

———. 1996. "Arab Muslim Families in the United States." In *Middle Eastern Diaspora Communities in America,* edited by Mehdi Bozorgmehr and Alison Feldman. New York: New York University, Hagop Kevorkian Center for Near Eastern Studies.

Aswad, Barbara C., and Barbara Bilge, eds. 1996. *Family and Gender Among American Muslims: Issues Facing Middle Eastern Immigrants and Their Descendants.* Philadelphia: Temple University Press.

Athar, Shahid. 1994. *Reflections of an American Muslim.* Chicago: KAZI Publications.

———. 1995. *Sex Education: An Islamic Perspective.* South Elgin, Ill.: Library of Islam.

Austin, Allan D. 1984. *African Muslims in Antebellum America: A Sourcebook.* New York: Garland.

———. 1997. *African Muslims in Antebellum America: Transatlantic Stories and Spiritual Struggles.* New York: Routledge.

Ayyub, Ruksana. 1998. "Survey on the Incidence of Domestic Violence in the Muslim Population." Unpublished data.

———. 2000. "Domestic Violence in the South Asian Muslim Immigrant Population in the United States." *Journal of Social Distress and the Homeless* 9(3): 237–48.

Badr, Hoda. 2000. "Al-Noor Mosque: Strength Through Unity." In *Religion and the New Immigrants: Continuities and Adaptations in Immigrant Congregations,* edited by Helen Rose Ebaugh and Janet Saltzman Chafetz. New York: Altamira Press.

———. 2002. "Re-Veiling Islamic Identity in the U.S. After September 11." Paper presented to the Conference on Muslim Minorities in Western Europe and North America After September 11, Duke University, Durham, N.C. (March 23).

Bagby, Ihsan A. 2001–2002. "A Profile of African-American Masjids: A Report from the National Masjid Study 2000." *Journal of the Interdenominational Theological Center* 29(1–2): 205–41.

Bagby, Ihsan, Paul M. Perl, and Bryan T. Froehle. 2001. *The Mosque in America: A National Portrait: A Report from the Mosque Study Project.* Washington, D.C.: Council on American-Islamic Relations.

Bakhtiar, Laleh. 1996. *Sufi Women of America: Angels in the Making.* Chicago: Institute of Traditional Psychoethics and Guidance.

Banner, Lois. 1998. *Finding Fran.* New York: Columbia University Press.

Barboza, Steven. 1994. *American Jihad: Islam After Malcolm X.* New York: Doubleday.

Barrier, N. Gerald. 2001. "Gurdwaras in the U.S.: Governance, Authority, and Legal Issues." *Understanding Sikhism* 4(1): 31–41.

Bayoumi, Moustafa. 2001. "East of the Sun (West of the Moon): Islam, the Ahmadis, and African America." *Journal of Asian American Studies* 4(3): 251–63.

Ba-Yunus, Ilyas. 1999. "Divorce." *Pakistan Link,* September 10, 42.

Ba-Yunus, Ilyas, and M. Moin Siddiqui. 1999. *A Report on the Muslim Population in the United States.* New York: Center for American Muslim Research Information (CAMRI).

Bayyah, Shaykh Abdullah bin. 2001. "Muslims Living in Non-Muslim Lands." Introduced by Shaykh Hamza Yusuf. Available at: *www.zaytuna.org/sh_bin_bayyah.html.*

Berg, Herbert. 1998. "Elijah Muhammad: An African American Muslim 'Mufassir'?" *Arabica* 45: 320–46.

———. 1999. "Elijah Muhammad and the Qur'an." *Muslim World* 89: 42–55.

Berri, Abdullatif. 1989. *Temporary Marriage in Islam.* Dearborn, Mich.: Az-Zahra International.

Bilge, Barbara. 1994. "Voluntary Associations in the Old Turkish Community of Metropolitan Detroit." In *Muslim Communities in North America,* edited by Yvonne Yazbeck Haddad and Jane Idleman Smith. Albany: State University of New York Press.

———. 1996. "Turkish-American Patterns of Intermarriage." In *Family and Gender Among American Muslims: Issues Facing Middle Eastern Immigrants and Their Descendants,* edited by Barbara C. Aswad and Barbara Bilge. Philadelphia: Temple University Press.

Bilgrami, Akeel. 1993. "What Is a Muslim?: Fundamental Commitment and Cultural Identity." In *Hindus and Others: The Question of Identity in India Today,* edited by Gyandra Pandey. New York: Viking.

Blank, Jonah. 2001. *Mullahs on the Mainframe: Islam and Modernity Among the Daudi Bohras.* Chicago: University of Chicago Press.

Boyarin, Jonathan, and Daniel Boyarin, eds. 1997. *Jews and Other Differences: The New Jewish Cultural Studies.* Minneapolis: University of Minnesota Press.

Bozorgmehr, Mehdi. 1996. "Diaspora in Microcosm: Middle Easterners in Los Angeles." In *Middle Eastern Diaspora Communities in America,* edited by Mehdi Bozorgmehr and Alison Feldman. New York: New York University, Hagop Kevorkian Center for Near Eastern Studies.

———. 1997. "Internal Ethnicity: Iranians in Los Angeles." *Sociological Perspectives* 40(3): 387–408.

Bozorgmehr, Mehdi, and Alison Feldman, eds. 1996. *Middle Eastern Diaspora Communities in America.* New York: New York University, Hagop Kevorkian Center for Near Eastern Studies.

Bozorgmehr, Mehdi, and Georges Sabagh. 1988. "High-Status Immigrants: A Statistical Profile of Iranians in the United States." *Iranian Studies* 21: 5–35.

———. Forthcoming. "Salient Identities of Iranian Muslims in L.A." in *American Muslim Identities,* edited by Karen Isaksen Leonard.

Bozorgmehr, Mehdi, Georges Sabagh, and Claudia Der-Martirosian. 1993. "Beyond Nationality: Religio-Ethnic Diversity." In *Irangeles: Iranians in Los Angeles,* edited by Ron Kelley, with Jonathan Friedlander. Berkeley: University of California Press.

Braude, Ann. 1997. "Women's History Is American Religious History." In *Retelling U.S. Religious History*, edited by Thomas A. Tweed. Berkeley: University of California Press.

Brodeur, Patrice. 2002. "The Changing Nature of Islamic Studies and American Religious History," and "The Changing Nature of Islamic Studies and American Religious Studies." Parts 1 and 2. *The Muslim World* 91: 1, 71–98; 92: 1, 185–208.

Brodkin, Karen. 1998. *How Jews Became White Folks and What That Says About Race in America*. New Brunswick, N.J.: Rutgers University Press.

Bukhari, Zahid. 2002. "Project MAPS Conducts the First Systematic American Muslim Poll." *Newsletter of the Project MAPS (Muslims in the American Public Square)* (spring): 1.

Bulliet, Richard W. 1994. *Islam: The View from the Edge*. New York: Columbia University Press.

Cainkar, Louise. 1991. "Palestinian-American Muslim Women: Living on the Margins of Two Worlds." In *Muslim Families in North America*, edited by Earle H. Waugh, Sharon McIrvin Abu-Laban, and Regula Burckhardt Qureshi. Edmonton, Can.: University of Alberta Press.

———. 1994. "Social Class as a Determinant of Adaptation and Identity Among Immigrant Palestinian Women." In *The Development of Arab-American Identity*, edited by Ernest McCarus. Ann Arbor: University of Michigan Press.

———. 1996. "Immigrant Palestinian Women Evaluate Their Lives." In *Family and Gender Among American Muslims: Issues Facing Middle Eastern Immigrants and Their Descendants*, edited by Barbara C. Aswad and Barbara Bilge. Philadelphia: Temple University Press.

———. 1999. "The Deteriorating Ethnic Safety Net Among Arabs in Chicago." In *Arabs in America: Building a New Future*, edited by Michael Suleiman. Philadelphia: Temple University Press.

———. Forthcoming. *Palestinian Immigrants in the United States: Gender, Culture, and Global Politics*. Philadelphia: Temple University Press.

Caldwell, Deborah. 2001. "Something Major Is Happening." Available at: *www.islamicvoice.com/december.2001/reformation.htm*.

Campo, Juan. 1996. "Islam in California: Views from *The Minaret*." *The Muslim World* 86: 3–4, 294–312.

Casanova, Jose, and Aristide Zolberg, eds. Forthcoming. *Religion and Immigrant Incorporation in New York*. New York: New York University Press.

Chaudhry, Lubna Nazir. 1997. "Researching 'My People,' Researching Myself: Fragments of a Reflective Tale." *Qualitative Studies in Education* 10(4): 441–53.

———. 1998. "We Are Graceful Swans Who Can Also Be Crows: Hybrid Identities of Pakistani Muslim Women." In *A Patchwork Shawl: Chronicles of South Asian Women in America*, edited by Shamita Das Dasgupta. New Brunswick, N.J.: Rutgers University Press.

———. 1999. "Fragments of a Hybrid's Discourse." In *Emerging Voices: South Asian American Women Redefine Self, Family, and Community*, edited by Sangeeta R. Gupta. New Delhi: Sage Publications.

Chittick, William C. 1994. "The Islamic Concept of Human Perfection." In *Jung and the Monotheisms: Judaism, Christianity, and Islam*, edited by Joel Ryce-Menuhin. New York: Routledge.

Collier, Jane F., Bill Maurer, and Liliana Suarez-Navaz. 1997. "Sanctioned Identities: Legal Constructions of Modern Personhood." *Identities* 2(1–2): 1–27.

Coombe, Rosemary J., and Paul Stoller. 1994. "X Marks the Spot: The Ambiguities of African Trading in the Commerce of the Black Public Sphere." *Public Culture* 7: 249–74.

Council on Islamic Education. 1998. *Teaching About Islam and Muslims in the Public School Classroom*. 3d ed. Fountain Valley, Calif.: Council on Islamic Education.

Curtis IV, Edward E. 1997. "Islam in Black St. Louis: Strategies for Black Liberation in Two Local Religious Communities." *Gateway Heritage* 17(4): 30–43.

———. 2002a. *Islam in Black America: Identity, Liberation, and Difference in African-American Islamic Thought*. Albany: State University of New York Press.

———. 2002b. "Islamizing the Black Body: Ritual and Power in Elijah Muhammad's Nation of Islam." *Religion and American Culture* 12(2): 167–96.

Curtis, R. M. Mukhtar. 1994. "Urban Muslims: The Formation of the Dar ul-Islam Movement." In *Muslim Communities in North America*, edited by Yvonne Yazbeck Haddad and Jane Idleman Smith. Albany: State University of New York Press.

Curtiss, Richard. 2000. "The Case for a Muslim and Arab American Bloc Vote." Talk given at the American Muslim Alliance National Convention, Irvine, California (September 30).

D'Alisera, Joann. 2001. "I Love Islam: Popular Religious Commodities, Sites of Inscription, and Transnational Sierra Leonean Identity." *Journal of Material Culture* 6(1): 91–110.

Dallalfar, Arlene. 1996a. "Immigration and Identity: Muslim and Jewish Iranian Women in Los Angeles." In *Middle Eastern Diaspora Communities in America*, edited by Mehdi Bozorgmehr and Alison Feldman. New York: New York University, Hagop Kevorkian Center for Near Eastern Studies.

———. 1996b. "The Iranian Ethnic Economy in Los Angeles." In *Family and Gender Among American Muslims: Issues Facing Middle Eastern Immigrants and Their Descendants*, edited by Barbara C. Aswad and Barbara Bilge. Philadelphia: Temple University Press.

Dannin, Robert. 1995. "Ethno-methodological Approaches to Studying Islam in America." In *The Diversity of the African-American Religious Experience: A Continuing Dialogue*. New York: New York Public Library, Schomberg Center for Research in Black Culture.

———. 1996a. "Understanding the Multi-ethnic Dilemma of African-American Muslims." In *Middle Eastern Diaspora Communities in America*, edited by Mehdi Bozorgmehr and Alison Feldman. New York: New York University, Hagop Kevorkian Center for Near Eastern Studies.

———. 1996b. "Island in a Sea of Ignorance: Dimensions of the Prison Mosque." In *Making Muslim Space in North America and Europe*, edited by Barbara Daly Metcalf. Berkeley: University of California Press.

———. 2002a. *Black Pilgrimage to Islam*. New York: Oxford University Press.

———. 2002b. "The Greatest Migration?" In *Muslim Minorities in the West: Visible and Invisible*, edited by Yvonne Yazbeck Haddad and Jane Smith. New York: Altamira Press.

David, Gary, and Kenneth K. Ayouby. 2002. "Being Arab and Becoming Americanized: Forms of Mediated Assimilation in Metropolitan Detroit." In *Muslim Minorities in the West: Visible and Invisible,* edited by Yvonne Yazbeck Haddad and Jane I. Smith. New York: Altamira Press.

DeCaro, Louis A., Jr. 1996. *On the Side of My People: A Religious Life of Malcolm X.* New York: New York University Press.

DeLorenzo, Yusuf Talal. 1998. "The Fiqh Councilor in North America." In *Muslims on the Americanization Path?,* edited by Yvonne Yazbeck Haddad and John L. Esposito. Atlanta: Scholars Press.

Denny, Frederick M. 1991. "The Legacy of Fazlur Rahman." In *The Muslims of America,* edited by Yvonne Yazbeck Haddad. New York: Oxford University Press.

———. 1994. "American Perceptions of Islam and Muslims." In *Towards a Positive Islamic World-view,* edited by Yaacob Rahman and Abdul Rahman. Kuala Lumpur: Institute of Islamic Understanding Malaysia (IKIM).

Denny, Walter. 1984. "Contradiction and Consistency in Islamic Art." In *The Islamic Impact,* edited by Yvonne Yazbeck Haddad, with Byron Haines and Ellison Findly. Syracuse, N.Y.: Syracuse University Press.

Diouf, Mamadou. 2000. "The Senegalese Murid Trade Diaspora and the Making of a Vernacular Cosmopolitanism." *Public Culture* 12(3): 679–702.

Diouf, Sylviane A. 1998. *Servants of Allah: African Muslims Enslaved in the Americas.* New York: New York University Press.

Duran, Khalid. 1993. "Homosexuality and Islam." In *Homosexuality and World Religions,* edited by Arlene Swidler. Valley Forge, Pa.: Trinity Press.

Dusenbery, Verne A. 1995. "A Sikh Diaspora?: Contested Identities and Constructed Realities." In *Nation and Migration,* edited by Peter van der Veer. Philadelphia: University of Pennsylvania Press.

Ebin, Victoria. 1996. "Making Room Versus Creating Space: The Construction of Spatial Categories by Itinerant Mouride Traders." In *Making Muslim Space in North America and Europe,* edited by Barbara Daly Metcalf. Berkeley: University of California Press.

———. 1990. "Commerçants et Missionnaires: Une Confrérie Musulmane Senegalaise à New-York." *Hommes et Migrations* (1128–38): 25–31.

Eck, Diana L. 2001. *A New Religious America: How a "Christian Country" Has Now Become the World's Most Religiously Diverse Nation.* San Francisco: Harper San Francisco.

Eickelman, Dale F., and Jon W. Anderson, eds. 1999. *New Media in the Muslim World: The Emerging Public Sphere.* Bloomington: Indiana University Press.

Eisenlohr, Charlene Joyce. 1996. "Adolescent Arab Girls in an American High School." In *Family and Gender Among American Muslims: Issues Facing Middle Eastern Immigrants and Their Descendants,* edited by Barbara C. Aswad and Barbara Bilge. Philadelphia: Temple University Press.

Elkholy, Abdo A. 1966. *The Arab Moslems in the United States: Religion and Assimilation.* New Haven, Conn.: College and University Press.

Emerson, Steven. 2002. *American Jihad: The Terrorists Living Among Us.* New York: Free Press.

Engineer, Asghar Ali. 1980. *The Bohras.* Delhi, India: Vikas Publishing House.

Esposito, John L. 2002. *Unholy War: Terror in the Name of Islam*. Oxford: Oxford University Press.

Essien-Udom, E. U. 1962. *Black Nationalism: A Search for an Identity in America*. Chicago: University of Chicago Press.

Evanzz, Karl. 1999. *The Messenger: The Rise and Fall of Elijah Muhammad*. New York: Pantheon.

Farrakhan, Louis. 1993. *A Torchlight for America*. Chicago: FCN Publishers.

Ferris, Marc. 1994. "To 'Achieve the Pleasure of Allah': Immigrant Muslim Communities in New York City 1893–1991." In *Muslim Communities in North America*, edited by Yvonne Yazbeck Haddad and Jane Idleman Smith. Albany: State University of New York Press.

Findley, Paul. 1989. *They Dare to Speak Out*. Chicago: Lawrence Hill Books.

Fischer, Michael M., and Mehdi Abedi. 1990. *Debating Muslims: Cultural Dialogues in Postmodernity and Tradition*. Madison: University of Wisconsin Press.

Fornaro, Robert J. 1984. "Asian Indians in America: Acculturation and Minority Status." *Migration Today* 12: 28–32.

Friedlander, Jonathan. 1994. "The Yemenis of Delano: A Profile of a Rural Islamic Community." In *Muslim Communities in North America*, edited by Yvonne Yazbeck Haddad and Jane Idleman Smith. Albany: State University of New York Press.

———. 2000. "Yemeni Farmworkers: From Ethnicity to Religion." Paper presented to the Conference on Muslim Identities in North America, University of California at Irvine (May 21).

Friedman, Jonathan. 1997. "Global Crises, the Struggle for Cultural Identity and Intellectual Porkbarrelling: Cosmopolitans Versus Locals, Ethnics and Nationals in an Era of De-hegemonization." In *Debating Cultural Hybridity: Multicultural Identities and the Politics of Anti-racism*, edited by Pnina Werbner and Tariq Modood. London: Zed Books.

Friedmann, Yohanan. 1989. *Prophecy Continuous: Aspects of Ahmadi Religious Thought and Its Medieval Background*. Berkeley: University of California Press.

Furlow, Christopher A. 1999. "Islam, Science, and Modernity: From Northern Virginia to Kuala Lumpur." Paper presented at the meeting of the American Anthropological Association, Chicago (November 21).

Gardell, Mattias. 1996. *In the Name of Elijah Muhammad: Louis Farrakhan and the Nation of Islam*. Durham, N.C.: Duke University Press.

Gerges, Fawaz A. 1999. *America and Political Islam: Clash of Cultures or Clash of Interests?* New York: Cambridge University Press.

GhaneaBassiri, Kambiz. 1997. *Competing Visions of Islam in the United States: A Study of Los Angeles*. Westport, Conn.: Greenwood Press.

Goldwasser, Elise. 1998. "Economic Security and Muslim Identity: A Study of the Immigrant Community in Durham, North Carolina." In *Muslims on the Americanization Path?*, edited by Yvonne Yazbeck Haddad and John L. Esposito. Atlanta: Scholars Press.

Gomes, Peter. 1996. *The Good Book: Reading the Bible with Mind and Heart*. New York: William Morrow.

Gomez, Michael A. 1994. "Muslims in Early America." *Journal of Southern History* 60(4): 671–710.

Gotanda, Neil. 2002. Talk on Asian Americans and racialization, given at the Conference on Asian Pacific Americans and Religion Research Initiative, Berkeley, Calif. (August 3).

Green, M. Christian, and Paul D. Numrich. 2001. *Religious Perspectives on Sexuality: A Resource Guide.* Chicago: Park Ridge Center.

Griggs, Khalid Fattah. 2002. "Islamic Party in North America: A Quiet Storm of Political Activism." In *Muslim Minorities in the West: Visible and Invisible,* edited by Yvonne Yazbeck Haddad and Jane I. Smith. New York: Altamira Press.

Haddad, Yvonne Yazbeck. 1983. "Arab Muslims and Islamic Institutions in America: Adaptation and Reform." In *Arabs in the New World: Studies on Arab-American Communities,* edited by Sameer Y. Abraham and Nabeel Abraham. Detroit: Wayne State University.

———. 1991. *The Muslims of America.* New York: Oxford University Press.

———, ed. 2002. *Muslims in the West: From Sojourners to Citizens.* New York: Oxford University Press.

Haddad, Yvonne Yazbeck, and John L. Esposito, eds. 1998. *Muslims on the Americanization Path?* Atlanta: Scholars Press.

Haddad, Yvonne Yazbeck, ed., with Byron Haines and Ellison Findly. 1984. *The Islamic Impact.* Syracuse, N.Y.: Syracuse University Press.

Haddad, Yvonne Yazbeck, and Adair T. Lummis. 1987. *Islamic Values in the United States: A Comparative Study.* New York: Oxford University Press.

Haddad, Yvonne Yazbeck, and Jane Idleman Smith, eds. 1993. *Mission to America: Five Islamic Sectarian Communities in North America.* Gainesville: University Press of Florida.

———. 1994. *Muslim Communities in North America.* Albany: State University of New York Press.

———. 2002. *Muslim Minorities in the West: Visible and Invisible.* New York: Altamira Press.

Haddad, Yvonne Yazbeck, John Obert Voll, and John L. Esposito. 1991. *The Contemporary Islamic Revival.* Westport, Conn.: Greenwood Press.

Hadhrami, Abu Amal. 2000. "Muslim Americans Need Own Outlook." *Islamic Horizons* (January-February): 48–53.

Haeri, Shahla. 1989. *Law of Desire: Temporary Marriage in Sh'i Iran.* Syracuse, N.Y.: Syracuse University Press.

Haider, Gulzar. 1996. "Muslim Space and the Practice of Architecture." In *Making Muslim Space in North America and Europe,* edited by Barbara Daly Metcalf. Berkeley: University of California Press.

Hall, Stuart. 1987. "Minimal Selves." In *Identity,* edited by Homi Bhabha. London: Institute of Contemporary Arts.

———. 1988. "New Ethnicities." *ICA Documents* (7): 27–31.

———. 1989. "Cultural Identity and Cinematic Representation." *Framework* 36: 68–81.

Halliday, Fred. 1996. *Islam and the Myth of Confrontation: Religion and Politics in the Middle East.* New York: I. B. Tauris Publishers.

Hanassah, Shideh. 1993. "Caught Between Two Cultures: Young Iranian Women in Los Angeles." In *Irangeles: Iranians in Los Angeles,* edited by Ron Kelley, with Jonathan Friedlander. Berkeley: University of California Press.

Hannerz, Ulf. 1992. *Cultural Complexity: Studies in the Social Organization of Meaning*. New York: Columbia University Press.

Harris, Michael S. 1995. "Bangladeshis in Babylon: Convenience Store Clerks and the Cultural Transaction." Paper presented at the meeting of the American Anthropological Association, Washington, November 19.

Hasan, Asma Gull. 2000. *American Muslims: The New Generation*. New York: Continuum.

Hasnat, Naheed. 1998. "Being 'Amreekan': Fried Chicken Versus Chicken Tikka." In *A Patchwork Shawl: Chronicles of South Asian Women in America*, edited by Shamita Das Dasgupta. New Brunswick, N.J.: Rutgers University Press.

Hathout, Hassan. 1995. *Reading the Muslim Mind*. Plainfield, Ind.: American Trust Publications.

Hathout, Maher. 2002. *Jihad Versus Terrorism*. Pasadena, Calif.: Dawn Books.

Hegland, Mary Elaine. 1999. "Iranian Women Immigrants Facing Modernity in California's Bay Area: The Courage, Creativity, and Trepidation of Transformation." In *The Iranian Woman and Modernity: Proceedings of the Ninth International Conference of Iranian Women's Studies Foundation*, edited by Golnaz Amin. Cambridge, Mass.: Iranian Women's Studies Foundation.

———. Forthcoming. "Women of Karbala—Moving to America." In *Women of Karbala*, edited by Kamran Aghaie. Austin: University of Texas Press.

Hermansen, Marcia K. 1991. "Two-Way Acculturation: Muslim Women in America Between Individual Choice (Liminality) and Community Affiliation (Communitas)." In *The Muslims of America*, edited by Yvonne Yazbeck Haddad. New York: Oxford University Press.

———. 1994. "The Muslims of San Diego." In *Muslim Communities in North America*, edited by Yvonne Yazbeck Haddad and Jane Idleman Smith. Albany: State University of New York Press.

———. 1997. "In the Garden of American Sufi Movements: Hybrids and Perennials." In *New Trends and Developments in the World of Islam*, edited by Peter B. Clarke. London: Luzac Oriental Press.

———. Forthcoming a. "Muslim Americans and Religious Healing." In *Religious Healing in America*, edited by Linda Barnes and Susan Sered. New York: Oxford University Press.

———. Forthcoming b. "What's American About American Sufi Movements?" In *Sufism in Europe and the United States*, edited by David Westerlund. London: RoutledgeCurzon.

———. Forthcoming c. "How to Put the Genie Back in the Bottle: Identity-Islam and Muslim Youth Cultures in America." In *Progressive Muslims: On Justice, Gender, and Pluralism*, edited by Omid Safi. Oxford: Oneworld Publications.

———. Forthcoming d. "Mystifying Identities in Muslim America: American Sufi Movements."

Hofman, Murad Wilfried. 1999. "Muslims in the Next Millennium." *Islamic Horizons* (January–February): 20–22.

Hollinger, David A. 1995. *Postethnic America: Beyond Multiculturalism*. New York: Basic Books.

Howell, Sally. 2000a. "Finding the Straight Path." In *Arab Detroit: From Margin to Mainstream*, edited by Nabeel Abraham and Andrew Shryock. Detroit: Wayne State University Press.

————. 2000b. "Politics, Pragmatism, and the 'Arab Vote': A Conversation with Maya Berry." In *Arab Detroit: From Margin to Mainstream*, edited by Nabeel Abraham and Andrew Shryock. Detroit: Wayne State University Press.

————. 2000c. "The Art and Artistry of Arab Detroit: Changing Traditions in a New World." In *Arab Detroit: From Margin to Mainstream*, edited by Nabeel Abraham and Andrew Shryock. Detroit: Wayne State University Press.

————. 2000d. "Cultural Interventions: Arab American Aesthetics Between the Transnational and the Ethnic." *Diaspora* 9(1): 59–82.

————. Forthcoming. "Arab and Islamic Arts in Detroit: New Experiments in Strategic Essentialism." In *American Muslim Identities*, edited by Karen Isaksen Leonard.

Huntington, Samuel P. 1993. "The Clash of Civilizations?" *Foreign Affairs* 72(3): 22–49.

Husain, Asad, and Harold Vogelaar. 1994. "Activities of the Immigrant Muslim Communities in Chicago." In *Muslim Communities in North America*, edited by Yvonne Yazbeck Haddad and Jane Idleman Smith. Albany: State University of New York Press.

Islam, Naheed. 1998. "Naming Desire, Shaping Identity: Tracing the Experiences of Indian Lesbians in the United States." In *A Patchwork Shawl: Chronicles of South Asian Women in America*, edited by Shamita Das Dasgupta. New Brunswick, N.J.: Rutgers University Press.

Jamal, Amaney A. 2002. "Individual Versus Group Rights: Mosques and Collective Identity Formation Among Arab Americans." Unpublished paper, Princeton University.

Jamal, Amaney, Ann Chih Lin, and Abigail J. Stewart. Forthcoming. "Patriarchy, Connection, and Individualism: Immigration and the Experience of Gender in Arab Immigrant Families." *Gender and Society*.

Jervis, James. 1997. "The Sufi Order in the West and Pir Vilayat 'Inayat Khan: Space-Age Spirituality in Contemporary Euro-America." In *New Trends and Developments in the World of Islam*, edited by Peter B. Clarke. London: Luzac Oriental Press.

Jiwa, Munir. 2002. "Imagining, Imaging, Identity: Ambiguous Aesthetics and 'Muslim' Visual Artists in New York City." Paper presented to the Conference on Muslim Minorities in Western Europe and North America After September 11, Duke University, Durham, N.C. (March 23).

Johnson, Steve A. 1991. "Political Activity of Muslims in America." In *The Muslims of America*, edited by Yvonne Yazbeck Haddad. New York: Oxford University Press.

————. 1994. "The Muslims of Indianapolis." In *Muslim Communities in North America*, edited by Yvonne Yazbeck Haddad and Jane Idleman Smith. Albany: State University of New York Press.

Jordan, Terry. 1982. *Texas Graveyards: A Cultural Legacy*. Austin: University of Texas Press.

Joseph, Craig. 2002. "Islamic Schools and Lawsuits in Chicago." Paper presented to the Conference on Muslim Minorities in Western Europe and North America After September 11, Duke University, Durham, N.C. (March 23).

Joseph, Suad. 1999. "Against the Grain of the Nation—The Arab." In *Arabs in America: Building a New Future*, edited by Michael Suleiman. Philadelphia: Temple University Press.

Kanji, Anise. 1990. " 'Oh My Sisters, Agitate': Aga Khan III and the Status of Isma'ili Muslim Women." Undergraduate thesis, Harvard College.

Karim, Jamillah. Forthcoming a. "African American Muslim Identity Formation: A Response to Difference."

———. Forthcoming b. "Voices of Faith, Faces of Beauty: Empowering American Muslim Women Through *Azizah* Magazine." In *Muslim Networks: Medium, Method, and Metaphor,* edited by Miriam Cooke and Bruce B. Lawrence. Chapel Hill: University of North Carolina Press.

Kassam-Remtulla, Aly. 1999. "(Dis)placing Khojahs: Forging Identities, Revitalizing Islam, and Crafting Global Isma'ilism." Honors thesis, Stanford University. Available at: *ismaili.net/~heritage/Source/1121b/main.html.*

Keddie, Nikki. 1997. "Secularism and the State: Towards Clarity and Global Comparison." *New Left Review* 226: 21–40.

Kelley, Robin D. G. 1994. *Race Rebels: Culture, Politics, and the Black Working Class.* New York: Free Press.

Kelley, Ron. 1993a. "Ethnic and Religious Communities from Iran in Los Angeles." In *Irangeles: Iranians in Los Angeles,* edited by Ron Kelley, with Jonathan Friedlander. Berkeley: University of California Press.

———. 1993b. "Wealth and Illusions of Wealth in the Los Angeles Iranian Community." In *Irangeles: Iranians in Los Angeles,* edited by Ron Kelley, with Jonathan Friedlander. Berkeley: University of California Press.

———. 1994. "Muslims in Los Angeles." In *Muslim Communities in North America,* edited by Yvonne Yazbeck Haddad and Jane Idleman Smith. Albany: State University of New York Press.

Kelley, Ron, with Jonathan Friedlander, eds. 1993. *Irangeles: Iranians in Los Angeles.* Berkeley: University of California Press.

Kepel, Gilles. 1997. *Allah in the West: Islamic Movements in America and Europe.* Cambridge: Polity Press.

Khalidi, Omar. 1998. "Approaches to Mosque Design in North America." In *Muslims on the Americanization Path?,* edited by Yvonne Yazbeck Haddad and John L. Esposito. Atlanta: Scholars Press.

Khan, Badruddin. 1997. *Sex Longing and Not Belonging.* Oakland, Calif.: Floating Lotus USA.

Khan, Mohommed A. Muqtedar. 1998a. "Muslims and American Politics: Refuting the Isolationist Arguments." *American Muslim Quarterly* 2(1–2): 60–69.

———. 1998b. "Muslims and Identity Politics in America." In *Muslims on the Americanization Path?,* edited by Yvonne Yazbeck Haddad and John L. Esposito. Atlanta: Scholars Press.

———. 2002. *American Muslims: Bridging Faith and Freedom.* Beltsville, Md.: Amana Publications.

Khan, Shahnaz. 2000. *Muslim Women: Crafting a North American Identity.* Gainesville, Fla.: University Press of Florida.

Khan, Surina A. 1998. "Sexual Exiles." In *A Patchwork Shawl: Chronicles of South Asian Women in America,* edited by Shamita Das Dasgupta. New Brunswick, N.J.: Rutgers University Press.

Kolars, Christine. 1994. "Masjid ul-Mutkabir: The Portrait of an African American Orthodox Muslim Community." In *Muslim Communities in North America,* edited by Yvonne Yazbeck Haddad and Jane Idleman Smith. Albany: State University of New York Press.

Kramer, Martin. 2001. *Ivory Towers on Sand: The Failure of Middle Eastern Studies in America*. Washington, D.C.: Washington Institute for Near East Policy.

Kulwicki, Anahid, and Penny S. Cass. 1996. "Arab-American Knowledge, Attitudes, and Beliefs About AIDS." In *Family and Gender Among American Muslims: Issues Facing Middle Eastern Immigrants and Their Descendants*, edited by Barbara C. Aswad and Barbara Bilge. Philadelphia: Temple University Press.

Kurien, Prema. 2000. "Constructing 'Indianness' in the United States and India: The Role of Hindu and Muslim Indian Immigrants." In *Asian and Latino Immigrants in a Restructuring Economy: The Metamorphosis of Los Angeles*, edited by M. Lopez-Garza and D. R. Diaz. Palo Alto, Calif.: Stanford University Press.

Lahaj, Mary. 1994. "The Islamic Center of New England." In *Muslim Communities in North America*, edited by Yvonne Yazbeck Haddad and Jane Idleman Smith. Albany: State University of New York Press.

Lang, Jeffrey. 1994. *Struggling to Surrender: Some Impressions of an American Convert to Islam*. Beltsville, Md.: Amana Publications.

———. 1998. *Even Angels Ask: A Journey to Islam in America*. Beltsville, Md.: Amana Publications.

Lawrence, Bruce B. 1998. *Shattering the Myth: Islam Beyond Violence*. Princeton, N.J.: Princeton University Press.

———. 2002. *New Faiths, Old Fears: Muslims and Other Asian Immigrants in American Religious Life*. New York: Columbia University Press.

Lawrence, Stewart J. 1999. "Religion and Immigration in the United States: A Bibliographic Report." Unpublished report to funders, Louisville Institute and the Pew Charitable Trusts.

Lee, Martha F. 1988. *The Nation of Islam: An American Millenarian Movement*. Lewiston, N.Y.: Edwin Mellen Press.

Leonard, Karen Isaksen. 1989–1990. "Mourning in a New Land: Changing Asian Practices in Southern California." *Journal of Orange County Studies* 34: 62–69.

———. 1992. *Making Ethnic Choices: California's Punjabi Mexican Americans*. Philadelphia: Temple University Press.

———. 1993. "Ethnic Identity and Gender: South Asians in the United States." In *Ethnicity, Identity, Migration: The South Asian Context*, edited by Milton Israel and N. K. Wagle. Toronto, Can.: University of Toronto, Center for South Asian Studies.

———. 1997. *South Asian Americans*. Westport, Conn.: Greenwood Press.

———. 2000. "State, Culture, and Religion: Political Action and Representation Among South Asians in North America." *Diaspora* 9(1): 21–38.

———. 2002a. "South Asian Leadership of American Muslims." In *Sojourners to Citizens: Muslims in Western Diasporas*, edited by Yvonne Yazbeck Haddad. New York: Oxford University Press.

———. 2002b. "American Muslims, Before and After September 11, 2001." *Economic and Political Weekly* 37(24): 2292–2302.

———. Forthcoming a. "American Muslim Discourses and Practices." *Ethnicities* 3: June 2003.

————, ed. Forthcoming b. *American Muslim Identities.*

Leonard, Karen, Alex Stepick, and Manuel Vasquez, eds. Forthcoming. "Religion, Immigration, and American Civic Life." Manuscript under preparation for the Social Science Research Council (SSRC).

Lin, Ann Chih, Alana Hackshaw, and Amaney Jamal. 2001. "When Does Discrimination Count as Discrimination?: Ideas About Discrimination from Arab Immigrants in Detroit." Paper presented at the meeting of the American Political Science Association, San Francisco (August 30–September 2).

Lin, Ann Chih, and Amaney Jamal. 2000. "Gender and Perceptions of State Authority Among Arab Immigrants to the United States." Paper presented at the meeting of the American Political Science Association, Washington, D.C. (August 31).

————. Forthcoming. "Muslim, Arab, and American: The Adaptation of Arab Immigrants to American Society." In "Religion, Immigration, and Civic Life," edited by Al Raboteau and Richard Alba. Manuscript under preparation for the Social Science Research Council (SSRC).

Lincoln, C. Eric. 1961. *The Black Muslims in America.* Boston: Beacon Press.

————. 1996. *Coming Through the Fire: Surviving Race and Place in America.* Durham, N.C.: Duke University Press.

————. 1997 [1983]. "The American Muslim Mission in the Context of American Social History." In *African-American Religion: Interpretive Essays in History and Culture,* edited by Timothy E. Fulop and Albert J. Raboteau. New York: Routledge. (Originally published in *The Muslim Community in North America,* edited by Earle H. Waugh, Baha Abu-Laban, and Regula B. Qureshi. Edmonton, Can.: University of Alberta Press.)

Lindkvist, Heather. 2002. "How to Restore Hope?: Life After September 11 for the Somali Community in Maine." Paper presented to the Conference on Muslim Minorities in Western Europe and North America After September 11, Duke University, Durham, N.C. (March 23).

Livezey, Lowell W. 2000. "Communities and Enclaves: Where Jews, Christians, Hindus, and Muslims Share the Neighborhoods." In *Public Religion and Urban Transformation: Faith in the City,* edited by Lowell W. Livezey. New York: New York University Press.

Lockwood, William G., and Yvonne R. Lockwood. 2000. "Continuity and Adaptation in Arab American Foodways." In *Arab Detroit: From Margin to Mainstream,* edited by Nabeel Abraham and Andrew Shryock. Detroit: Wayne State University Press.

Lotfi, Abdelhamid. 2001. "Creating Muslim Space in the USA: Masajid and Islamic Centers." *Islam and Christian-Muslim Relations* 12(2): 235–54.

Lotfi, Abdul Hamid. 2002. "Spreading the Word: Communicating Islam in America." In *Muslim Minorities in the West: Visible and Invisible,* edited by Yvonne Yazbeck Haddad and Jane I. Smith. New York: Altamira Press.

Lovell, Emily Kalled. 1983. "Islam in the United States: Past and Present." In *The Muslim Community in North America,* edited by Earle H. Waugh, Baha Abu-Laban, and Regula B. Qureshi. Edmonton, Can.: University of Alberta Press.

Lowe, Lisa, 1991. "Heterogeneity, Hybridity, Multiplicity: Marking Asian American Differences." *Diaspora* 1(1): 24–44.

Mahdi, Muhsin. 1997. "The Study of Islam: Orientalism and America." In *Mapping Islamic Studies: Genealogy, Continuity, and Change,* edited by Azim Nanji. New York: Mouton de Gruyter.

Mahmud, Tayyab. 1995. "Freedom of Religion and Religious Minorities in Pakistan: A Study of Judicial Practice." *Fordham International Law Journal* 19(1): 40–100.

———. Forthcoming. "Fractured Identities, Contingent Interests: South Asian Muslims in the U.S." In *American Muslim Identities,* edited by Karen Isaksen Leonard.

Majaj, Lisa Suhair. 1996. "Arab American Literature and the Politics of Memory." In *Memory and Cultural Politics: New Approaches to American Ethnic Literatures,* edited by Amritjit Singh, Joseph T. Skerrett Jr., and Robert E. Hogan. Boston: Northeastern University Press.

Malcolm X, and Alex Haley. 1966. *The Autobiography of Malcolm X.* New York: Ballantine.

Malkki, Liisa. 2003. "Beyond Cultural Fundamentalism and Evangelical Imperialism." Unpublished paper.

Mamiya, Lawrence H. 1982. "From Black Muslim to Bilalian: The Evolution of a Movement." *Journal for the Scientific Study of Religion* 21(2): 138–52.

———. 1983. "Minister Louis Farrakhan and the Final Call: Schism in the Muslim Movement." In *The Muslim Community in North America,* edited by Earle H. Waugh, Baha Abu-Laban, and Regula B. Qureshi. Edmonton, Can.: University of Alberta Press.

———. 1988. "The Black Muslims as a New Religious Movement." In *Conflict and Cooperation Between Contemporary Religious Groups.* Tokyo: Chuo Academic Research Institute.

———. 2001–2002. "Faith-Based Institutions and Family Support Services Among African-American Muslim Masjids and Black Churches." *Journal of the Interdenominational Theological Center* 29: 1–2, 25–61.

Marsh, Clifton E. 1984. *From Black Muslims to Muslims: The Transition from Separatism to Islam, 1930–1980.* Metuchen, N.J.: Scarecrow Press.

Martin, Richard C. 1985. *Approaches to Islam in Religious Studies.* Tucson: University of Arizona Press.

Masud, Muhammad Khalid. 1990. "The Obligation to Migrate: The Doctrine of Hijra in Islamic Law." In *Muslim Travelers: Pilgrimage, Migration, and the Religious Imagination,* edited by Dale F. Eickelman and James Piscatori. Berkeley: University of California Press.

Mattson, Ingrid. 1999. "Muslim Women: A Force of Change in Muslim Society." Available at: *www.islam21.net/pages/conferences/april99-22.htm.*

Maurer, Bill. Forthcoming. "Islamic Finance and 'America': A Tale in Three Acts." In *American Muslim Identities,* edited by Karen Isaksen Leonard.

Mazrui, Ali A. 1996. "Islam in a More Conservative Western World." *American Journal of Islamic Social Sciences* 13(2): 246–49.

McAlister, Melani. 2001. *Epic Encounters: Culture, Media, and U.S. Interests in the Middle East, 1945–2000.* Berkeley: University of California Press.

McCloud, Aminah Beverly. 1991. "African-American Muslim Women." In *The Muslims of America,* edited by Yvonne Yazbeck Haddad. New York: Oxford University Press.

———. 1995. *African American Islam.* New York: Routledge.

———. 1996. " 'This Is a Muslim Home': Signs of Difference in the African-American Row House." In *Making Muslim Space in North America and Europe,* edited by Barbara Daly Metcalf. Berkeley: University of California Press.

Melton, Gordon, and Michael Koszegi, eds. 1992. *Islam in North America: A Sourcebook.* New York: Garland.

Messick, Brinkley. 1997. "Genealogies of Reading and the Scholarly Cultures of Islam." In *Cultures of Scholarship,* edited by S. C. Humphreys. Ann Arbor: University of Michigan Press.

Metcalf, Barbara Daly. 1996. "New Medinas: The Tablighi Jama'at in America and Europe." In *Making Muslim Space in North America and Europe,* edited by Barbara Daly Metcalf. Berkeley: University of California Press.

Michalak, Laurence. 1989. "The Arab in American Cinema: A Century of Otherness." *Cineaste* 17: 3–9.

Modood, Tariq. 1988. " 'Black,' Racial Equality, and Asian Identity." *New Community* 14(3): 397–404.

———. 1994. "Political Blackness and British Asians." *Sociology* 28(4): 859–76.

Mohammed, Warith Deen. 1991. *Al-Islam: Unity and Leadership.* Chicago: The Sense Maker.

Mohammad-Arif, Aminah. 2000. *Salam America: l'islam indien en diaspora.* Paris: CNRS Editions.

Moore, Kathleen M. 1991. "Muslims in Prison: Claims to Constitutional Protection of Religious Liberty." In *The Muslims of America,* edited by Yvonne Yazbeck Haddad. New York: Oxford University Press.

———. 1995. *Al-Mughtaribun: American Law and the Transformation of Muslim Life in the United States.* Albany: State University of New York Press.

———. 1998. "The Hijab and Religious Liberty: Anti-discrimination Law and Muslim Women in the United States." In *Muslims on the Americanization Path?,* edited by Yvonne Yazbeck Haddad and John L. Esposito. Atlanta: Scholars Press.

———. 1999. "A Closer Look at Anti-terrorism Law: *American-Arab Anti-discrimination Committee v. Reno* and the Construction of Aliens' Rights." In *Arabs in America: Building a New Future,* edited by Michael Suleiman. Philadelphia: Temple University Press.

———. 2002a. "American Attitudes Toward Immigration and Muslim Presence in the United States Since September 11." Paper presented to the Conference on Muslim Minorities in Western Europe and North America After September 11, Duke University, Durham, N.C. (March 23).

———. 2002b. "Representation of Islam in the Language of Law: Some Recent U.S. Cases." In *Muslims in the West: From Sojourners to Citizens,* edited by Yvonne Yazbeck Haddad. New York: Oxford University Press.

Muhammad, Akbar. 1984. "Muslims in the United States: An Overview of Organizations, Doctrines, and Problems." In *The Islamic Impact,* edited by Yvonne

Yazbeck Haddad, with Byron Haines and Ellison Findly. Syracuse, N.Y.: Syracuse University Press.

Murray, Stephen O., and Will Roscoe, eds. 1997. *Islamic Homosexualities: Culture, History, and Literature.* New York: New York University Press.

Naber, Nadine. 2000. "Ambiguous Insiders: An Investigation of Arab American Invisibility." *Ethnic and Racial Studies* 23(1): 37–61.

———. Forthcoming. "Muslim First, Arab Second: A Strategic Politics of Race and Gender." In *American Muslim Identities,* edited by Karen Isaksen Leonard.

Naff, Alixa. 1985. *Becoming American: The Early Arab Immigrant Experience.* Carbondale: Southern Illinois University Press.

Naficy, Hamid. 1993a. "Popular Culture of Iranian Exiles in Los Angeles." In *Irangeles: Iranians in Los Angeles,* edited by Ron Kelley, with Jonathan Friedlander. Berkeley: University of California Press.

———. 1993b. *The Making of Exile Cultures: Iranian Television in Los Angeles.* Minneapolis: University of Minnesota Press.

———. 1998. "Identity Politics and Iranian Exile Music Videos." *Iranian Studies: Bulletin of the Society for Iranian Cultural and Social Studies* 31(1): 52–64.

———. 1999. "Between Rocks and Hard Places: The Interstitial Mode of Production in Exilic Cinema." In *Home, Exile, Homeland,* edited by Hamid Naficy. New York: Routledge.

———. 2001. *An Accented Cinema: Exilic and Diasporic Filmmaking.* Princeton, N.J.: Princeton University Press.

Naim, C. M. 1995. "Ambiguities of Heritage." *Toronto Review* 14(1): 1–5.

Naipaul, V. S. 1998. *Beyond Belief: Islamic Excursions Among the Converted Peoples.* Boston: Little, Brown.

Nance, Susan. 2002. "Mystery of the Moorish Science Temple: Southern Black and American Alternative Spirituality in 1920s Chicago." *Religion and American Culture* 12(2): 123–66.

Nanji, Azim. 1983. "The Nizari Isma'ili Muslim Community in North America: Background and Development." In *The Muslim Community in North America,* edited by Earle H. Waugh, Baha Abu-Laban, and Regula B. Qureshi. Edmonton, Can.: University of Alberta Press.

———, ed. 1997. "Introduction." In *Mapping Islamic Studies: Genealogy, Continuity, and Change,* edited by Azim Nanji. New York: Mouton de Gruyter.

Nasr, Seyyed Hossein. 1987. *Traditional Islam in the Modern World.* New York: KPI.

Nazir-Chaudhry, Lubna. Forthcoming. "Aisha: An Ethnographic Montage of a Pakistani Muslim Immigrant." In *American Muslim Identities,* edited by Karen Isaksen Leonard.

Niaz, Anjum. 2002. "Blasphemy!" *Pakistan Link,* November 2, PL32.

Nimer, Mohamed. 2002a. "Muslims in American Public Life." In *Muslims in the West: From Sojourners to Citizens,* edited by Yvonne Yazbeck Haddad. New York: Oxford University Press.

———. 2002b. *The North American Muslim Resource Guide.* New York: Taylor and Francis/Routledge Publishers.

Nu'man, Fareed H. 1992. *The Muslim Population in the United States.* Washington, D.C.: American Muslim Council.

Numrich, Paul D. 1997. "Recent Immigrant Religions in a Restructuring Metropolis: New Religious Landscapes in Chicago." *Journal of Cultural Geography* 17(1): 55–76.

———. 2000a. "Change, Stress, and Congregations in an Edge-City Technoburb." In *Public Religion and Urban Transformation: Faith in the City,* edited by Lowell W. Livezey. New York: New York University Press.

———. 2000b. "Recent Immigrant Religion and the Restructuring of Metropolitan Chicago." In *Public Religion and Urban Transformation: Faith in the City,* edited by Lowell W. Livezey. New York: New York University Press.

Nuruddin, Yusuf. 1994. "The Five Percenters: A Teenage Nation of Gods and Earths." In *Muslim Communities in North America,* edited by Yvonne Yazbeck Haddad and Jane Idleman Smith. Albany: State University of New York Press.

———. 1998. "African-American Muslims and the Question of Identity: Between Traditional Islam, African Heritage, and the American Way." In *Muslims on the Americanization Path?,* edited by Yvonne Yazbeck Haddad and John L. Esposito. Atlanta: Scholars Press.

Nyang, Sulayman S. 1991. "Convergence and Divergence in an Emergent Community: A Study of Challenges Facing U.S. Muslims." In *The Muslims of America,* edited by Yvonne Yazbeck Haddad. New York: Oxford University Press.

———. 1998. "Islam in America: A Historical Perspective." *American Muslim Quarterly* 2(1): 7–38.

———. 2002. "Continental African Muslim Immigrants in the United States: A Historical and Sociological Perspective." In *Muslims in the West: From Sojourners to Citizens,* edited by Yvonne Yazbeck Haddad. New York: Oxford University Press.

Palmer, Susan, and Steve Luxton. 1997. "The Ansaaru Allah Community: Postmodernist Narration and the Black Jeremiad." In *New Trends and Developments in the World of Islam,* edited by Peter B. Clarke. London: Luzac Oriental Press.

Peek, Lori A. 2002. "Religious and Ethnic Issues After September 11, 2001: Examining Muslim University Student Experiences." Available at: *www.colorado.edu/ hazards/qr/qr156/qr156html.*

Perry, Donna L. 1997. "Rural Ideologies and Urban Imaginings: Wolof Immigrants in New York City." *Africa Today* 44(2): 229–60.

Pipes, Daniel, and Khalid Duran. 2002. "Muslim Immigrants in the United States." Available at: *www.cis.org/articles/index.html#Backgrounders.*

Poston, Larry. 1991. "Da'wah in the West." In *The Muslims of America,* edited by Yvonne Yazbeck Haddad. New York: Oxford University Press.

———. 1992. *Islamic Da'wah in the West: Muslim Missionary Activity and the Dynamics of Conversion to Islam.* New York: Oxford University Press.

Project MAPS (Muslims in the American Public Square). 2002. Poll conducted by Zogby International in November-December 2001. Available at: *www. projectmaps.com/PMReport.htm.*

Qureshi, Regula Burckhardt. 1995 [1986]. *Sufi Music of India and Pakistan: Sound, Context, and Meaning in Qawwali.* Chicago: University of Chicago Press.

Raboteau, Al, and Richard Alba, eds. Forthcoming. *Religion, Immigration, and Civic Life.* Manuscript under preparation for the Social Science Research Council (SSRC).

Rahimieh, Nasrin. 1990. *Oriental Responses to the West: Comparative Essays in Select Writers from the Muslim World*. New York: E. J. Brill.

Rapoport, David C. 2001. "The Fourth Wave: September 11 in the History of Terrorism." *Current History* (December): 419–24.

Rashid, Samory. 2000. "Divergent Perspectives on Islam in America." *Journal of Muslim Minority Affairs* 20(1): 75–90.

Rasmussen, Anne. 2000. "The Sound of Culture, the Structure of Tradition." In *Arab Detroit: From Margin to Mainstream*, edited by Nabeel Abraham and Andrew Shryock. Detroit: Wayne State University Press.

Read, Jen'nan Ghazal. 2002. "Challenging Myths of Muslim Women: The Influence of Islam on Arab-American Women's Labor Force Activity." *Muslim World* 92(1–2): 19–38.

Rignall, Karen. 2000. "Building the Infrastructure of Arab American Identity in Detroit: A Short History of ACCESS and the Community It Serves." In *Arab Detroit: From Margin to Mainstream*, edited by Nabeel Abraham and Andrew Shryock. Detroit: Wayne State University Press.

Rippin, Andrew. 1990–93. *Muslims: Their Religious Beliefs and Practices*. New York: Routledge.

Ross-Sheriff, Fariyal, Mali Dhanidina, and Ali S. Asani. 1996. *Al-Ummah: Handbook for an Identity Development Program for Immigrant Muslim Youth in North America*. New York: Al-Ummah Corporation, Aga Khan Foundation.

Roy, Asim. 1996. *Islam in South Asia: A Regional Perspective*. New Delhi: South Asian Publishers.

Ruthven, Malise. 1997. "Aga Khan III and the Isma'ili Renaissance." In *New Trends and Developments in the World of Islam*, edited by Peter B. Clarke. London: Luzac Oriental Press.

Ryce-Menuhin, Joel, ed. 1994. *Jung and the Monotheisms: Judaism, Christianity, and Islam*. New York: Routledge.

Sabagh, Georges, and Mehdi Bozorgmehr. 1994. "Secular Immigrants: Religiosity and Ethnicity Among Iranian Muslims in Los Angeles." In *Muslim Communities in North America*, edited by Yvonne Yazbeck Haddad and Jane Idleman Smith. Albany: State University of New York Press.

Sachedina, Abdulaziz Abdulhussein. 1988. *The Just Ruler (al-sultan al-'adil) in Shi'ite Islam*. New York: Oxford University Press.

———. 1994. "A Minority Within a Minority: The Case of the Shi'a in North America." In *Muslim Communities in North America*, edited by Yvonne Yazbeck Haddad and Jane Idleman Smith. Albany: State University of New York Press.

Saeed, Agha. 2000. "National Council on Islamic Affairs Announces Merger with American Muslim Alliance." *Pakistan Link*, February 25, 20.

———. 2002. "The American Muslim Paradox." In *Muslim Minorities in the West: Visible and Invisible*, edited by Yvonne Yazbeck Haddad and Jane I. Smith. New York: Altamira Press.

Safi, Omid, ed. *Progressive Muslims: On Justice, Gender, and Pluralism*. Oxford: Oneworld Publications.

Safizadeh, Fereydoun. 1996. "Children of the Revolution: Transnational Identity Among Young Iranians in Northern California." In *Middle Eastern Diaspora Communities in America*, edited by Mehdi Bozorgmehr and Alison Feldman. New York: New York University, Hagop Kevorkian Center for Near Eastern Studies.

Said, Edward. 1986. *After the Last Sky: Palestinian Lives*. New York: Pantheon Books.
——. 1997. *Covering Islam*. 2d ed. New York: Vintage Books.
——. 1999. *Out of Place: A Memoir*. New York: Alfred A. Knopf.
Sakata, Hiromi Lorraine, and Karen Leonard. Forthcoming. "Indo-Muslim Music, Poetry, and Dance in America." In *American Muslim Identities*, edited by Karen Isaksen Leonard.
Samhan, Helen Hatab. 1999. "Not Quite White: Race Classification and the Arab-American Experience." In *Arabs in America: Building a New Future*, edited by Michael Suleiman. Philadelphia: Temple University Press.
Sanyal, Usha. 1999. "The [Re]Construction of South Asian Muslim Identity in Queens, New York." In *Expanding Landscapes: South Asians in Diaspora*, edited by Carla Petievich. Delhi: Manohar.
Schimmel, Annemarie (translated by Susan H. Ray). 1997. *My Soul is a Woman: The Feminine in Islam*. New York: Continuum.
Schmidt, Garbi. 1998. *American Medina: A Study of the Sunni Muslim Immigrant Communities in Chicago*. Lund, Sweden: University of Lund.
——. 2002a. "The Complexity of Belonging: Sunni Muslim Immigrants in Chicago." In *Muslim Minorities in the West: Visible and Invisible*, edited by Yvonne Yazbeck Haddad and Jane I. Smith. New York: Altamira Press.
——. 2002b. "A Visible Change: Young Muslims in Denmark and the United States After September 11." Paper presented to the Conference on Muslim Minorities in Western Europe and North America After September 11, Duke University, Durham, N.C. (March 23).
——. Forthcoming a. "Muslim Social Activism: An American and Transnational Phenomenon." In *American Muslim Identities*, edited by Karen Isaksen Leonard.
——. Forthcoming b. "Sufi Charisma on the Internet." In *Sufism in Europe and the United States*, edited by David Westerlund. London: RoutledgeCurzon.
Schopmeyer, Kim. 2000. "A Demographic Portrait of Arab Detroit." In *Arab Detroit: From Margin to Mainstream*, edited by Nabeel Abraham and Andrew Shryock. Detroit: Wayne State University Press.
Segal, Daniel A. 2002. Review of Karen Brodkin. *American Ethnologist* 29(2): 470–73.
Seikaly, May. 1999. "Attachment and Identity: The Palestinian Community of Detroit." In *Arabs in America: Building a New Future*, edited by Michael Suleiman. Philadelphia: Temple University Press.
Shaheen, Jack G. 2001. *Reel Bad Arabs: How Hollywood Vilifies a People*. New York: Olive Branch Press.
Shain, Yossi. 1994. "Marketing the Democratic Creed Abroad: U.S. Diasporic Politics in the Era of Multiculturalism." *Diaspora* 3(1): 85–111.
Shakir, Evelyn. 1997. *Bint Arab: Arab and Arab American Women in the United States*. Westport, Conn.: Praeger.
Shryock, Andrew. 2000. "Family Resemblances: Kinship and Community in Arab Detroit." In *Arab Detroit: From Margin to Mainstream*, edited by Nabeel Abraham and Andrew Shryock. Detroit: Wayne State University Press.
——. 2002. "New Images of Arab Detroit: Seeing Otherness and Identity Through the Lens of September 11." *American Anthropologist* 104(3): 917–22.
Siddiqi, Muzammil H. 1986. "Muslims in a Non-Muslim Society." *Islamic Horizons* (May–June): 22.

Silvay, Lucy. 2002. "Gay and Muslim: The Ultimate Oxymoron?" *Gay and Lesbian Times: Southern California's Newsmagazine,* September 5, 38–41. Available at: *www.gaylesbiantimes.com.*

Simmons, Gwendolyn Zoharah. 2000. "Striving for Muslim Women's Human Rights—Before and Beyond Beijing." In *Windows of Faith: Muslim Women Scholar-Activists in North America,* edited by Gisela Webb. Syracuse, N.Y.: Syracuse University Press.

Slyomovics, Susan. 1996. "The Muslim World Day Parade and 'Storefront' Mosques of New York City." In *Making Muslim Space in North America and Europe,* edited by Barbara Daly Metcalf. Berkeley: University of California Press.

Smith, Jane Idleman. 1984. "The Experience of Muslim Women: Considerations of Power and Authority." In *The Islamic Impact,* edited by Yvonne Yazbeck Haddad, with Byron Haines and Ellison Findly. Syracuse, N.Y.: Syracuse University Press.

———. 1999. *Islam in America.* New York: Columbia University Press.

Sollors, Werner. 1986. *Beyond Ethnicity: Consent and Dissent in American Culture.* New York: Oxford University Press.

Sonbol, Amira El-Azhary. 2000. "Rethinking Women and Islam." In *Daughters of Abraham: Feminist Thought in Judaism, Christianity, and Islam,* edited by Yvonne Yazbeck Haddad and John L. Esposito. Gainesville: University of Florida Press.

Sonn, Tamara. 1994. "Diversity in Rochester's Islamic Community." In *Muslim Communities in North America,* edited by Yvonne Yazbeck Haddad and Jane Idleman Smith. Albany: State University of New York Press.

Starrett, Gregory. 1999. "Muslim Identities and the Great Chain of Buying." In *New Media in the Muslim World: The Emerging Public Sphere,* edited by Dale F. Eickelman and Jon W. Anderson. Bloomington: Indiana University Press.

———. 2002. "Suffering and Citizenship in African-American Responses to September 11." Paper presented to the Conference on Muslim Minorities in Western Europe and North America After September 11, Duke University, Durham, N.C. (March 23).

Stepick, Alex. Forthcoming. "God Is Apparently Not Dead: The Obvious, the Emergent, and the Unknown in Immigration and Religion." In *Religion, Immigration, and American Civic Life,* edited by Karen Leonard, Alex Stepick, and Manuel Vasquez. Manuscript under preparation for the Social Science Research Council (SSRC).

Suleiman, Michael W., ed. 1999. *Arabs in America: Building a New Future.* Philadelphia: Temple University Press.

Suleri, Sara. 1992. *The Rhetoric of English India.* Chicago: University of Chicago Press.

Swedenborg, Ted. 1996. "Transnational Islamic Rap." Paper presented at the meeting of the American Anthropological Association, Chicago, (November 3).

———. 2002. "Snipers and the Panic over Five Percent Islamic Hip-Hop." MERIP press information note 111, November 10, 2002. Available at: *www.merip.org.*

Taha, Mahmud Muhammad. 1987. *The Second Message of Islam (Risalah al-thaniyah min al-Islam),* translated by Abdullahi Ahmed An-Na'im. Syracuse, N.Y.: Syracuse University Press.

Takim, Liyakat. 2002. "Multiple Identities in a Pluralistic World: Shi'ism in America." In *Muslims in the West: From Sojourners to Citizens*, edited by Yvonne Yazbeck Haddad. New York: Oxford University Press.

Taylor, Charles. 1999. "Two Theories of Modernity." *Public Culture* 11(1): 153–74.

Tipton, Steven M. 1982. *Getting Saved from the Sixties: Moral Meaning in Conversion and Cultural Change.* Berkeley: University of California Press.

Tohidi, Nayereh. 1993. "Iranian Women and Gender Relations in Los Angeles." In *Irangeles: Iranians in Los Angeles*, edited by Ron Kelley, with Jonathan Friedlander. Berkeley: University of California Press.

Trix, Frances. 1994. "Bektashi Tekke and the Sunni Mosque of Albanian Muslims in America." In *Muslim Communities in North America*, edited by Yvonne Yazbeck Haddad and Jane Idleman Smith. Albany: State University of New York Press.

Turner, Richard Brent. 1997. *Islam in the African-American Experience.* Bloomington: Indiana University Press.

Tweed, Thomas A. 1997. "Introduction: Narrating U.S. Religious History." In *Retelling U.S. Religious History*, edited by Thomas A. Tweed. Berkeley: University of California Press.

Tweed, Thomas A., and Stephen Prothero. 1999. *Asian Religions in America: A Documentary History.* New York: Oxford University Press.

Vasquez, Manuel. Forthcoming. "Historicizing and Materializing the Study of Religion: The Contributions of Migration Studies." In *Religion, Immigration, and American Civic Life*, edited by Karen Isaksen Leonard, Alex Stepick, and Manuel Vasquez. Manuscript under preparation for the Social Science Research Council (SSRC).

Viswanathan, Gauri. 1998. *Outside the Fold: Conversion, Modernity, and Belief.* Princeton, N.J.: Princeton University Press.

Vitalis, Robert. 2002. "International Studies in America." *Items and Issues* (SSRC bulletin) 3(3–4): 1, 2, 12–16.

Voll, John. 1980. "Hadith Scholars and Tariqahs: An Ulama Group in the Eighteenth-Century Haramayn and Their Impact in the Islamic World." *Journal of Asian and African Studies* 15(3–4): 264–73.

Waardenburg, Jacques. 1997. "Islamic Studies and the History of Religions: An Evaluation." In *Mapping Islamic Studies: Genealogy, Continuity, and Change*, edited by Azim Nanji. New York: Mouton de Gruyter.

Wadud, Amina. 1999. *Qur'an and Woman: Rereading the Sacred Text from a Woman's Perspective.* New York: Oxford University Press.

———. 2000. "Alternative Qur'anic Interpretation and the Status of Muslim Women." In *Windows of Faith: Muslim Women Scholar-Activists in North America*, edited by Gisela Webb. Syracuse, N.Y.: Syracuse University Press.

Walbridge, Linda S. 1996a. "Sex and the Single Shi'ite: Mut'a Marriage in an American Lebanese Shi'ite Community." In *Family and Gender Among American Muslims: Issues Facing Middle Eastern Immigrants and Their Descendants*, edited by Barbara C. Aswad and Barbara Bilge. Philadelphia: Temple University Press.

———. 1996b. "Five Immigrants." In *Family and Gender Among American Muslims: Issues Facing Middle Eastern Immigrants and Their Descendants*, edited by Barbara C. Aswad and Barbara Bilge. Philadelphia: Temple University Press.

———. 1997. *Without Forgetting the Imam: Lebanese Shi'ism in an American Community*. Detroit: Wayne State University Press.

———. 1999. "A Look at Differing Ideologies Among Shi'a Muslims in the United States." In *Arabs in America: Building a New Future*, edited by Michael Suleiman. Philadelphia: Temple University Press.

Walbridge, Linda, and T. M. Aziz. 2000. "After Karbala: Iraqi Refugees in Detroit." In *Arab Detroit: From Margin to Mainstream*, edited by Nabeel Abraham and Andrew Shryock. Detroit: Wayne State University Press.

Walbridge, Linda, and Fatimah Haneef. 1999. "Inter-ethnic Relations Within the Ahmadiyya Muslim Community in the United States." In *The Expanding Landscape: South Asians and the Diaspora*, edited by Carla Petievich. Delhi: Manohar.

Warner, R. Stephen, and Judith G. Wittner, eds. 1998. *Gatherings in Diaspora: Religious Communities and the New Immigration*. Philadelphia: Temple University Press.

Waugh, Earle H. 1999. *The Islamic Tradition: Religious Beliefs and Healthcare Decisions*. Chicago: Park Ridge Center.

Waugh, Earle H., Baha Abu-Laban, and Regula B. Qureshi, eds. 1983. *The Muslim Community in North America*. Edmonton, Can.: University of Alberta Press.

Waugh, Earle H., Sharon McIrvin Abu-Laban, and Regula Burckhardt Qureshi, eds. 1991. *Muslim Families in North America*. Edmonton, Can.: University of Alberta Press.

Wax, Emily. 1999. "The Mufti in the Chat Room: Islamic Legal Advisers Are Just a Click Away from Ancient Customs." *Washington Post*, July 31.

———. 2000. "Gay Muslims United in Face of Rejection." *Houston Chronicle*, April 15.

Webb, Gisela. 1994. "Tradition and Innovation in Contemporary American Islamic Spirituality: The Bawa Muhaiyaddeen Fellowship." In *Muslim Communities in North America*, edited by Yvonne Yazbeck Haddad and Jane Idleman Smith. Albany: State University of New York Press.

———, ed. 2000. *Windows of Faith: Muslim Women Scholar-Activists in North America*. Syracuse, N.Y.: Syracuse University Press.

Webb, Mohammed Alexander Russell. 1893. *Islam in America*. New York: Oriental Publishing.

Weightman, Barbara A. 1993. "Changing Religious Landscapes in Los Angeles." *Journal of Cultural Geography* 14(1): 1–20.

Werbner, Pnina. 1998. "Diasporic Political Imaginaries: A Sphere of Freedom or a Sphere of Illusions?" *Communal/Plural* 6(1): 11–31.

———. 1999. "Global Pathways, Working-class Cosmopolitans, and the Creation of Transnational Ethnic Worlds." *Social Anthropology* 7(1): 19–20.

———. 2002. "On Moral Panics and Diasporic Vulnerabilities: Multicultural Dilemmas in the Face of Global Terror." Talk given at the University of California at Irvine, February 5.

Werbner, Pnina, and Tariq Modood. 1997. *Debating Cultural Hybridity: Multicultural Identities and the Politics of Anti-racism*. London: Zed Books.

Williams, Raymond Brady. 1988. *Religions of Immigrants from India and Pakistan: New Threads in the American Tapestry*. New York: Cambridge University Press.

———. 1991. "Asian-Indian Muslims in the United States." In *Indian Muslims in North America,* edited by Omar Khalidi. Watertown, Mass.: South Asia Press.

Wilson, Peter Lamborn. 1993. *Sacred Drift: Essays on the Margins of Islam.* San Francisco: City Lights Books.

———. 1997. "The Strange Fate of Sufism in the New Age." In *New Trends and Developments in the World of Islam,* edited by Peter B. Clarke. London: Luzac Oriental Press.

Wolfe, Michael. 1998. *The Hadj: An American's Pilgrimage to Mecca.* New York: Grove-Atlantic Press.

Wong, Sau Ling. 1995. "Denationalization Reconsidered: Asian American Cultural Criticism at a Theoretical Crossroads." *Amerasia Journal* 21(1–2): 1–27.

Wormser, Richard. 1994. *American Islam: Growing Up Muslim in America.* New York: Walker and Co.

Wuthnow, Robert. 1988. *The Restructuring of American Religion: Society and Faith Since World War II.* Princeton, N.J.: Princeton University Press.

Yang, Fenggang, and Helen Rose Ebaugh. 2001. "Transformations in New Immigrant Religions and Their Global Implications." *American Sociological Review* 66(April): 269–88.

Zarcone, Thierry. 2000. "Freemasonry and the Related Trends in Muslim Reformist Thought in Turko-Persian Area." Paper presented to the Conference on Iran and the Surrounding World Since 1500, University of California at Los Angeles (April 15).

= Index =

Aafreen, Sabah, 123
AAI (Arab American Institute), 12
AAUG (Association of Arab American University Graduates), 12
Abdullah, Omer Bin, 23
Abdullah, Zain, 55, 58, 74
Abdul-Rauf, Muhammad, 88–89
Abdur-Rahim, Tarajee, 33, 70
Abedi, Mehdi, 56, 80
Abou El Fadl, Khaled, 26, 89–90, 91, 92, 97–99, 111, 137, 156n8
Abraham, Nabeel, 11, 62, 63–64, 64
Abrahamic religions, partnering of, 59
Abusharaf, Rogaia Mustafa, 109, 157–58n9
ADC (American-Arab Anti-Discrimination Committee), 12, 19
affirmative action programs, 116
Afghanistan, 13, 17, 28
African American Muslims: absence from political debates, 20, 24; and African immigrants, 57–58, 80; Ahmadi sect, 6–7, 40; as black nationalists, 6, 17, 53, 57, 152n2; domestic spaces of, 74; educational efforts, 112–13; evangelistic role of, 71; gender issues, 78, 96, 123, 154n6; generational issues, 62–63, 111, 122; identity politics of, 53–54, 57–58; vs. immigrants, 17, 20, 33, 40, 55, 57–58, 93, 103, 112, 117, 137; and Iranian immigrants, 44; and marriage rules, 66–67, 68; mosque

community, 73, 76–77, 78–79; music, 116–17, 124; national organizations of, 145; and Persian Gulf states, 81–82; political participation of, 7, 17, 19, 30, 32, 103; profile of, 5–9; research issues, 22, 30–33, 130, 132–33, 153n7; roots of movement, 107
African immigrants, 41, 57–58, 74, 80
African Muslims, 41, 55, 74, 84
Aga Khan, 22, 26, 36–38, 53
Aga Khan III, 37, 68
Aga Khan IV, 37–38, 79, 84, 85
Ahmad, Mirza Ghulam, 39
Ahmadi (Qadiani) Muslims: African Americans, 6–7, 40; discrimination against, 84–85; history of, 151n9; identity issues, 53, 54, 149n5; multiracial communities, 58; and music, 116–17; religious practices, 39–40, 148n5; research issues, 22
Ahmed, Karen Hunt, 62
Aidi, Hisham, 117
Akram, El-Hajj Wali, 63
Alalwani, Taha, 89–90
al-'Aql, Shaykh, 39
Al-Faruqi, Isma'il, 55, 88, 115
Al Hakim, 39
Ali, Noble Drew, 5, 6
Ali, Syed Faiz, 122
Al-Johar, Denise, 66, 122
Alkhateeb, Sharifa, 95
Allen, Edward, Jr., 6

185